LOCATION LOCATION LOCATION

LOCATION LOCATION LOCATION

The Complete Guide to Buying and Selling Your Home

FANNY BLAKE

First published 2002 by Channel Four Books,
an imprint of Pan Macmillan Ltd,
Pan Macmillan, 20 New Wharf Road, London N1 9RR
Basingstoke and Oxford
Associated companies throughout the world
www.panmacmillan.com

ISBN 0 7522 6521 0

Text © Fanny Blake, 2002

The right of to be identified as the author of this work has been asserted
by her in accordance with the Copyright, Designs and Patents Act 1988.

5 7 9 8 6 4

A CIP catalogue record for this book is available from the British Library.

Designed and typset by seagulls
Printed and bound by Mackays of Chatham plc, Chatham, Kent

This book accompanies the television series *Location Location Location*
made by Ideal World Productions for Channel 4.

CONTENTS

FOREWORD

Over the last three years we have made seven series of *Location, Location, Location* for Channel 4 and its popularity just keeps on growing. During each programme, we go through as many stages in the property-buying process as we can. If an offer is accepted during a show, it means we can take our buyer and viewers through every step of the way, showing them how to look, how to prioritize, how to sacrifice some of their criteria, how to make a decision between two properties they really like and, very importantly, how to negotiate – something of which many people have little experience.

The aim of the programme is to be as informative as possible about every aspect of buying a house and some aspects of selling since, unless you are a first-time or lucky second-home buyer, the majority of house purchases involve both. What both the programme and this accompanying book do is help guide and advise buyers to show them that the whole process does not have to be the nightmare it is so often made out to be.

We have both been in the home-search business for over five years. In addition, Kirstie is the child of addicted movers and Phil is a qualified surveyor. We believe that as a result we can offer a unique perspective on the business of home-buying to share with you. We are also attempting to expand and increase recognition of the home-finding industry, which we believe will help to create a more efficient property market. Currently, we have a very inefficient and biased property market, where all the professional help is for the seller. There is no other market in the world, whether it is dealing in Wellington boots or stocks and shares, where this is the case.

Few people have our experience of moving house simply because they do not do it that often. As a result, we are only too aware of the principal hurdles you may have to overcome. Our first tip would be preparation, preparation, preparation: before you even begin your hunt, make sure you know how much you can spend and how much the hidden costs will be, such as solicitor's fees, surveys, costs of moving and so on. Secondly, remember to be nice to the estate agent. For instance, if you are in town, take them a cup of coffee from the nearest coffee shop. A simple thing but they will remember you as a result. If you make an enemy of them you won't get anywhere. Thirdly, do not expect the estate agent to point out any of the downsides to a property, you must find those out for yourself. Fourthly, do not let a deal fall through because of a disagreement over what is included on the fixtures and fittings list. Keep your sense of perspective at all times. Finally, always keep on your solicitor's back. In this country it traditionally takes six to eight weeks to exchange contracts. There's no earthly reason why it should. Searches aside, it should be possible to exchange in three weeks. If you regard the whole process as a military operation, it should not be painful.

Throughout the series, we have been able to learn about the property market countrywide – an experience that few are fortunate enough to have. However without any shadow of a doubt, the greatest pleasure is in searching out properties people were not expecting to find, matching their brief and saving them money. For instance, about a month ago we managed to find a couple the unexpected but ideal property and saved them £25,000 that they were prepared to spend. It was a joy to be able to do that for someone and we hope this book will help do the same for you.

Happy house-hunting.

Kirstie and Phil

1   FINDING YOUR PROPERTY

Buying a home is likely to be one of the largest, if not the largest, investment most of us will make in our lifetime. Unfortunately, it is also one of the greatest causes of stress. For these simple reasons it is vital to make sure that the property you choose is the right one. Before you take your first steps through the estate agent's door and plunge into the property market, there are a number of factors to take into account. If you are clear in your mind about what it is you are looking for, then you will be less likely to fall under the spell of the estate agent's spin and buy somewhere unsuitable. House-hunting can be a nightmare, but if you prepare yourself carefully it should go like a dream, with minimum stress and maximum success.

THE RIGHT PROPERTY

Before embarking on your search, think carefully about exactly what sort of property you hope to buy. Pounding the pavements hunting for a home can be a time-consuming and wearisome business, but if you plan ahead, you can make the process easier on yourself. Starting with a clear idea of the area in which you would like to live, the kind of property you are hoping to find and your budget means you will be able to scythe through the estate agent's long and daunting lists. Looking at properties that are the wrong size, in the wrong place and beyond your means may make great entertainment on a wet Sunday afternoon but they are a serious distraction. You must remain focused on your requirements, possibly adapting them in the light of what you discover in your searches, but never letting yourself lose sight of your main goal. Consider the possible options and draw up a list of the things you would like to find in your perfect property, marking those you cannot live without.

Primary or secondary home?

The majority of people buying property are buying homes in which they intend to live permanently. However, if you are looking for a second home or a property that is purely for investment purposes, you will almost certainly have different criteria governing your final choice. Think about each of these carefully. Your primary home has to fulfil a number of practical considerations including being close to your work, schools and the local amenities that matter to you. A second home is more of an indulgence, where you can lead a kind of fantasy life during weekends and holidays, but there are considerations to be taken into account here too. Does it need to be within a certain distance of your primary home, or close to a particular railway station or motorway? Do you want a garden, a tennis court, stables? Should a *pied à terre* in town be particularly close to the centre, so you can walk to and from the theatre or art galleries? Draw up your own list of requirements.

For how long?

How long do you intend to keep the property? If you are thinking of keeping the place long term, then its idiosyncrasies may matter less, whereas with a short-term buy, it is more important to consider the resale potential. To ensure the maximum number of potential buyers will view your home when you come to sell, you will need to consider their likely needs in terms of proximity to public transport and local amenities, car parking availability, as well as your own.

Town or country?

If you are buying in a town, think about how close you need to be to work, schools, shops, local transport and friends. The busy centre of town, close to cinemas, theatres, galleries, restaurants and bars, may appeal more than the leafier suburbs. Car owners will need somewhere to park their car. Dog walkers, joggers or those with small children may want to be near a park. You will probably have a wide variety of properties to choose from, but they will certainly be more expensive than in the country and you may have to compromise more to find your ideal home.

If buying in the country, question how isolated you want to be. A remote cottage miles from anywhere might be the ideal place for a two-week holiday but could be less practical on a long-term basis. Think about how close you want to be to amenities and how much you may want to become involved in the local community. It may be more difficult to join in if you are living miles from other people. A country life is one with a slower pace and a more healthy environment, but it is also one where winters can be inhospitable and your social life more restricted.

House or flat?

Do you want the convenience of living on one floor, or would you prefer the idea of going upstairs to bed? If you can stretch your finances to a house, you will not have to put up with noise from people living above or below you and may even be fortunate enough not to have them immediately on either side. Owning a house almost certainly means you will own the freehold of the property and have control of its upkeep, unlike a leaseholder whose property ultimately belongs to someone else (see Freehold vs. Leasehold on page 148).

If you want to buy a flat, you will need to make slightly different considerations. Do you want to live in a service block with a caretaker or doorman to look after your needs, or in a block where each individual flat owner has their own responsibilities. A modern purpose-built block may be more efficient in terms of space and function than a conversion, although a conversion may have more character. If the property is lease-hold, find out how long the lease is. It may make a difference to your decision. If the lease runs for less than sixty years, it could be difficult to get a mortgage and it may affect the ease with which you sell the property at a later date.

Old or new?

Decide whether you prefer an old property or something modern. The original period features of an old property lend character, but could involve a higher degree of maintenance. The design, modern conveniences and energy-saving facilities in a contemporary home may be more attractive. A new house should come with a ten-year NHBC or Zurich insurance registration, ensuring that any structural problems within that time will be rectified by the builder. An old house may be difficult to modify to your requirements while a new one can be tailor-made for you. It may be easier to get a mortgage on a new house – possibly even for 100% if necessary. See Typical Period Features on page 154 for more details.

Size?

Be realistic about how many people will be living in the house and whether that might change over the period you are in it. For instance, if you are thinking of starting a family, you will need a minimum of two bedrooms, and if you are expecting to have visitors, plan for a spare room even if it doubles as something else while empty. How many bathrooms and reception rooms will you need? Do you need to think about having enough room for a nanny or grandparent? If so, will it be a self-contained flat, a bedsit or a room where they can retreat away from the family? Remember that the bigger the house, the more expensive it will be to run.

A house may come up that is beyond your budget but has space that is, or could be, converted into a flat or bedsit. If the potential rental income would cover the extra mortgage payments, it might make it a viable financial proposition and enable you to make a good investment (see Letting A Room on page 64).

Outside space

Some people find a small, easy-to-manage patio garden enough while others yearn for something larger. A garden is a commitment, so be realistic about who is going to look after it unless you want it to be turned over to the children as a playground and football pitch. Other considerations outside the house might include a garage, a pool, stables or games room.

Buying to rent

This has become a hugely popular form of investment over the last few years. If you are buying a place to let, your thoughts must be entirely with your prospective tenant and his needs. The location is paramount, depending whether you are aiming at students, city slickers or families. Take advice from a local lettings agent as to the must-have features, be they stripped wood floors, *en suite* bathrooms, an optimum number of bedrooms and so on. Be clear who your target market is and provide exactly what is needed – not what *you* want.

HOW MUCH TO SPEND

Work out your budget

Before going to the estate agent with your detailed brief, you also need to work out a budget (see Checklist 2, page 265). In the heat of the moment you may be tempted to go above it, so it is very important to know exactly how much you have to play with, particularly since some estate agents are very good at tempting you along to see something slightly out of your range. A way to avoid this is, of course, to give them a slightly lower budget than you really have. It is important to be realistic about what you can and cannot afford to avoid overstretching yourself.

Mortgage

If you need to borrow money to buy the property, you should fix up a mortgage in principle before beginning your search for a property so you know how much you can borrow. The various types of mortgage and the way to get them are explained in Chapter 3 About Mortgages. Work out how much you can afford to borrow by looking at your monthly income and expenditure. Is the difference enough to cover the repayment costs? If not, you will need to look at ways of cutting down on other things in order to cover the payments.

Deposit

When the time comes, you will need a certain amount of capital (usually between 5% and 10% of the purchase price) available when the contracts are exchanged.

Extra costs

Remember, you will inevitably incur a number of additional costs over and above the cost of the property itself. You will have to pay the cost of the survey, your solicitor's fees, the cost of the local searches, stamp duty, a valuation fee for the mortgage lender and the set-up costs of the mortgage. There will also be the cost of the move itself. You will be paying a removal company, and possibly for telephone, electricity or gas connections. You may want to reserve a contingency sum in case anything goes wrong, or for decorating and buying new furniture.

Restoration/renovation

If you are planning on buying somewhere that will need renovation or any kind of building work, make sure you get all estimates for any work involved *before* contracts are exchanged.

Independent Financial Adviser (IFA)

If you are buying a property for investment then it may be wise to talk to an independent financial adviser who will be able to guide you through issues concerning mortgages and tax.

WHEN TO LOOK

If you are moving a long distance and your move is governed by your career or by school terms, then you will have little or no choice about timing. However, for those looking for a different house within roughly the same area or those without such stringent ties, there is the freedom to look at the property market, see what it is doing and judge whether it is the right time or not.

The busiest times for the property market tend to be spring, when people are coming out of their winter hibernation and looking for a new start, and autumn, when their energy levels are renewed from summer holidays, along with their resolve to find a new home before Christmas. Although it may be worth looking for a place in the off-peak seasons, you may find that sellers hold back their property until they can be sure of a clutch of potential buyers. In recent years, a property boom has affected most parts of the country, with prices rising from month to month and doom merchants predicting a slump at any time. Buying in a boom is not ideal, simply because prices are inflated and the value of your property may drop or at best remain the same when the market changes. There is also the danger of running into negative equity (ie when you have a large mortgage and prices drop so far that the property is effectively worth less than the amount you borrowed). The ideal time to buy is when the market is depressed or just going up. All that said, buying property is always a gamble, since it is impossible to predict surely the way the market will go. The only thing to do is to take the best advice you can, read the financial and property pages, do your research carefully and plunge in.

WHERE TO LOOK

The scatter-gun effect of looking all over a wide area rarely pays off. It is far better to focus on a couple of districts that you like most or that you think will be most suitable and concentrate your search within them. That way you will develop a knowledge of a particular area, the types of property to be found there and of the comparative prices they are fetching. It will give you a chance to find out the advantages and disadvantages to living there, getting to know it at different times of the day and night. Even moving a few streets away can be like moving to another country. If you do the groundwork, you will have more chance of finding the right property at the right price.

The internet can provide you with a certain amount of hard information on an area and the activities of its local council, the performance of local schools, etc, but there is nothing like walking round and exploring for yourself to get the feel of the place. Buy the local newspapers to see what is going on in the area, get a sense of how friendly and safe it feels and what resources it provides.

If you are moving from one town to another, or thinking of abandoning the rat-race for the peace and quiet of the countryside, it is well worth renting for six months or a year to begin with. This will enable you to get the feel of your new surroundings. It will buy you time to see whether or not you like the place. If your move is not connected with the demands of your work, you will have a chance to see whether or not this new way of life is for you. It is easier to give up rented accommodation and move back home or on to somewhere else than it is to sell another property.

Estate agents

Most people's first port of call for buying property is still the high street estate agents. If you are already in the area in which you want to buy, or know it well, you will probably know the local estate agents' offices. If you are moving to somewhere unfamiliar, the National Association of Estate Agents (NAEA) will be able to put you in touch with member agents in the area in which you are interested. Alternatively, look in the national and local papers to see which local agents advertise there or browse the internet.

As in all professions, there are good estate agents and bad ones. A good one will help you find the right property as quickly as possible. They will fix up a number of viewings together and will take notice of your requirements. They will act as a liaison point between you and the vendor. But how do you know the difference between a reputable one and a fly-by-night? Membership of the NAEA binds estate agents to a vigorously enforced Code of Practice and insists they adhere to professional Rules of Conduct. This does not guarantee you will not be ripped off, but it at least gives you some comeback. Further protection is offered by their membership of the Ombudsman for Estate Agents (OEA). It is worth visiting several agents to judge who you feel might have the right sort of property for you and whom you can trust. There is no charge, so use as many as you can manage.

However, the agent is taken on by the vendor to sell his property in return for a commission that is a percentage of the sale price. It is important that you remember that he is working for them and not 'for you. He is obliged to answer your questions truthfully but he does not have to inform you of any problems connected with the property. Those are for you and your solicitor to find out. When dealing with an agent, you do not want to be inundated with details of properties that are of no interest to you, so it is important that you do your homework and be 100% clear about the location and type of property you are looking for and your budget. If they take you to somewhere you do not like, say so and explain why so that it is less likely to happen again. Do not be browbeaten into going to view properties that you know you cannot afford or that are in areas in which you know you do not want to live. Agents' memories can be short, so they may need regularly reminding that you are still looking for somewhere. It is not enough to wait for the latest particulars to drop through your door, particularly during a property boom when the market is extremely fast-moving. You will want to be told of a suitable property the moment it comes on the market, not five or ten days later when two people are already considering making offers. Befriend the agents you are using and gently badger them until you are top of their phone list.

A good estate agent should:
- ➤ Introduce serious potential purchasers
- ➤ Keep you informed on his progress
- ➤ Guide you through the negotiation of the offer

➤ Act as the liaison point for both parties
➤ Help through the selling process to completion
➤ Assist with the handover of keys

In the wake of the recent property boom, some estate agents have resorted to various unorthodox tactics to attract buyers and hike up prices. This goes further than stories of removing one another's 'For Sale' boards at dead of night or erecting 'Sold' boards outside properties not on the market to attract other potential vendors. At the time of writing, the Office of Fair Trading is investigating various allegations made against agents. These include encouragement of publishing inaccurate details, gazumping, charging exorbitant fees, inventing non-existent bidders to force up the price and forcing buyers to take in-house mortgages. Although the government proposed sellers' packs to make the vendor commission a basic survey and prepare some of the legal work before the property is put on the market, the legislation has not yet gone through. *Caveat Emptor* – buyer beware.

Property shops

In Scotland and some parts of England, there are property shops that are frequently (almost always in Scotland) run by solicitors. They display details of the houses and flats on offer and a potential buyer can make an appointment directly with the vendor to view and subsequently negotiate. An advantage of this is that, if run by solicitors, they will often offer a conveyancing package as part of the deal.

Internet

There are hundreds of websites that claim to sell homes in the UK. Some belong to individual estate agencies, while others use groups of agents to organise properties by area, period, price or size of home. The advantage of some of the better sites is that they often provide a virtual tour of the property, meaning you would see more of the rooms than you would on a standard estate agent's sheet. They often offer floor plans that are helpful in assessing the flow and size of the property. Some of the sites are first-rate and others appalling. The only way to find out which is which is by trial and error, and word of mouth. It is worth looking to see if they provide an address and phone number so you will have some means of recourse if things go wrong.

Private sales

It is always worth looking in the local and national property pages for private sales. Many people prefer to sell their home this way because they will not have to pay an estate agent's commission. However, they are an unknown quantity so when visiting their home, it is advisable to take someone with you. If you are desperately keen to live in a particular street, or even in a specific house, try writing to the owner, informing them of your interest in the property should it ever come on the market. Occasionally it pays off and the letter arrives in time to tip the balance just as the owner is considering whether to sell.

Search agencies

If you are moving from one part of the country to another and are thwarted by the logistics of finding a new home so far away, or are too busy to conduct a thorough search in your home town, it may be more convenient to use a property finding service. The Association of Relocation Agents will provide a list of suitable firms in the right area. They will view properties on your behalf, following your detailed brief, negotiate the purchase price, organise surveys, oversee the conveyancing and generally make sure the purchase goes without a hitch. They will charge a registration fee that may be refundable in the event of a purchase and a fixed percentage, usually between $1^1/_2$% and 2% of the purchase price, to be paid at exchange of contracts. The point to remember is that, unlike an estate agent, they are working for you and it is in their interests to find a property that meets as many of your criteria as possible.

Auctions

Properties sold at auction are frequently repossessions from a mortgage company or bank. They may also be unusual properties that are difficult to value on the open market, or alternatively they may have been inherited by beneficiaries who want to be sure that the property has been sold fairly for the best possible price. Occasionally, you may find there is a problem with the property that has made it difficult to sell by private treaty. The problem might be structural, or to do with its location, or it may have a sitting tenant. Auctions are also a way of selling property quickly, since once the bid is accepted, the deal is legally binding. These are generally advertised in the press or you might notice a sign outside the property. Visit some auctions to see how they work. If you decide to buy the property, you must have everything in place before the hammer falls (see Chapter 2 Buying Your Property for further information on buying at auction).

Right to buy

If you are a secure tenant of a council registered landlord and have lived in the property for more than two years, you are probably eligible to buy it at a considerable discount. You can either buy it outright or buy it to rent on mortgage terms. If you buy, the discount on a flat will be between 44% and 70% of its value on the open market. The discount on a house is between 32% and 60%. If you move within three years after the purchase the discount must be repaid.

Buying to rent on mortgage terms entails the payment of an initial sum, which will be less than the right-to-buy price. A mortgage company will lend this, charging repayments that are no more than the current rent you pay. If you sell within the first year, the discount must be repaid. If you sell in the second or third year, two thirds or one third of the discount must be paid respectively.

For full details of this scheme, read *Your Right to Buy and Other Help to Buy* published by the Department for Transport, Local Government and the Regions or see www.housing.odpm.gov.uk/order/rightbuy.

Housing associations

Another way of getting your foot on the first rung of the property ladder is to buy with an independent housing association. They work mostly with local authority tenants, but not necessarily exclusively. They operate various shared ownership schemes whereby a Housing Association builds a number of flats or houses and the buyer takes out a mortgage of between 25% and 75%, paying rent on the rest with the option to increase the amount they own whenever they can. They can also sell their share in the property before reaching full ownership. Contact your local authority to find out about schemes in the area.

Home swapping

Occasionally it is possible to exchange homes with someone. It may involve one party paying extra to make up the difference in value, but it could cut out any estate agent's fees if you have met through personal contacts or online. It also has the benefit of avoiding any chain, with both parties motivated to get on with the sale so they can have the other house. The snag is that it all depends on finding someone with the right property who wants to move at exactly the same time as you.

House swapping usually happens when one of the two parties is trading down or up, or when they are swapping location from town to country and vice versa. The parties often meet by coincidence, although there is no harm in advertising in local papers or online at www.webswappers.com. Although it should not be beyond the wit of most estate agents to recognise a likely pairing on their books, they rarely do. If you are trading down and receive a substantial cash payment of the difference in value of the properties, you are not liable to stamp duty – a worthwhile saving. Some of the major property developers will take your home in part-exchange for another. It is unlikely you will achieve the full value of your house by doing this, since they invariably take a discount.

Buying off-plan

Builder and developers are constantly at work on new schemes. Use all the usual methods to find them – estate agents, the internet, newspapers and property magazines, word of mouth. Most particularly, watch out for hoardings as you drive around. There is likely to be a show house that can be viewed. Make sure you understand which are standard features and which are optional extras. Do not assume everything you see is included in the asking price, and check exactly what is. Get as much background information as you can about the builder, asking about their reliability and the standard of their workmanship. If you have to rely on a floor plan for information, have the size of the rooms confirmed and study the specifications carefully so that you make the right decisions about the different finishes, fixtures and fittings on offer. It may be pos-sible to change the heating or cooking specifications if you have strong feelings about using gas or electricity. Make sure that everything you agree is confirmed in writing so there can be no misunderstanding.

FINDING THE RIGHT PROPERTY

It may be stating the obvious, but it is important that you visit a property before purchasing it, so that you can be sure it meets all your requirements and that you are aware of any defects. The estate agent may take you round it, or will make an appointment for you with the owner. If you know immediately that it is not for you, leave as quickly as you can without wasting any more of anyone's time, and clearly explain your reasons to the agent so he does not waste any more of yours.

The first viewing

Once you have seen a number of houses, they tend to blend into one another and important features may get forgotten. To avoid this happening, take a notebook with you or even a Polaroid camera to record the good and bad points and to jog your memory later. It is important to view a good number of properties so that you get an idea of the sort of things available and of their comparative prices. Use Checklist 3 on page 266.

Make sure you know what exactly is included in the purchase price. Will you be expected to pay extra for additional land or outbuildings? Are any of the furniture or the carpets and curtains included in the sale?

Do not be distracted by the décor. Try to ignore the owner's possessions and focus on the space itself. Look at the size of the rooms and the amount of natural light they receive. If you are having trouble getting a sense of the space, lie on the floor and look upwards. It is surprising how much it helps. Visualise your own possessions in place and imagine how you might feel living there. Take into account the cost of redecoration.

Look at the layout of the house. Could it be improved to meet your needs? Can the function of some rooms be changed to suit your lifestyle? For example a small bedroom could become a bathroom, a study or a gym. Knocking down an internal wall can transform some houses, lending them considerable extra space and light. Would an extension make the difference to any downstairs living space? Alternatively, is there scope for a loft extension or converting a cellar? Make a note of any improvements you think might be made. Unless your pockets are very deep, you will need to get an estimate for any work before making an offer.

Do not be taken in by the homely atmosphere provided by the smell of coffee, scented candles, the sound of music or an outdoor water feature. Are they disguising the smell of damp, the sound of the neighbours' motorbike revving or the children next door? It may not come naturally to you but it pays to be suspicious. Do not take anything at face value.

The kitchen and bathroom are the two rooms that can cause problems. If they need replacing, the additional outlay can be prohibitive if your budget is tight. You will need to add this into your calculations, bearing in mind the disruption of having them replaced when you move in.

Is there any storage space? It is useful to know whether or not you will easily be able to hide away your clothes, kitchen utensils, sports equipment and so on. Do not be embarrassed to have a good poke around – open cupboards and drawers, checking they work properly.

Look very carefully at the general condition of the house. If it appears uncared for, with rooms undecorated and DIY jobs unfinished, it is quite possible that the owner has not paid enough attention to the more major aspects of its upkeep. If you can, lift up the floor coverings to see if they are hiding any horrors, or even better a fabulous old wood or tiled floor.

Look at the windows, check they open and shut properly and show no signs of rot. Is there double glazing? Similarly check whether the doors fit properly and are properly secure. Note any cracks in the walls. They may just be superficial cracks in the plasterwork or something more serious (see Cracks in Walls on page 193).

How is the house heated? Installing central heating might be a huge expense on top of the purchase. Make a note of any signs of damp so that you remember to check them out if you return for a second viewing (see Damp – Does It Matter? on page 234).

Once you are happy that you have had a thorough look at the inside of the house, step outside and take stock of what you see. If there is a garden, be realistic about the amount of time you will have to tend it. If there is a garage, measure it to make sure that your car will fit and check whether or not there are any power points. What other parking provision is there, if any?

There are a number of things it is worth trying to establish with the owner, either directly or through the estate agent. It may be useful to know why they are selling. They are unlikely to admit that it is because of the neighbours from hell or the smell of the pigsty over the fence that wafts through the house whenever the wind blows from the west. These are things that you must find out, but the owners may have a reason for moving that is relevant to your purchase. Find out how long the house has been on the market and if there have been any offers that have fallen through. If so, ask why. The answers may strengthen your position when you come to make an offer. It is important to know how soon the owners want to move and whether they are in a chain of house purchasers that may lead to the date slipping. It is possible that the owners may have got planning permission for work they have not carried out. It is likely they will volunteer the information, so ask to see the plans. You may want to do the work yourself or reapply with changes.

If a house meets most but not all the criteria you have listed, consider whether it makes up for it in other ways. Few people end up buying a house like the one of which they had dreamed in the first place. If you are buying during a boom in the property market, to stand a chance of buying the property at all you may have to move quickly and skip any second viewing before you make an offer. In that case you must be vastly more thorough in your one and only visit, taking into account the things that, in an ideal world, you would check in a second viewing before making a final decision.

The second viewing

Once you have seen a number of houses and weighed up the various pros and cons, it is time to make a shortlist of favourites and return to look at them again, this time with a cold objective eye, making sure that you have covered all the above points thoroughly and looking in more detail at others. Often, going back for a second time you will find something that went unnoticed before. If buying alone, it is often wise to take along a friend you can rely on to be completely objective and to raise any problems you are trying to ignore. It is also wise to return at a different time of the day and week. This will enable you to see whether or not it is affected by rush hour traffic, passing trains, parking problems or planes flying directly overhead. It will also let you see how the light changes within the house and garden at different times of the day. If near a public venue such as a pub, a football club or a college you would be well advised to return during an appropriate time to see if the noise level will affect you.

This time, double check that the accommodation is really what you want. Is there room for all your belongings? For instance, if you have a bike, is the only place to house it the narrow hall? Will you have to lug your buggy up any stairs to the front door? Take a tape measure and make sure that your king-size bed, dining table, chest freezer or large chesterfield sofa will fit the intended rooms. If there is no dining room, where are you going to eat? Are the bedrooms really large enough? Are you going to be able to live with the views from all the windows? How overlooked are they by neighbours? How well soundproofed are the rooms? Can you hear any of the neighbours? The direction the property faces is a key factor in determining how much sunlight enters the rooms at which time of day.

Examine the lighting, heating and other services. An old house may need to be rewired or have a decent heating system installed. Does any existing heating work properly? Ask if it can be turned on so that you can feel the radiators. Ask about the vendor's annual heating costs. Is the attic space insulated? Establish where the water tank and boiler are. Are they in good condition or will they need replacing? Find out about the water supply and related charges. It is useful to know where the power points are located, whether you will need more, and which rooms have television, cable or phone sockets. Urban houses will all be connected to the main drains but in the country you may need to find out if there is a septic tank or cess pit.

Keep a sharp eye out for signs of damp, especially around windows, under the roof or along the basement or ground floor walls. Are there any cracks that look significant?

Were your ideas for renovation on the first visit completely mad? Take another close look at the possibilities and their pros and cons. Ask an architect or builder to visit it with you to give their professional opinion and an estimate for the work involved.

Go into the garden to see how overlooked it is and how easy to main-tain. Ask whether or not there are any rights of access through it and, if there are shared facilities such as gardens, walls, drives, roofs or garages, find out who is responsible for their upkeep. Check the state of any boundary walls or fences. If the boundaries to the property are not clear, ascertain where exactly they are and whether there has been any prob-lem with the neighbours over acknowledging them. Your solicitor will check these aspects out later, but having the information at this stage may be useful. How much sun does it get? Is it safe for children?

Look at the brickwork of the house to see, among other things, whether or not it has been recently repointed and, if not, whether it needs it. Look round the base of the house to see if there is evidence of a damp-proof course, and if there are air bricks ventilating any closed-up chimney breasts or under-floor areas. Are any of the walls bowing at all? Watch out for cracks in the brickwork that may suggest subsidence or be causing damp inside. Look at the roof for slipped slates, damage to the flashings and the condition of the chimneys. Check the drainpipes, guttering and the wall behind or below them for signs of leaking. Look at the window frames to see what sort of condition they are in and whether they fit properly. Does the exterior need painting or re-rendering? If it has just been painted, make sure as far as you can that it is not because anything is being hidden. If recent work has been done on the house, ask to see any relevant guarantees or warranties. If there is an extension or loft conversion ask to see the planning permission. (If they did not apply for it when necessary, you should ask that they reapply retrospectively as a condition of the contract.)

If there is a garage, make doubly sure your car will fit, that it is easily accessible and is properly secure. If there is not, look at the alternatives, which may involve the additional cost of residential parking, meters and an increased insurance premium. If you do not have a car, a garage could be used for another purpose, such as a playroom, studio or study.

If the property is near a river, ascertain what risks there are of flooding. Check when the last flood occurred and what, if any, damage was caused. If near the sea, look into any fears of coastal erosion.

Once you have assessed the house and its immediate surroundings, it is time to look at the neighbourhood. The condition of the neighbouring properties will give you a clue as to how hard it might be to sell your property at a later date. Confirm how near the house is to local amenities that may be important to you, whether shops, schools, hospitals or leisure facilities. Is the area well serviced by public transport, and how close does it come to the property? Try to find out about the neighbourhood in general, also assessing if it has a high crime rate. Ask whether there are any developments planned in the area. If there is a wide open space opposite the house, you will not be happy if you move in and discover a block of flats going up right in the middle of your view. Do not be embarrassed to knock on the neighbours' doors to introduce yourself and ask any pertinent questions. If you look around to see signs of loft, back or side extensions, then you are likely to get planning permission for something similar. It is always much harder to be the first in the street to get permission. In the country, a local pub may be the ideal source for information about the place, people who live there and any difficulties householders may have had with planning permission, flooding and so on.

Make copious notes, using Checklists 3 and 4 on pages 266 and 272, and take photographs so that you can go home and make an informed decision as to whether the property is the one for you. Do not let your heart rule your head.

BUYING A FLAT

If you are buying a flat, almost all of the above applies. However, there are a number of different considerations also to be borne in mind. Firstly, you need to know whether the flat is shared freehold or leasehold and, if the latter, who the freeholder is. Establish what the ground rent and service charges are and what the latter covers. It would be useful to know if a sinking fund exists to cover any major repairs or expenditure, and if not, you should bear in mind that you may be asked for an unbudgeted large payment for such things as repair work on the roof, redecoration of the common parts or the exterior.

Remember to look closely at the common parts, including any shared outside space, to see how well they are looked after and ask whose responsibility it is to keep them in good order. You will also want to know what rights you have to use them. If there is a lift, find out from neighbours or the owner how reliable it is. Talking of neighbours – check out the soundproofing between flats above below and beside yours. You should also ask about the arrangements for rubbish disposal and cleaning windows, particularly if your flat is high up the building.

DONALD BAILEY, ABERDEEN

Wanted: 'A traditional property with period features, with at least two bedrooms so I can possibly rent one to my brother, a student at the university. I think I'll be able to do a reasonable job renovating a property. I'm certainly always on the lookout for a bargain and if I can make a bit of money on the property as well, I'd be very happy. My budget is around £135,000.'

Being a shrewd investor with an eye for potential is one thing, but finding investment potential, space for a lodger and a chance to dabble in DIY in the most desirable part of the city was a tall order. However, company executive Donald Bailey had decided to leave the bright lights of London and move to the west end of Aberdeen, where he rented with a couple of friends. He was determined to find himself a new home that met those requirements.

> TIP: Renting is a good way to up your buying power. Work out the initial costs to make sure they will be covered by the rental income. It is worth investing in quality fittings that will last. Inform your mortgage lender and the tax man about the arrangements.

Aberdeen is on the north-east coast of Scotland between the mouths of the rivers Don and Dee. Once famous for the clippers that sailed to India in the nineteenth century, its prosperity was revived in the 1970s when offshore oil was discovered and the city became the oil capital of the north. Since then, house prices have reflected the success of the oil industry year by year. There is a wide range on offer, from fishermen's cottages in old Aberdeen to grand west-end properties (many of which were designed by royal architect John Smith around the time Prince Albert asked him to design Balmoral). The thing they have in common is that they are all built of granite. The distinctive grey stones give the city a silvery sheen on a sunny day, but can seem gloomy on a cloudy one.

TIP: The Scottish system for buying property is quite different from that in the rest of the UK. (See pages 57 and 172)

The first property Donald saw was in tree-lined Whitehall Place, a four-bedroom house on the market at offers over £117,000. Extremely spacious, if a bit dated, the property seemed something of a bargain. Though it was hard to see beyond the furniture and décor, there was scope for improvement and the potential for more than one lodger if need be. 'The house itself has got certain things that put me off in terms of the room size and décor. A whole house is a bit too "housey" for me. Not really the kind of swanky bachelor pad I'm looking for.'

Ten minutes south of the city centre is the popular area of Ferryhill, and a church that had been converted into thirteen flats. One on the ground floor was for sale at offers over £95,000. It had two large bedrooms and two bathrooms, one *en suite*, but the interior bore absolutely no reference to the fact that it was in a church. It might have been possible to remove a stud wall to expose the original wall, however. A telephone call to the council revealed that although they did not know what was behind the plasterwork, they would encourage any owners to restore the features of the church.

> TIP: **When thinking of making changes, phone the planning office, especially with unusual or historic properties that may have hidden restrictions.**

Property three was in Hamilton Terrace in the city's west end, and packed with the period features Donald is so keen on. An end-of-terrace flat, it had two huge bedrooms and a garden, with offers over £115,000. The living room had high ceilings and was typically well proportioned, but the bathroom was comparatively small. The main bedroom was much bigger than the second with an elegant bay window. All the woodwork had been painted but Donald could have it stripped back to the natural wood for a more authentic look. 'It's really the sort of thing I'm looking for. My only concern is the size of the bathroom, especially if I am going to have a lodger.'

Then it was back to Ferryhill, to a much grander property in Braemar Place. A four-bedroom house with a couple of reception rooms, a new kitchen and bathroom and shared garden was on the market at offers over £135,000.

> TIP: **If a property includes a communal garden, meet the neighbours before buying and make sure you are on the same wavelength about the sort of use you will have. Check with your solicitor about access. There are horror stories about people who buy gardens and cannot get to them.**

There was also potential for adding a second bathroom for a lodger that would increase the property's value. 'I really like it. It's been done out very nicely but it's a different prospect from the other two-bedroom flats that we've seen. Since it is at the top end of my budget, it does make me feel slightly uncomfortable.'

A cheaper alternative was found further down the same road. This flat had its own front door, four bedrooms and loads of potential. Offers were asked for over £86,000. The kitchen badly needed updating, although the old-fashioned double Belfast sink was a bonus. Similarly, the bathroom basin was a period piece but the rest of the room needed a makeover, including removal of the panelling round the freestanding bath. It would be a big job to get the place up to scratch, and what Donald might save in the purchase price would be lost in the cost of time and effort involved.

The final property he saw was in Stanley Street – a large ground-floor flat with two bedrooms, a sunny hall and a large living room with high ceilings and bay windows, at offers over £98,000. The contemporary blue-and-white kitchen was a strong selling point too. Slightly concerned about the size of the second bedroom, Donald was delighted to discover there was an unconverted basement the same size as the flat itself. The ceiling height was low but there was a lot of space that could be connected to the flat above by a spiral staircase. 'There's a good feeling about this place. It's done out very nicely, it's a good location, it's got a garden and the extra space in the basement does make up for my other worry. With the price, I should have enough left over to do any renovation.'

> **TIP:** Good presentation should not swing a sale. Keep a cool head when assessing a property.

His final decision came down to Hamilton Place or Stanley Street. Taking his brother Kenneth for support, Donald revisited Stanley

Street with a quantity surveyor. The verdict on the basement was that the floor would have to be lowered which might possibly uncover a damp problem. If all went well, the initial cost would be around £18,000. If it was found that the foundations were not deep enough then another £6,000 would be needed to underpin the house. But the work would add around £50,000 to the value. Returning to Hamilton Place, Donald was reminded of its larger rooms and the option of installing a second bathroom in the master bedroom, the cost of which should be covered by any subsequent rental income.

Ultimately, Donald decided to put in a note of interest on Stanley Street, had it surveyed to his satisfaction, then put in his offer. Sadly, a number of other people realised the opportunity it presented and he lost out to someone else. There is always a risk that some properties will appeal across the board and competition will be fierce, but he was not disheartened and returned to his hunt for a shrewd investment.

RELOCATING TO A NEW CITY

Moving to a new city can be problematic if you do not know it well and do not have the time to visit it and explore the different areas, getting a feel for which would be most suitable for you.

In the first instance, it might be worth putting your furniture in storage and renting a property while you find your bearings. This will give you a chance to find out which parts of the city are within easy commuting distance from your work, where the good schools are, and where the quieter, busy, fashionable or up-and-coming areas are so you make an informed choice about your move.

If you want to buy immediately, contact local estate agents, look on the internet or use a home search agency. The latter will do the initial legwork for you, visiting the place with your explicit brief in mind and weeding through likely properties so that you can visit for a short time and see them all. It cuts out weeks of traipsing up and down motorways, despairing of ever finding the right place.

Research about an unfamiliar town can easily be done on the internet. Check out the relevant council site to get a sense of the area, looking at their plans and priorities. Investigate the area through sites such as www.upmystreet.com, which is packed with information on everything from schools to shops, council tax to crime rates and the others listed on page 281. Look up school league tables and Ofsted school reports from the comfort of your home.

Use local surveyors to look at the property. They will be familiar with the lie of the land and know of any problems particular to the area that they might have to cover. There is no substitute for hands-on experience.

JEFF AND CARINE HEENAN-JALIL, BATH

Wanted: 'Four bedrooms and two bathrooms. Something that's big on the inside, light and airy with high ceilings and maybe some open-plan living and with good indoor/outdoor flow. The other thing we want is to be close to the city. All of this for £300,000.'

It is a long way from Australia to Bath, but Jeff Heenan-Jalil, a telecoms executive, and his wife Carina, a lawyer and now a full-time mother, had upped sticks from the Antipodes and decided to make it their home. Bath is famous for its hot springs, Roman baths and elegant Georgian stone crescents. Its status as a World Heritage Site has meant that few new homes have been built. The advantage of this is that most of the properties available are both original and attractive, but the disadvantage is lack of supply and consequent high prices.

Jeff and Carina had clear ideas about the sort of home they wanted to find for themselves and their two children. The first house they looked at was in Weston, a popular area five minutes drive from the city centre, where a three-bedroom Regency house was on the market for £275,000. The house was on three floors and retained many original features such as the cupboards, cornicing and fireplaces. However,

Jeff and Carina were not impressed by the period details or the size of the rooms, particularly the kitchen. They moved swiftly on to the next property.

> **TIP: If you do not like original features, remember they are adding to the price of the property. Ask yourself whether it is worth paying that bit extra or not.**

From the façade, the Victorian terraced house in Berkeley Place looked as if it was only on two floors. In fact, two more floors descended the hill at the back of the house. A Grade II listed building, it was priced at £298,000. Again, Carina found it hard to see the potential: 'It doesn't have that "wow" factor.' While the garden and views were spectacular, the house itself was spoilt by uPVC windows, a dated kitchen and unimpressive décor. Jeff agreed. 'I can't get over the internal decoration, it just hits me straight in the face.'

Not far away in Upper Camden Place stood another period townhouse with four reception rooms and an asking price of £340,000. Although over budget, it was worth seeing to try to define more clearly what they wanted in a house. Below the grand upper floors was a big open-plan living room/kitchen. Original wood floors and a country kitchen complete with Aga and open shelving did not convince the couple the house was for them. They appreciated the size but were not impressed by the style. Beyond the kitchen was a study/playroom that had been dug under the garden, tanked and sealed, adding extra space. On the first floor was an extremely spacious living room with a bathroom leading off it – potential for an *en suite* bedroom. The icing on the cake had to be the panoramic views of Bath that must have added between £10,000 and 20,000 to the price of the house, but Jeff was not impressed. 'I must admit, it's nothing that's going to say, "Pick me, pick me".' That plus the steep steps up to the house and the lack of easy parking finally decided them against it.

> **TIP: Lie on the floor of a room to get an idea of the space without the existing furniture.**

Although their friends may have advised them to buy Georgian, the style did not seem to be grabbing Jeff and Carina, so the next house they saw was a good-sized detached four-bedroom modern home with its own garage, being sold for £298,000. The quiet neighbourhood in north Bath would be ideal for bringing up children and the house offered plenty of space and a large kitchen where Jeff would be in his element. But the verdict? 'I think what it does to me is absolutely crystallise the fact that we want period.'

On then to Thomas Street in the city itself, where a four-bedroom Georgian townhouse was for sale at £275,000. An imposing entry led into a stone-flagged hallway with a stone staircase that ran the height of the house. The two reception rooms on the ground floor could be knocked through for open-plan living and by updating the basement kitchen, the house would increase in value. 'It's got a nice feel even though it's dated. But it's something we could stamp our own identity on.' The master bedroom impressed with its proportions, the sunlight adding to its feeling of airiness and spaciousness. The snag was that the only bathroom existed at the very top of the house. If they were interested, a way would have to be found of incorporating another bathroom or shower room. Again, the perennial Bath parking problem existed.

Finally, they went fifteen minutes out of the city to look at a renovated sixteenth-century barn. At £320,000 it was in negotiating range and required no work. Boasting original wooden beams, exposed internal stonework, good-sized rooms, plenty of free-flowing space and a rustic-style kitchen, the house had a lot to offer.

> **TIP: Find out whether wooden beams have been treated for beetle attack and ask for guarantees/certificates for that and any electrical or plumbing work.**

Jeff was particularly taken by the kitchen range: 'sex on wheels'. Carina would have liked more windows in the bedroom, and in the south-east facing courtyard and shared parking area, it was unclear who had rights to park where, and a van could completely block the light to their ground floor windows.

> **TIP: If there is a shared parking area, check what rights you have over the plot.**

Jeff and Carina decided to return to Thomas Street for a second look. 'When I first walked in there, it was the ideal home for me,' said Jeff. 'It met probably 80% of our requirements. It's got the location, the four bedrooms, wonderful kitchen space and living on two floors.' Looking at the wall that separated the two living rooms, they would have to check with the relevant authorities before any work could be carried out in this Grade II listed building. Whatever changes are made, the original use of the room must still be visible so it was likely that only part, not all, of the wall could go. The question of the bathroom could be solved by converting the bedroom beneath the existing bathroom, or by using the space by the basement toilet to install a shower. Finally, they looked into the access to the back of the property and realised they would need a solicitor to check their rights of way across some common land to their back gate. Encouraged by the signs of it being in an up-and-coming area, they decided to make an offer of £235,000, bearing in mind they would need to budget an additional £25,000 for a new kitchen floor, second bathroom and general decoration. Their offer was rejected, and as they raised their offer nearer the asking price, the vendor took the property off the market. So the disappointed family had to begin their search again from square one.

TIP: Under English law, until contracts are exchanged, the vendor can walk away from the deal at any time.

REDUCING THE RISK WHEN BUYING A PROPERTY

Make the task of finding the right property easier, and reduce the risks of making one of the most expensive mistakes of your life by working out what you really want before you start.

> **Budget**. Have the house you are selling valued. Arrange a mortgage in principal for a new property. Assess your monthly income and expenses to check you can afford the repayments. Factor in legal fees, the cost of a survey and stamp duty. Do not overstretch yourself.
> **Location**. Decide exactly in which area you want to live. Have a focus so that you can see what you can get for your budget in the place you want to be. If you are unable to find what you want within those limits, you may have to broaden your search later on.
> **Local amenities**. List those that you want to be easily accessible from your property. You may want good local transport links with your office, or you may want to be in easy reach of a gym or leisure centre. How important is it for you to be near the shops, a school, hospital or doctor's surgery? List them in order of importance.

➤ **The property**. Prioritise what is important to you. Town or country; house or flat; period or modern; number of bedrooms; number of bathrooms; any special requirements such as a home office, a pool, a billiards room, space for the grand piano; an additional room/flat to let; garage; garden. Work out what is essential and where you would be prepared to compromise.

➤ **Estate agent**. Do not rely on seeing their lists. Go in and talk to them so that they understand exactly what it is you are after. Cajole them into putting you at the top of their telephone list so that you are called the moment anything suitable comes on the market. If you do not like a property, try and explain why so that they do not make the same mistake again.

➤ **Viewing**. Take a notebook and camera to prevent the properties from getting confused in your mind. If you think you have found the right place, return to it more than once if need be to look at it more clinically. Ask someone with an objective eye to accompany you to help point out potential problems. Go back at different times of the day and week. If necessary, take a tape measure to check any bulky furniture will fit. If planning renovations, get estimates for the work before making an offer.

➤ **Ask the right questions**. Make sure you quiz the owner or estate agent about every aspect of the purchase, and make a note of their replies.

➤ **Survey**. A mortgage lender's valuation does not substitute either a Homebuyer's Survey or a full structural survey. Depending on the age and condition of the property, you can cover yourself with either of those. If the surveyor raises any problems, follow them up with the relevant professionals, getting quotes for any necessary work before you make an offer or exchange contracts.

STEVE AND HELEN BROCKINGTON, CARDIFF

Wanted: 'The perfect house is semi-rural with somewhere to park the car. Somewhere where you lock the gate on the world, as opposed to the front door, with nice big rooms and lots of light coming in. We're looking at a budget of £96,000.'

Childhood sweethearts Steve and Helen Brockington, who both work for CHSS Health & Safety, were looking for their first married home. They hoped to move in after their marriage in eight weeks, so time was of the essence. They were keen to move from their present home, away from the roar of traffic past their front door, to a quieter part of Cardiff. As Europe's fastest growing city, Cardiff has experienced huge recent investment in redevelopment and new building, with Cardiff Bay bringing new jobs and waterfront living.

Their search started in Whitchurch, four miles north of the city centre, where a busy, village-like atmosphere gives way to quiet, leafy side-streets. The first property was a two-bedroom Victorian terrace house in Old Church Road with a price tag of £95,950. The ground floor boasted various period features and had been opened up to be light and comfortable. The builder who had owned the house for nine years had gradually done it up, and the quality of the workmanship was first rate throughout, although the unusual extension was unfinished.

> **TIP: If attention has been paid to small details, it is possible that the owner has skimped on the more major items.**

Though the owner assured them that the work would be completed before the sale went through, any buyer would be advised to ask his solicitor to draw up a specification of works, detailing the work to be done. A hidden staircase led the way to an attic room with dormer windows that offered bags of potential as a spare room or office. The garden was on the small side, thanks to a large shed that offered considerable storage space. 'It's right up to the maximum we can spend so we'd have to live with everything that's here.'

> **TIP: A 'Specification of Works' should be drawn up by your solicitor to provide a list of the work to be done before completion.**

Closer to the city is the up-and-coming area of Canton, where what were originally basic houses for dock workers have been converted into desirable homes. As an investment, a terraced house on Severn Road needed lots of work, but at £90,000, presented a golden opportunity. The house was structurally sound though it needed rewiring, new windows, and a new kitchen and upstairs bathroom. An estimate for the work came in at £8,000 plus VAT. The concrete roof tiles seemed to be too heavy for the joists, so the ceiling showed ominous signs of leaking. There was lots of space and potential, but Steve and Helen were apprehensive about the amount of work necessary.

Across Cardiff Bay is the Victorian seaside town of Penarth, recently woken up by the arrival of a new marina and stylish £350,000-plus waterfront houses. Upper Cliff Drive offered a slightly older three-bedroom property for £95,000. The spacious double-aspect living room shared a hatch with the 'classic' melamine kitchen. It would be possible to make it bigger so that a breakfast bar/work surface could be installed. Although there was a garage, it did not make Steve's eyes light up. 'I don't see it as a buying point. I would never go out and look for a place like this but now I'm in it, it's fresh and quiet.' The sense of light and space made up for the unprepossessing exterior. They were both surprised by how much they liked it, but in the end thought it might be a bit too quiet for them.

One of their favourite areas was Dinas Powys, six miles from Cardiff centre with a rural atmosphere that makes prices high and property scarce. In Chamberlain Row, a three-bedroom Victorian end-of-terrace house had an asking price of £92,500. A large garden, bright kitchen and dining room had them excited until they noticed the bad cracks in the exterior brickwork, possibly caused by the frequent trains running close by. Considering the time it would take to get the opinion of a structural engineer and the amount of work that might be involved, the house was no longer a contender.

Back in Penarth, a three-bedroom terraced house near the seaside was made affordable by the flats that blocked the view of the bay. At £95,000, it was a real possibility. All the rooms felt light and airy, decorated in brilliant colours and stylishly presented. Helen was impressed, but Steve had his heart set firmly on the first house they had seen.

> **TIP: Always see a property for a second time, and analyse it clearly so that you can make a balanced decision.**

They returned to Whitchurch for a second viewing during the morning rush hour to discover that the road had become much busier. Only

Steve could manage to put a positive spin on that. 'We're used to having a traffic jam outside our house at this time in the morning as opposed to traffic filtering through.' He was still reacting emotionally to the house, but the second viewing is about coming back to analyse things that may have concerned you before, and making a balanced decision. 'I have a very warm feeling inside. I feel at home here.' Helen was still concerned that the garden was too small, although removing the shed would add an extra ten feet (3m). A larger garden would most likely be an additional selling point when the house came up for resale in years to come. It is often worth phoning around to see what prices other properties in the area have fetched. In this instance, research showed that this house was priced on the high side, but the information could be useful as a negotiating tool.

> **TIP: It is a worthwhile exercise to gauge the market before offering on a property. View a number and try to discover what similar properties in the area have fetched.**

Steve was reluctantly dragged back to Penarth, where they discovered that the flats obscuring the view of the bay were due for demolition. Even so, Steve was not to be won round. 'This place did something for me yesterday, but it's not doing it for me today. I'm still not getting anything out of this kitchen.' This time, Helen was less convinced, even seeing a carpet she did not like (matching one in their rented flat) as a bad sign. Together, they decided to offer on Old Church Road.

The asking price of £95,950 seemed steep. £92,000 would be fair, but a tactical opening bid would be £87,500. Steve and Helen were in a strong negotiating position, being chain-free, with their mortgage in place and able to exchange contracts quickly. As expected, their first offer was turned down so they revised it to £90,000 which was again refused. Finally they agreed to the vendor's suggested price, but he suddenly took the house off the market. Helen and Steve were dreadfully disappointed, and with the wedding so close it would be impossible to buy somewhere in time. Instead, they resolved to enjoy themselves and postpone their search until after their marriage when they would be able to start again with a clearer idea of the property they wanted to find.

CHOOSING PROPERTY AS AN INVESTMENT

Every property bought should represent a long-term investment. We all hope that when we come to sell our home, it will be worth more than when we bought it. Putting money into property is increasingly being seen as a real alternative to investing in the stock market. It is possible not only to increase your capital growth but also to achieve high returns in terms of rental income. Just how quick a turnaround you achieve depends on the state of the housing market and how shrewd, or just plain lucky, you have been.

Location

Be clear about whether capital return or regular income is your prime interest. It may well determine the area in which you look. For instance, areas favoured by students will bring regular income but the properties may expect less increase in their capital growth. However much you improve a property, there may be a ceiling on its value if it is poorly situated. A railway line, motorway, prison, factory or pub will all work against it. If a property does have a ceiling price, for whatever reason, either walk away or do not financially over-stretch yourself doing it up. Do not necessarily buy somewhere you would like to live yourself, and make sure it is well located with regard to transport links and local amenities. Try to find an up-and-coming area, where you can buy reasonably, fix it up and sell for a profit.

Condition

How much effort are you prepared to put in? If you buy a wreck that needs a lot of work, make sure you budget so that the expense of renovation does not wipe out any profit. When it comes to selling the place on, the better it looks the better you will do. But remember that it should not be done up according to your taste for ethnic interiors or retro chic. To appeal to the broadest sweep of buyers, kitchens should be modern, clean and functional, bathrooms pristine and, if possible, more than one of them if it is a large house. Keep colours light and neutral. Keep floor coverings neutral.

Buy to let

Over the last few years, this has been an area that has experienced extraordinary growth in both cities and less prosperous areas. Mortgage lenders have schemes that, thanks to low interest rates, have enabled many people to invest in this way. When buying a property to let, have a clear idea of what type of person your tenant will be so that you second guess all his needs and provide them. Student accommodation will be very different from that required by a young city broker. With that in mind you must pick the right area, find out from lettings agents the sort of requirements your future tenant will have in terms of decoration, fixtures, fittings and furnishings, then do up the property accordingly. Remember to take into account the amount of wear and tear likely to be inflicted on the property, and budget for repairs and redecoration.

See Chapter 7 Making Money From Your Property and Chapter 8 Letting Your Property.

2 BUYING YOUR PROPERTY

At last – you have found the property that fulfils most if not all of your dreams, your mortgage is in place and you are ready to move. It is time to make an offer. The system in Scotland is different to that in England, Wales and Northern Ireland, so if you are buying a property in Scotland, skip to the end of this chapter.

MAKING AN OFFER

If it is a private sale your offer should be made directly to the owner of the property, otherwise it should be to the estate agent who is acting on their behalf. When deciding how much to offer, remember the seller will be asking as much as he dares, given the conditions of the property market at the time. However, the estate agent should be able to give you an indication of whether he is open to negotiation and an idea of what he is realistically expecting. Before making your offer, there are a number of factors that will govern the amount with which you open.

The state of the market

If you are buying during a property boom, in all probability you will find yourself in a sellers' market with little room to manoeuvre. When there is stiff competition among buyers for available property, you may have to go in at the asking price or even higher if you are determined to beat off any competition immediately. If the market is steady or depressed, then you may be in a position to offer below the asking price.

Your budget

Do not overstretch yourself. However good the condition of the property is, leave yourself enough for the inevitable expenses that will occur when you move in.

Your position

Never forget to use any bargaining power you have to improve your position in competition with other buyers. If you have sold your previous home, are a first-time buyer or cash buyer, you are in a position to move with speed – always appealing to someone selling their house. The fact that you are not dependent on selling a property, or on a chain of buyers and sellers behind you, will put you ahead of the pack.

The seller's position

Before you offer, take into account how long the house has been on the market and how quickly the vendor wants to sell. If he is anxious to get things done quickly, you may be in a strong position if you can oblige. If the price has already been lowered, it may be an indication that they would accept a lower offer than the current asking price. Find out if there have been any other offers and why they have fallen through. Again, this may be information you might use to your advantage.

Your attitude

However desperate you feel, however much you have lost your heart to a property, on no account show it. You will be revealing a weakness that can be exploited by the seller or an unscrupulous estate agent to raise the price.

The offer

Assuming you are not in a competitive situation, an initial offer could reasonably be between 15% and 20% below the asking price. Make it clear that any offer is subject to contract and survey. You are not committed to anything until the contracts are eventually exchanged, after your solicitor, surveyor and mortgage company have made their checks and you have received any relevant estimates. You may want to ask for a 'lock-out' agreement. This means the property must be removed from the market for an agreed period while you get your paperwork in place. The estate agent will put your offer to the seller who may react in a number of ways. He may accept it. He may negotiate through the estate agent to reach a price that is mutually acceptable. He may reject it out of hand, in which case you must decide whether or not you can or want to offer more and, if so, how much.

If you offer exactly the same as another buyer, there are a number of possible outcomes. The vendor may accept one rather than the other because that buyer is in a stronger position in terms of speed of purchase and reliability. Alternatively, he may initiate what is called a contract race. This means that whichever of the buyers is able to exchange contracts first is the one to purchase the property. This is an advantage to the vendor because it will encourage the property to be sold faster. However, if you do agree to go down this course, it is a high stakes business. If you do not win the race, the money you will have spent in getting that far will be wasted. So only go ahead if you are confident that you have a better than reasonable chance of winning.

An estate agent is not allowed to conduct any kind of bidding war, so in the event of two identical offers, he is entitled to ask for sealed bids. In this case, you must decide on your last and best offer, remembering to put forward any advantages you may have over other buyers. Some estate agents will accept these bids over the phone, but the correct way to make them is in writing, sealed in an envelope and delivered to the agent by an agreed time. The buyer will then decide which one he wishes to accept.

Once the offer is accepted, a deposit may be asked for. You are under no legal obligation to pay this, but you may feel it is a sign of good will to do so. Should the sale fall through, the deposit will be returned.

The estate agent will ask for the name and address of your solicitor, and you will move on to the next phase of the process.

AUCTIONS

The advantage of buying at auction is that once the hammer falls, the property in question is legally yours. No one can slip in and gazump you. But there is no room for mistakes as they will cost you dear. This means that you must prepare yourself properly before you set off for the auction room even though there is a chance you may not get your chosen property.

You must have a survey done to alert you to any structural problems and get estimates for any work that may need to be done. Appoint a solicitor and ask him to obtain and check the title deeds, carry out the local searches and check for any special conditions of sale. Ensure you have the funds available to pay for it, remembering that, if successful, you will be liable to pay a deposit, usually 10%, on the day of the auction. Make sure you find out why the property is being sold at auction. Decide the top price you are prepared to pay – and stick to it.

Properties can be withdrawn from sale and sold outside the auction. The proviso 'unless previously sold' may appear in the details. You may want to try this, having discovered the price the seller is hoping to reach. Otherwise, make sure the property is still available before you go to the auction.

Come the day of the sale, get to the auction rooms early, get a good seat and make sure you are clear as to which lot you are bidding for. You should go to a few auctions previously to familiarise yourself with the proceedings. It is advisable to take your solicitor with you, and if you are at all nervous about bidding or know that a rush of blood to the head could lead to disastrous consequences, ask your solicitor to bid for you. If you decide to bid yourself, above all keep calm. Remember your top bid and be prepared to lose the property. Do not let yourself get carried away and bid more. You may regret it later.

If you are successful, you will have to sign the auction contract – you are bound to buy the property even if you do not – and pay a deposit. Then go and treat yourself to a celebratory drink.

WHAT HAPPENS NEXT

Why do you need a solicitor?

Unless you are knowledgeable or determined enough to carry out the conveyancing procedures yourself, you will need the services of a solicitor or a licensed conveyancer (a qualified professional offering the same services as a solicitor but limited to house purchasing). It is not recommended for a layman to attempt to conveyance anything other than a vacant freehold property. Conveyancing property with sitting tenants or leasehold property can be a minefield, so it is better to leave it in the experienced hands of a professional. Once your offer has been accepted, a solicitor will oversee the necessary legal work involved in cleanly transferring the property from the vendor to the buyer.

How to find a solicitor/licensed conveyancer

The best way to find a solicitor or licensed conveyancer is unquestionably through personal recommendation from someone who has successfully used them. It is advisable to use someone local to the area in which you are buying simply because they will know the area and probably be familiar with planning restrictions. The National Solicitors' Network, the Law Society's regional directory or the Council for Licensed Conveyancers will all provide names of those practising there. Your estate agent or your building society may give you names, although they are not generally keen on giving recommendations. There are plenty of high street solicitors' offices that will have specialists in conveyancing. If having to take potluck, visit several so that you can compare costs. They will either charge a percentage of the purchase price of the property or a fixed fee. Make sure it is clear whether those fees include search fees. Clarify how they operate and how long they think the whole procedure may take. Try to get a sense of their efficiency, professionalism and courtesy – you may have to deal with them over a number of months. Never rely on good will. Make sure everything is agreed in writing.

The estate agent will pass the details of the vendor's solicitor on to yours and vice versa. Your solicitor will wait to receive a draft contract before initiating his preliminary inquiries. The contract will include the particulars and conditions of sale, including a description of the property, whether it is freehold or leasehold, details of any access rights over the property or of the owner over another property, any covenants and charges on the land. It will also give the terms of the proposed sale, including a proposed sum for the deposit, date of completion and insurance. It should also detail exactly what is included in the sale price in terms of fixtures and fittings. It may be that there will be provision to buy certain fittings such as curtains and carpets for an additional sum.

Having received this, and armed with any anxieties you may have about the property, your solicitor will make preliminary inquiries by returning a standard questionnaire asking for certain information such as the name of the freeholder (if a flat), who has responsibility for the boundaries of the property, what service charges are payable, the amount of ground rent, details of mains services, disputes relating to the property, guarantees for any structural work, details of sitting tenants and so on. When you receive any guarantees for such things as damp-proof course or rot treatment, check they are worth the paper on which they are written by confirming the firm that carried out the work is still in business and, if they are, ask if they will transfer the guarantee from one owner to another. If the firm has gone bust, the guarantee is worthless and there may be a case for renegotiating the purchase price.

Your solicitor will simultaneously undertake a local search on the property. Once he has received a plan of the property, he submits a standard questionnaire to the local authority. The answers will reveal any problems that might affect the property. These may include such things as road widening proposals, sewer or mains works, planning difficulties, planning enforcements, noise abatement orders, tree preservation orders or compulsory purchase orders. Remember that the searches only relate to the house and that it may be necessary to inquire separately if there are any proposals to develop neighbouring land. Since your solicitor will not visit the property to see any such possibilities, it is up to you to raise any such questions with him. It may also be necessary to make separate searches with the Water Authority regarding sewers and drainage, with Railtrack regarding restrictive covenants if the property is near a railway line or with British Coal if the property is within a mining area. Local searches vary in cost, depending on the local authorities, and can take anything between two days and six weeks to be returned.

If the seller's solicitor decides to conduct the sale according to the Law

Society Transaction Protocol, as well as a draft contract, he will send a 'Fixtures, Fittings and Contents' form, copies of the entries if registered with the Land Registry or copies of earlier title deeds (if unregistered) and a property information form which answers a standard set of enquiries relating to the property. Licensed conveyancers are not currently allowed to use these forms. There will still be inquiries your solicitor will want to make, but the process will be speeded up considerably. Remember that local searches become invalid after about three months, so it may be worth taking out insurance in order to cover you against any changes in circumstances that may arise or having it updated.

At the time of writing, the government is pushing for the introduction of a Seller's Pack to speed up the whole buying process (see Chapter 5 Selling Your Property). This would require the vendor to put together a pack of extensive information on the property, including the results of the local searches. The cost of this would be transferred to the buyer at the time contracts are exchanged.

While all this is going on, you should contact your mortgage lender to arrange a valuation of the property and confirm their offer to you. They need to ensure that the property is adequate security against their loan. Usually, the fee for this will be paid when submitting your initial application. Lenders lend on the basis of the valuation not the purchase price. If this means they offer to lend you less than they had originally indicated as a result, you may have to renegotiate the purchase price at this stage or drop out of the deal. It is most common for the buyer's solicitor to act on behalf of the mortgage lender for the transaction. Assuming this is the case, he will prepare a mortgage deed that will be the contract between you and the lender.

The valuation is not a thorough survey. It will not necessarily throw up all the defects of the property, nor even tell you whether or not it is worth the price being paid. The lender only wants to know that his money is safe, should you falter in your payments and they have to dispose of the property. So it is only sensible to commission a thorough survey of your own. Apart from assuring you that the property is sound, it may also give you a tool with which to renegotiate the price. The one most commonly used by home buyers is the Home-buyers' Survey and Valuation (HSV). Your estate agent may be able to recommend a surveyor. Your mortgage lender may offer a service that combines the HSV with their own valuation. Alternatively, the RICS (Royal Institute of Chartered Surveyors) will give you a list of surveyors in the area.

In any event, you should use a qualified surveyor who is a member of either the RICS, the Architects and Surveyors Institute or the Association of Building Engineers. It is wise to use one who knows the area and is familiar with any local conditions that might be relevant. Fees vary depending on the age of the property and the purchase price. An HSV is intended for houses, flats and bungalows that are conventionally built and in reasonable condition. It concentrates on any urgent repairs, suggesting estimates for the work are acquired before proceeding to contract, as well as pointing out matters such as subsidence which need further, immediate investigation, providing other information on less urgent repairs and any inconveniences that may be of interest to the buyer with regard to location, environment or insurance or legal matters that should be included in the legal inquiries. It will also give an opinion on the open market value of the flat and an estimate of the cost of rebuilding it in its current form (useful for insurance purposes). It will inspect all parts of the property that are accessible or visible from ground or floor level and the services.

If you are buying a property that is unusually built, rundown, has been radically altered or is one that you wish to extend, then a Building Survey, or full structural survey, is a more expensive but more thorough inspection. Unlike the HSV, it is not presented on a standard form, but includes extensive technical information on the construction of the building, materials used, condition of the foundations, walls, roof, floors, plumbing, drains, electrical wiring, outbuildings and garden as well as all major and minor defects. Costs will depend on the nature of the building and the time taken to carry out the report.

Whether you have an HSV or a Building Survey, remember that if there is any aspect of the property you are particularly anxious about, you can ask the surveyor to pay particular attention to it. Some surveyors, in an effort not to be negligent, will detail every little fault. Do not panic, but make an effort to distinguish what is genuinely serious and what is not.

At this stage, you may need to get estimates for any work that will need to be done. Find two or three builders through personal recommendation and ask them to quote for you. If you are using an architect to rebuild or extend the property, he will see to this. When you have a clear picture of the amount of money you will need, there may be a case to renegotiate the purchase price. You will have to tell the vendor of the flaw you have discovered and the unforeseen cost of putting it right.

If you are planning to make substantial alterations to a house and may require planning permission, it is a good idea to apply for it now. Planning permission belongs to the property concerned, not to the person applying for it. It may take weeks to come through, so this will save you time later. If the sale falls through, however, you will have wasted money.

When all the above procedures have been satisfactorily carried out and acted upon, and the buyer and seller are both completely happy with the contract, it is time to exchange contracts. At this point, a deposit (usually 10% of the purchase price) is paid, a completion date is agreed and the contract is legally binding. When deciding on the completion date, do not just plump for the nearest date possible. Check what day of the week it is. If you choose to move on a Friday, you may find yourself spending the weekend unable to get something you really need. If the oven you inherit does not work, or there is a leaking pipe, you may have to wait until Monday to get them fixed unless you pay for expensive emergency repairs. Also make sure that if the owner has agreed to complete any repairs before the move it is agreed in the contract and *not* in a letter of agreement, as this will make it more binding. There is no backing out now. This is also the point when the buyer becomes responsible for the insurance of the property.

Keep in touch with your solicitor after exchange because he still has work to do before completion. There is the investigation of title, which may involve checking previous transactions dating back fifteen years to ensure the vendor has clean title to the property. If the property is registered, the information should be easily available from the Land Registry. If the property is unregistered, then he will have to register the title with this conveyance. At this point he will receive a draft transfer from the seller's solicitor or a conveyance, depending on whether the property is registered or unregistered respectively. Once he has approved it, he will prepare or 'engross' the final deeds for your and the seller's signatures. At the same time he will ask you for the balance of the purchase money or he will sign the mortgage deed and apply to the lender to make sure the monies will be available on the day of completion. On the agreed date, the seller receives the money and you get the keys to your new home.

All that remains is for your solicitor to have the deed stamped by the Inland Revenue. This is when stamp duty, a government tax payable on property purchases over £60,000, is paid. The deeds will then be lodged with your mortgage lender or with you if you do not have a mortgage. Land registry fees are payable when the property is registered or when the transfer of title is recorded. These are charged on a variable scale that begins at £40 for a house worth £40,000 to £800 for those over a million.

BUYING A LEASEHOLD PROPERTY

Although the procedure for buying a leasehold property is principally the same as for buying a freehold property, there are a number of additional things to bear in mind and for your solicitor to check. If the property is leasehold, there is other documentation required. In the preliminary inquiries, your solicitor will ask for the name and address of the freeholder and to whom the ground rent should be paid; what service charges are payable; details of any insurance policy governing the property; whether any covenants been broken. These last might include the previous tenant subletting the property, or not paying ground rent when due. Equally, it might show the landlord has not looked after the property or that he has tried to evict a previous tenant. The freeholder may have to consent to the property being sold, in which case, your solicitor will want to know that consent has been granted. He will also want to see the Memorandum and Articles of Association of the management company together with the last three years of management accounts and service charge demands. It is crucial to go through the leasehold agreement with a fine-tooth comb, being aware of any potential problems. Your solicitor should have an experienced eye and be able to help you.

If you are buying a leasehold property with a lease that is running out, you are entitled to buy the freehold or extend the lease for a further fifty years *if* you have lived in it for the last three years or three of the last ten years. To do this, notice must be served on the landlord before the lease expires.

BUYING WITH SOMEONE ELSE

If buying with another person, there are two forms of joint ownership. Talk to your solicitor if you have any doubt as to which arrangement would be most suitable for you.

If you are joint tenants, neither of you can sell your share without the agreement of the other. The property will be owned in equal shares. If one of you dies, the other automatically inherits the deceased's share. This is a common arrangement for married couples or committed partnerships. However, if you are buying with a friend it is generally preferable to be tenants in common. This means that each of you is entitled to dispose of your share as you wish. It also allows the owners to have unequal shares in the property, depending on the amount of money they have been able to contribute to the purchase.

If you are buying with a friend, it is essential that your solicitor draw up an agreement between you that covers all eventualities and specifies your financial arrangements. If every expense is to be split 50/50, things should be pretty straightforward. If not, think of all possible ramifications and provide for them. What begins as a great adventure can end in disaster if all these things are not agreed at the very beginning.

HOW LONG DOES IT ALL TAKE?

It is impossible to give a hard and fast rule. Each sale depends on the individuals involved and the particular building. If nothing goes wrong and all parties act efficiently, contracts can be exchanged within two months of an offer being accepted. Completion takes place whenever it is agreed, anything from a few days to weeks later. But what can go wrong?

Gazumping

Gazumping usually occurs in a rising market. It is what happens when, after having accepted an offer, a vendor accepts a higher offer from another buyer and reneges on his deal with you. He is legally within his rights to do this. There is absolutely nothing you can do except try to gazump the second buyer yourself or look for another property. A way of getting round this is to agree to a 'lockout' agreement, in exchange for your guarantee of exchanging contracts within a certain period. In any event, the sooner you can exchange contracts the less likely you are to be gazumped.

Property is taken off the market

Until contracts are exchanged, both you and the seller are able to back out of the deal. If the vendor decides for any reason that he does not want to sell his house after all, there is absolutely nothing you can do about it.

Survey results

Sometimes a survey may reveal something as major as subsidence or dry rot that will be too time-consuming and expensive to put right. In which case you may decide the only course of action is to back out of the deal.

Valuation results

If the mortgage lender's valuation values the property less than the agreed purchase price, the percentage they lend you will be of their value, not yours, so you may find yourself without enough money to complete the purchase.

The chain

If you are one in a long line of people all dependent on the successful purchase and sale of each other's houses, it is likely that at some time or another it will break. If one person drops out of the chain, it will delay the sale of your property or the purchase of the new one. If it looks as though your purchase is in jeopardy, one course of action is to hang on and hope your vendor does not decide to sell to another buyer able to move faster than you. While hanging on, prepare your-self for the possibility of having to go back to square one and look for another house. If desperate, you could take out a bridging loan but this is extremely risky and can be very expensive if your house does not sell quickly.

SCOTLAND

The process of buying property in Scotland is quite different from the rest of the UK. For a start, there is no such concept as leasehold property. Most property, including flats, is owned on feudal tenure. This means they are owned absolutely and the owner can dispose of them freely. However, the original land owner or developer, known as the superior, may have set out conditions regarding its use or prohibiting alterations. These 'feuding' conditions can remain in place for ever unless the supe-rior agrees to waiving or modifying them.

When buying a flat, it is particularly important to examine the whole building for any defects and to establish that the costs for any repairs to the structure or the common parts is shared equally among the flat owners.

If you need a Scottish solicitor and have no word-of-mouth recom-mendations, the Law Society of Scotland provides a Directory of General Services that lists them. Remember, they do not set fixed charges so it is worth shopping around to compare fees.

The property will have been advertised and the offers over price given will represent the lowest offer acceptable. Of course, if the market is sluggish there is nothing to stop you putting in a lower bid but you may run the risk of losing the property having incurred various associated expenses. Occasionally, a property will be offered at a fixed price, in which case you have to move quickly, because the first acceptable bid at that price gets it. Before offering you must let your solicitor know of your intent, and he will inform the vendor's solicitor. Never agree to anything in writing or sign any documents without consulting your solicitor. You should have a survey carried out at this stage for your own benefit and make sure your finances are in place. Your mortgage company will have the property valued and confirm how much it will lend you. You must not make an offer without your lender's approval, otherwise you may find yourself legally committed to buying a property without the necessary finance.

The offer itself is prepared by your solicitor. The amount you choose to offer will depend on the results of your survey and the state of the market. If you can, you should familiarise yourself with the prices fetched by similar properties in the area. The offer is a formal document that not only spells out the price you wish to offer but also any conditions under which the property is to be bought, eg a moving-in date, and what contents are to be included. Normally, the seller will set a date by which all offers must be in. Once an offer has been put forward, there is no pulling out. If accepted, it forms a legally binding contract ensuring neither party can back out of the transaction. The advantage of this system is that it precludes the possibility of being gazumped. The disadvantage is that, if unsuccessful, you have wasted considerable sums of money.

If the offer is accepted, you are immediately responsible for insuring the property. Your solicitor will examine the title deeds and initiate procedures towards completion. If you are buying jointly with anyone else, ask for advice about the terms of the title. It is important that it states the fact clearly if you do not own equal shares, and it needs to make provision for either party selling. On completion day, settlement takes place whereby the solicitors meet and exchange a cheque for the keys.

After completion, stamp duty of 1% is payable and the title must be registered with either the Register of Sasines or the Land Register.

IAN GODFREY, CHELTENHAM

Wanted: 'I'd like to live within ten or fifteen minutes' walk of the town centre. I am quite fussy when it comes to location and although I don't really expect to find anything with a garage, if I do it will be a big plus. House prices have been shooting up in Cheltenham, and I realised that if I don't move fairly soon, I'm never going to be able to afford the jump from my flat up to the sort of period house I would like to live in. I would pay up to about £450,000 for the right house.'

Trading up can be expensive, but renting part of the property can be a way to meet the mortgage repayments. Anaesthetist Ian Godfrey lived in a good-sized flat in Cheltenham's Pittville, but he was aware that if he did not make the move into a period house now, the differential between flat and house prices would soon become too great for him to bridge. As it was, the only way to manage it was to buy a house with a flat he could rent out, enabling him to borrow an extra £100,000. His friend James, who works in PR, had already agreed to be his tenant, so it was a question of finding a property that would suit them both.

The regency elegance of Cheltenham has been one of its major attractions since the eighteenth century, when people flocked to the town for its spa waters. Today, it attracts tourists to both its festival and to its racecourse. Even newer buildings have been built in period style so the centre of the town is uniformly designed. Towards the south-west, there is an attractive mix of Victorian and more recent urban styles. Properties in the centre and close to the parks command the highest prices, the larger houses often offering large basements with good rental potential. This was the sort of property on which Ian had set his heart.

The first house he saw was a recently renovated end-of-terrace, four-bedroom property in Albion Street, close to his current home. On the market for £445,000, it offered well-proportioned rooms and a separate two-bedroom flat. The house was ideal, with plenty of space, a drawing room with huge sash windows and original cornicing. The only kitchen was in the basement, but the developer was prepared to put in a second one upstairs or reduce the price. The major drawback was the fact that the town ring-road ran right past the front door. The noise was constant, but double-glazing was a possible remedy. Nonetheless Ian was adamant. 'The house is absolutely what I want. If I could move it somewhere else, it would be perfect.'

Moving on, another recently developed Regency terrace in Portland Street might have been the answer. In a quieter residential area, the house had four bedrooms and a one-bedroom basement flat, and was on the market at £395,000. The restored period features, including the original wooden shutters, banisters and cornicing contrasted effectively with modern fixtures such as contemporary fireplaces and recessed lighting. The blue/brown kitchen was not expensive but had been fitted extremely well and benefitted from good quality appliances. The master bedroom had an *en suite* shower, cleverly installed into the available space. All the main living rooms presented a pleasing blank canvas to any buyer, with magnolia walls and neutral carpets. Downstairs, the flat had a sleek minimalist kitchen and a light airy living room. But Ian still had reservations, despite the coveted secure parking area outside. 'It's nice, the only thing that counts against it is its location on the main road out of Cheltenham.'

TIP: If a piece of cornicing is missing, have a mould made from the existing cornicing to make a new section that can be pieced in.

Still concentrating on the location, he viewed a three-bedroom detached villa in St Anne's Road, Fairview. It did not have a flat but a studio room in the garden. However, the price was £350,000, giving him £100,000 for developing the studio. The house itself was fake pebble-dashed and Ian was reassured to hear that it could be removed, although it would be a time-consuming, expensive process. Again, the proportions of the rooms were good, including a formal dining room and a very contemporary kitchen. The bathroom was the *pièce de résistance*, with a cast-iron roll-top bath taking centre stage. There was even a fireplace – all it needed was to have the chimney swept and a hearth put in. The attic was huge and, at a later date, could be turned into a bedroom to add value. Despite its attractions, however, it did not have the Regency feel that Ian really wanted.

TIP: If you are considering an attic conversion, decide whether the space is going to be habitable or just for storage. Check the building regulations, including strength of floor joists, fire regulations and standing room.

So it was back to Pittville's Clarence Road where a four-bedroom house was for sale at £349,000 with its three-bedroom basement flat for sale separately at £169,950. This was the biggest house Ian had seen, in a superb location opposite Pittville Park. But he immediately knew it was not for him. However much space there was, it was right by the main pedestrian route out of Cheltenham and Miles. 'It looks like an absolutely beautiful house but I don't think I could ever live in this particular location.'

It was time to look at something completely different. Eight miles from Cheltenham, in the idyllic village of Deerhurst, was a spectacular barn conversion, priced at £445,000. The accommodation was upside down, with four bedrooms on the ground floor and two splendid reception rooms and a kitchen under the high beamed ceiling upstairs. The views were stunning and the place was full of character, enhanced by the existing decoration and furniture. Creating a flat downstairs would just be a matter of adding a second front door and reorganising the partition walls. 'I've always had it in the back of my mind that I'd move to the country. I just thought I was a little bit young, but it's a beautiful house and Cheltenham's not that far.'

TIP: With barn conversions, always have a full structural survey to make sure everything is sound.

Just as Ian was deliberating, a Regency house came on the market in Clarence Square, with an asking price of £550,000, way over his budget. It did not have a basement flat but did have four reception rooms and four bedrooms. It was on the quieter side of the square with a south-facing garden. The house was superb with many original features, a perfect first-floor drawing room next door to the master bedroom, a huge bathroom and a decent kitchen in the basement, the obvious place to a create a separate rental flat. Bingo. 'Lovely house, fabulous location, really nice feel. I feel really at home here. It's just whether I can make it work financially.'

Having taken stock of all the properties he had seen, Ian decided to take James back to the houses in Portland Street and Clarence Square for a closer second look. In Portland Street he noticed an old damp patch that signified some remedial work had been done to the house – something to point out to a surveyor.

> TIP: Make a list of things you want the surveyor to check. Do not assume they will see what you see.

There were fewer period features than he said he wanted, but the contemporary dash made quite an impact. James was extremely keen on the flat. 'It's nice and clean, nice big space and the kitchen is excellent. It's a really good kitchen and I do lots of cooking.' There were one or two minor problems including a leaking bathroom radiator, but nothing that the developer would not fix.

> TIP: If considering a newly renovated property, make a snagging list of any problems, however minor, and make sure they are all sorted out by the developer before you exchange contracts.

However, Clarence Square still had the edge over it for Ian. To convert the basement at a basic level would cost a minimum of £5,000. 'Portland Street ticks most of the boxes but I'm looking for a house I'm going to live in for the next ten or fifteen years. I have a feeling that I'd be getting itchy feet after five years or so and be wanting to move. For that reason I think Clarence Square is actually the perfect house for me.'

He put in an offer of £510,000 that was not enough to swing it. But before he had time to despair, another house came on to the market in the same square for £450,000. To his delight, his offer was accepted. 'I'm really excited. I've got a house in the square I wanted, and I just can't wait to move.'

LETTING A ROOM

If your heart is set on a large house that you know will be a sound investment for the future but the asking price is beyond your means, consider the possibility of renting out a room to help offset the cost of the mortgage. If you do decide to go down this road, you must notify your mortgage lender.

Fixing the rent

When fixing a rent, take into account how much you need to cover the mortgage repayments, not forgetting the additional insurance and related bills including electricity (heating and lighting) and gas.

Rent-a-room scheme

The rental you receive from the room is taxable. However, the government's rent-a-room scheme allows you to earn up to £4,250 of rental income a year tax-free. Anything above that will be taxed. If you share joint ownership of the house, whichever person is receiving the rent will be granted the total exemption. If you both receive the rent or both let separate rooms then the exemption is split between you.

You can elect not to join the scheme, in which case you must inform your tax office within twenty-two months of the end of the tax year. If you have carried out extensive renovations on the room, you may find that having offset those expenses against your tax, the rental income is no longer taxable. Ask for advice from a financial advisor or visit www.inlandrevenue.gov.uk.

Tenancy agreement

Even if the tenant is your oldest friend, it is essential that you have a legal agreement between you stating clearly the terms under which you are letting them the room. It is also important to make it clear which other parts of the house they have free access to, and if you are limiting their use of the kitchen or bathroom to certain times. Agree whether they can entertain in their room and whether or not their visitors can stay overnight. After all, this is first and foremost your home and wherever possible this arrangement should not detract from your enjoyment of it. Take good legal advice to ensure that you are covered should you want, at any time, to evict your tenant.

Extra income

If you want to make more money from your tenant, it is legitimate to charge for providing meals or doing their washing. The income from these services can be incorporated into the rent-a-room scheme provided you are not qualified in it as a trade. If in doubt, a lawyer or accountant should be able to advise you.

Telephone

One of the causes of immense friction between tenant and landlord in this situation can be over the phone bill. The simplest solution is to provide them with a separate line for which you pay the rental charges and they pay the bills. This also means that your line is always free for you to use whenever you need it.

Bathroom

The other area of conflict is often the bathroom, particularly when everyone is trying to get out of the house at the same time. If you can provide your lodger with their own shower room at least, it will ease that pressure and further raise the rental value.

PETER AND CLARE O'SULLIVAN, CORNWALL

Wanted: 'We're looking for a property with some kind of potential, something we can utilise to make some extra money. In a nutshell, our ideal would be a wonderful family home with enough room for all five of us to knock about without being on top of each other. It would be nice to be near a beach for the children so they can play and get into the boarding culture. We've got about £240,000 to spend but could push it a little if we find a real dream house.'

Many of us dream of escaping the pace of city life and moving to the country, but how tough is it to turn the dream into reality? Peter O'Sullivan, a website designer, and his wife Clare, a full-time mother, had sold their house in London and decided to move to Cornwall with their three children. Fortunately for them, they had made enough on the sale to make them cash buyers. Currently renting on Cornwall's north coast, they were getting to know the area well and were aware that it was fast becoming a popular choice for people wanting an all-year-round improvement in their quality of life.

Their search began in the picturesque harbour town of Port Isaac.

Just a short walk up the hill was a semi-detached, stone-built, four-bedroom farmhouse with a separate two-bedroom holiday cottage and an asking price of £240,000. Clare's initial reaction was that it might be too isolated for the children to make friends easily. A pretty building on the outside, it had been done up inside in a range of decorative styles with exposed stonework, wood panelling, wallpaper and border, and swirling seventies carpet. The house had been used as a Bed & Breakfast, so all the bedrooms were decorated with delicate floral prints, and each had a bathroom. There was no need for all those bathrooms, so the possibility existed of enlarging a couple of the bedrooms. Removing the bathrooms would also mean getting rid of much of the unattractive exterior pipework.

> **TIP: Sometimes, having a redundant room can increase the value of a property.**

The holiday cottage would rent for £250 per week in the low season, going up to £350 in the high season – a good income generator along with the static caravan and paddock in front of the house. Scary décor aside, the house had definite potential, but it just did not have the right vibes for Peter and Clare.

They had been dreaming of sea views, and the property they saw next in Porthcothan had just that. The four-bedroom house was slightly over budget at £250,000 but there was a lot of house for the money, plus another promising money-maker. The house itself had a real family feel and was in good repair, with a view right down to the beach below. The 33-foot (10m) living room was impressive but could be improved further by replacing the obtrusive central staircase with a more discreet spiral one. The bedrooms were a good size, with the low attic room perfect for the children.

> **TIP: Remember, your children may understand the dangers of a swimming pool, but other people's may not. Safety is your responsibility.**

Outside was a small pool that would bring up the key costs by about £35 per month for the chemicals. About 100 yards from the house, at the entrance to the beach, was a building plot with planning permission for two houses that would have an asking price of £400,000 each. This was definitely good news for the values of the area.

> **TIP: A nearby building plot is not always bad news. In some instances, the new houses may push up property values in the area.**

Outside Padstow they saw a chocolate-box, four-bedroom house with a stylish modern interior, priced at £220,000. The kitchen was on the small side, but of the two reception rooms, one could be used as a children's room. A bright light stairway led up to attractive attic bedrooms in the eaves. There were a lot of original features, particularly the two fireplaces. The fact that they were neatly laid gave the impression that they were working but was no guarantee.

> **TIP: Even if a fireplace has been neatly arranged with kindling and paper, it is not an absolute guarantee. Always double check with the owner.**

It was important that Peter and Clare kept their heads and did not confuse a perfect holiday destination with the reality of life there out of season. Peter was absolutely clear. 'I think it's a lovely little house. It could have been just plucked out of Fulham and dropped down here. It's got the right number of rooms, the vibes and the style, but it hasn't got the room.'

On to the picture-postcard village of St Mawgan, where a house near the beach was waiting. It had stables and impressive views down to the sea, but was just over budget at £265,000.

> **TIP: If you are buying a property for its view, you must check that it is safeguarded. Your solicitor will conduct a local search which should reveal any up-and-coming planning applications.**

The entrance led straight into the large, open kitchen with modern fittings, a range and a dining table. The master bedroom had a luxurious *en suite* bathroom and plenty of space for an armchair or *chaise longue*. One of the children's bedrooms was tiny but could be compensated for by converting the garage into a playroom. Outside, knowing that Clare would be keener than him, Peter considered the possibilities of using the stables for livery which would bring in about £200 per week. Alternatively they could rent the stabling and paddock for about £30 per week. Another opportunity presented itself in the form of an old static caravan. Since there was one on the berth already, the council, reluctant to give permission for new statics, would not object to replacing old with new. An initial outlay of £1,500 to £2,000 would bring £400 to £500 rental return per week in high season.

Before making up their mind, they were determined to take a look at an imposing seven-bedroom Victorian villa, currently used as a care home. There was no question that the electrics, plumbing and heating would have been regularly checked and therefore reliable. However, buying a property this size and in this condition would be a huge commitment. It was likely that the council would permit an exterior staircase, similar to the one on the house next door, to be built as access to a rented top-floor flat but the restoration inside would be extensive and time-consuming, which worried Clare. 'It's a gorgeous house. It could be absolutely fantastic, but could we ever finish it?'

It was back to St Mawgan for a second viewing and a chance to check out the village and local facilities, most importantly the local school. The house itself felt as friendly as before and still looked big enough for the family. The planning authorities had no problem with any alterations to be made to the garage, either walling up the door space, including a big window, insulating the walls and adding insulation and double glazing or just rubber painting the floor, boxing the door in with plywood and adding a couple of night storage heaters. They made up their minds to offer only to discover that an offer of £280,000 had already been made. As cash buyers ready to move quickly it was worth offering what the house was worth to them, but before they did, the other offer was accepted.

When you find a property you like it pays to move swiftly. Peter and Clare did find their Cornish dream in the end, both spacious and £35,000 under their budget so they had enough left over for another small rental property. 'We're looking forward to moving in, settling in and having a different life in Cornwall.'

RELOCATING TO A HOLIDAY AREA

A word of warning. Buying a property in a place where you have enjoyed countless holidays may not necessarily bring you all the instant happiness you expect. Two weeks along a beaten track in a remote part of the world may have its charms when you have nothing to do but drive for the shopping, explore and enjoy your escape from the rat race. When confronted with it every day, however, through rain and shine, with few neighbours and none of your old friends, things may begin to look a little bleak. Similarly, the enjoyment shared by a family on a beach holiday may be diminished when they find themselves there out of season, when the tourist attractions are closed and the tourists have gone home, leaving it virtually dead.

There are legions of people who have upped sticks for another way of life, only to discover that without cinemas, friends and the buzz of city living, it is not what they wanted after all. But by this time they have moved off the property ladder and cannot afford to move back.

If you are determined to make the move, there are number of things you might include in your planning. In the first place, consider letting your current home and renting another in or near the place where you think you want to live for a period of a year. This will give you and the children a chance to see what it is like throughout the seasons, and to sound out the local transport and facilities that you may not have needed to pay much attention to before. Renting a property should not prevent you from continuing or starting up a business. In fact, it gives you the opportunity to return to square one if things do not work out as successfully as planned.

It is probably wise to choose an area that is not entirely governed by the tourist season so that you will be able to find new friends and occupations that are there all year round. Will you want to return frequently to your old home town for work reasons? If so, make sure you live reasonably near a mainline station to cut the travelling time. Is there enough room for you or your partner to have a separate office? If you have school-age children, think about their daily journey back and forth. Will you be driving them every day or would it make more sense to be in easier reach of a bus stop or local train station?

If you are proposing to let part of the property or convert outbuildings for letting, consult local holiday homes rental companies to see what income you might hope to generate. It will almost certainly be more cost effective to buy a property where any conversions have already been done and where you will be inheriting a clientele rather than having to build one up from scratch. The nearer you are to the local attractions, the higher the potential rental income unless you are offering a very superior sort of accommodation. You must notify your mortgage lender if you are letting any part of your home.

SIOBHAN AND DANILO MELANDRI, EDINBURGH

Wanted: 'Two bedrooms, a garden to relax and in a very nice area, somewhere I could be quite homely and happy for some time. In theory, we've got a budget of £200,000.' Siobhan

'I really, really want a garage so I can pursue my hobby which is to get myself a classic car. That is absolutely not negotiable.' Danilo

Edinburgh is Scotland's number one tourist attraction, a buzzing metropolis offering chic café culture alongside neo-classical architecture and brooding Celtic mystery. And it is a city where the property market is exploding. Thanks to the establishment of the Scottish parliament and the rapid influx of new businesses, it is now second to London as the UK's most expensive area for home buyers. Properties range from stately Georgian and busy Victorian near the centre to open-plan, purpose-built living in the docks area. House hunters Danilo, a software engineer, and Siobhan, a marketing manager for an advertising agency, had definite ideas about what they wanted and had already looked at over thirty properties. Their budget of £200,000 might sound high, but looking for a garage and a garden in the centre of Edinburgh, they were almost certainly restricting their choices. A further six properties offering a range of possible solutions were lined up for them to view.

The first was in Dalrymple Crescent, part of The Grange, an exclusive conservation area two miles south of the city centre. Here, a three-bedroom garden flat was on the market for offers over £160,000. The layout of the flat had remained virtually the same since its days as 'below stairs'. For a basement flat, it was remarkably light and airy with two bathrooms and a large garden leading from a small conservatory. However, the rooms were on the small side and the kitchen units would have to be raised about six inches at an estimated cost of £200. But the biggest minus was the carport. Inquiries to the planning office revealed that it was in a conservation area so there were no guarantees that Danilo would be able to build a private garage.

Given that garages are at a premium in a city centre, Danilo agreed that buying a separate lock-up garage close by might be a viable alternative. Having found one for sale at £15,000, it was only a short walk to an elegant two-bedroom drawing-room flat in Clarendon Road. Recently renovated and on sale at offers over £145,000, it left enough in their budget to afford the garage too. It was a typical Edinburgh flat with high ceilings and large windows that had been recently renovated for sale. There were signs that the renovation was unfinished – some of the skirting in the hall was missing and plastic sheeting was still attached to the glass doors. These were small things to fix but, combined with the flat's distance from the garage, they were enough to put off Danilo and Siobhan.

> **TIP: It is possible to specify in your offer that any incomplete jobs are attended to before you exchange contracts.**

Going further afield in search of the elusive garage, they headed to Trinity in the north of the city, close to the up-and-coming docklands but three miles from the city centre. A 1920s' two-bedroom semi on sale at offers over £125,000 presented an unattractive (to Danilo and Siobhan) pebble-dash exterior to the world. Inside, it was surprisingly spacious with two bathrooms and a separate dining room. It had heaps of potential, with the possibility of creating a great open-plan living area where a wooden floor and white walls would maximise the sense of space. Adding a new bathroom and shower would complete the transformation. Danilo and Siobhan were not convinced.

> TIP: Never assume everything is included. Your solicitor will have a list of what is staying and what is not. If you want something – ask.

A three-bedroom Victorian villa was for sale in Laverock Road, only a short walk away. Designed by Hippolyte Blanc, who created some of the interiors at Edinburgh Castle, it would stretch the couple's budget at offers over £195,000. A corner house with superb original features including fireplaces, cornicing and banisters, it also benefitted from windows on three sides. A master bedroom with an *en suite* power shower, a luxurious bathroom, a beautifully fitted kitchen (although with little work space), a small decked garden and a garage were the major selling points. Siobhan loved it, but Danilo was less sure.

> TIP: Measure a garage carefully to check your car will fit, and allow for additional space if it is to be used as a workshop.

Further from the city centre, the couple were likely to get more for their money, so they travelled to Corstorphine, where a three-bedroom bungalow offered space, a garage and a good-sized garden for offers over £175,000. Siobhan's verdict? 'It's all very well done, loads of

LOCATION LOCATION LOCATION

space, perfect family home – it's just everything I'm not. I stayed in a house that was quite similar in the suburbs before and it says every-thing to me that's negative that I don't want to be.' A strong personal reaction is enough of a reason for not wanting to buy a house, so with surburbia given a definite thumbs down, it was back into town.

Dean Village is one of the most sought-after areas in Edinburgh, a rural idyll less than ten minutes walk from Siobhan's work. A modern weir-side mews house arranged over three floors complemented the older properties opposite. It had a strong cottage feel, an internal garage, utility room, snug kitchen and separate dining room. The biggest room was the living room with a balcony over the rushing waters of Leith, with two attic bedrooms above. Five years old, it should have had most of a new-build's teething problems sorted out but there was a crack in the hall ceiling. Investigation revealed the sili-cone round the shower tray had perished and was causing a leak. Danilo was smitten, but Siobhan was still unsure. 'I'm not looking for cool. I'm looking for nests and homes for the next fifteen to twenty years.' Her heart was still set on Laverock Road.

> **TIP: If you see ceiling cracks or something suspicious, think what is above it and immediately investigate.**

Both houses were priced close to their budget, and they would almost certainly sell for £30,000 or so more. A second view of the properties, taking an unemotional look at the pros and cons, ultimately convinced Siobhan that Laverock Road was not for her after all. Returning to Dean Village, Siobhan began to appreciate the advantage of the central location and the potential of the interior to be opened up into a loft-style space by removing the internal kitchen wall. That combined with the rural feel in the heart of the city and the peaceful garden won her over. In the end, they made a bid of £275,000 (£75,000 over their declared budget) and to their absolute delight won it by only a couple of thousand pounds. The house was theirs.

MORTGAGES – WHAT TO ASK

➤ What is the standard interest rate (SVR)?

➤ What are the interest rates available on different types of mortgages?

➤ What will the monthly repayment per £1,000 borrowed be?

➤ When and how must payments be made?

➤ Can you defer payments at any time?

➤ What happens when interest rates change?

➤ Is there an arrangement fee?

➤ Are there early redemption penalties?

➤ What other conditions are there in taking out the loan?

➤ Can you extend the initial arrangement after the agreed number of years?

➤ What percentage of the valuation will they offer as a normal maximum loan?

➤ Do you have to buy insurance as a condition of the loan?

➤ Do they provide a mortgage certificate?

3 ABOUT MORTGAGES

WHAT IS A MORTGAGE?

A mortgage is a sum of money borrowed in order to buy a property. It is generally lent over a fixed term, during which the borrower will make appropriate payments to pay it off. The lender holds the deeds as security against the loan. The loan is taken out against the property so that, if the borrower is unable make the repayments, the property may be repossessed by the lender and sold.

WHEN DO I NEED IT?

Most people are not fortunate enough to be able to pay for a property outright. If you want to buy a house or flat, it should be possible to borrow most, if not all, of the money required. The amount you can borrow will depend on the condition of the property and on your financial situation.

HOW MUCH CAN I BORROW?

If you are buying alone, most mortgage lenders will usually be prepared to lend three times your annual gross income. Recently, however, building societies have started lending salary multiples of five or even six to compensate for the high property prices.

If you are proposing to buy with a partner, they will usually either lend:

3 x major annual gross income + 1 x minor annual gross annual income
> or

2.5 x joint annual gross income

If you are self-employed the same rules apply, but based on your income over the previous three years.

When deciding how much to borrow, do take into account your other annual expenditure. Do not borrow more than you can safely afford to pay back. The lender will not be sympathetic to the fact that you run an expensive racehorse, pay school fees or enjoy exotic holidays. Is it worth giving up the pleasures of life to buy your dream home? Think carefully.

It is generally possible to borrow up to 95% of the purchase price *if* the lender's valuation coincides. Some lenders will lend up to 100% on a new build. If, however, the lender values the house at less than the purchase price, they will only offer the agreed percentage of the price it is valued at (the LTV, or loan-to-value). The valuation is not a full survey but acts as an assurance to the lender that his loan is recoverable should anything go wrong. If that happens you will have to either make up the difference in cash or look elsewhere.

HOW MUCH SHOULD I PAY AS A DEPOSIT?

A deposit can be as low as 5%, and more commonly 10%. The more equity you have in the property, the better. The less you need to borrow, the wider the range of mortgage possibilities open to you. It is also worth bearing in mind that over the years, as you improve the property and it increases in value, your equity will increase too, making the purchase a sound investment. If you take a 100% mortgage, pay no deposit, and the housing market tumbles, you will find yourself in the unfortunate position of having negative equity (ie you owe more than the house is worth), which may make it impossible for you to sell until the market recovers.

WHERE DO I GET A MORTGAGE?

There are a wide variety of potential lenders. The traditional option is a building society, but all the major high street banks have got in on the act, and offer similar services. You could also turn to specialist lenders, local authorities if you are buying a council property, or developers if you are buying a new property. Some estate agents also arrange finance. If you are unsure about whom to approach, try looking at some of the specialist internet sites (see page 282), which will give you an overview of the market and provide calculators to help you work out the real cost of your loan over the period you realistically expect to stay in the property. If you prefer the more personal touch, visit a mortgage broker or Independent Financial Adviser (IFA). Mortgage brokers should be able to answer all your questions, demystifying a financial maze. They may be able to help if you are finding it hard to get a mortgage, if you need a particularly large loan, or are trying to buy an unconventional property. Anyone can claim the title 'mortgage broker', so it is important you find a professional, preferably by personal recommendation.

WHAT DO I NEED TO GET A MORTGAGE?

To qualify for a mortgage you will have to produce proof of identity and of your financial situation, showing you are in a position to repay the loan. You may have to provide some or all of the following:

- Passport, birth certificate, driving licence
- Proof of address
- Landlord's reference, previous mortgage statements
- Up to a year's worth of bank statements
- Proof of three years' earnings

The lender may want to communicate with your employer to verify your earnings. If you are self-employed, you should expect to have to provide three years' worth of your most recent accounts.

WHEN SHOULD I APPLY?

Ideally, you should apply for a mortgage before you start looking for a property. Having worked out your budget, you will know how much you can afford to borrow. The lender will give you Approval in Principal, which means that they are prepared to lend the money subject to their valuation of whichever property you choose. Many companies provide a mortgage certificate valid for a certain length of time. Having this approval puts you in a strong position when you make your offer for a property. It shows the seller that you are serious and have the necessary funds available. If the property market is booming, this may give you an advantage over another potential buyer.

HOW MUCH DOES IT COST?

You will be responsible for paying:

➤ The valuation fee

➤ Your solicitor for handling the mortgage

➤ The lender's solicitor for handling the application

➤ An arrangement fee (if your mortgage requires it)

➤ A mortgage indemnity guarantee if the loan is over 75%

➤ A mortgage protection policy

➤ Costs arising from stipulations for repairs arising from the valuation

➤ Fees for any inspections that take place during the building of a new house.

WHICH MORTGAGE?

There are a dizzying array of mortgage products on the market. Competition between lenders is high, so they are constantly redefining their offers to attract new customers. Before approaching a lender, it is best to acquaint yourself with the basic formulae so that you will not be blinded by jargon.

Essentially, there are only two distinct types of mortgage:

➤ Repayment (capital and interest)

➤ Interest-only (endowment, ISA or pension).

Repayment mortgages

Each month, your repayments will go towards paying off both the interest on the loan and the loan itself. The repayments are based on the amount borrowed, the length of the mortgage period (usually twenty or twenty-five years) and the Bank of England's base rate of interest. Repayments are made over the specified period and, assuming you do not default for any reason, by the end of the term the whole amount should be paid off. To begin with, most of each monthly payment goes towards paying the interest but as the term of the mortgage progresses, the amount of the loan paid off increases.

Advantages

➤ Assuming the borrower keeps up with the repayments, the loan will be fully paid off at the end of the repayment period.

➤ It is possible to make extra payments or pay in a lump sum to reduce both the interest and the capital owed.

➤ Negative equity is less of a threat because the capital is being paid off month by month.

➤ As the loan is paid off, the level of equity in the property increases.

➤ It is not always necessary to take out life assurance cover.

➤ This type of mortgage is not reliant on the twists and turns of the stock market.

Disadvantages

➤ If you die before the mortgage is paid off without having taken out any life assurance cover, the property may have to be sold by the lender to repay the outstanding debt.

➤ If you move within a few years of taking out the mortgage, it is likely little of the loan will have been paid off. If a further twenty-five-year mortgage is required for a different property, you will extend the period for repaying the debt.

➤ Some arrangements may invite financial penalties if extra lump sums are used to pay off the debt.

➤ This type of mortgage does not benefit from a rising stock market.

Interest-only mortgages

This differs from a standard repayment mortgage because the monthly repayments only pay off the interest on the loan. In addition, you will have to set up a 'repayment vehicle' or investment plan into which you will pay a sum each month in order to save enough to pay off the loan in full at the end of the mortgage term. The repayment vehicle is usually one of three things: an endowment, a pension or an ISA. If you cannot keep up the payments into the repayment vehicle, you will not be able to pay off the loan.

Advantages

➤ Some vehicles are more tax efficient than others.

➤ If the investment growth rate is faster than predicted at the outset, you may be able to pay off your mortgage early, or you may receive a tax-free lump sum when the debt is repaid at the end of the mortgage term.

➤ You can generally shift your investments to a new mortgage should you move.

Disadvantages

➤ If the investment plan under-performs, you will not have enough saved to pay off the mortgage in full. Both you and the lender should monitor its performance so that you can make extra payments into the policy to compensate for any anticipated shortfall.

➤ Financial penalties may be incurred if the plan is cashed in early.

LOCATION LOCATION LOCATION

➤ Financial penalties may be incurred if you stop paying the premiums.

➤ Throughout the mortgage period, your debt to the lender remains constant.

Endowment mortgages

The repayment vehicle is in the form of an endowment policy. This involves monthly payments to a life insurance company, who invest the money in a savings plan. The payments are based on the amount of the loan and the time over which you have agreed to pay it back, your age and health. The idea is that when the term is up, the investment will have matured and will realise enough to pay off the mortgage and, if you are lucky, give you a bonus. However, because of the nature of the stock market, there is no guarantee that when the policy matures, there will be enough money to pay off the mortgage. Life insurance is automatically provided by this arrangement so that should you die before the policy matures, your loan will be paid off. If you want to cash one in early, take professional independent financial advice first.

There are various forms of endowment policy. The two most commonly used are 'with profits' and 'unit-linked'. 'With profits' aims to pay off the loan plus give you a share in the profits made by the company investing your premiums. An annual reversionary bonus is guaranteed if you do not cash in the policy early. When the policy matures, a terminal bonus may be paid depending on the performance of the fund. A 'unit-linked' policy depends on the value of the investment plan when it reaches the end of the mortgage period.

Advantages

➤ If the investment performs beyond expectations, you may enjoy a terminal bonus or be able to pay off the mortgage early.

➤ It is usually an economic way of obtaining life insurance cover.

➤ The mortgage can be transferred to another property if you move.

Disadvantages

➤ There is no guarantee you will be able to pay off the mortgage at the end of the term.

➤ Premiums can be high, especially if you are not in the first flush of youth or have health problems.

➤ This is the least flexible type of investment, with little room to manoeuvre once you have signed on the dotted line.

ISA mortgages

The repayment vehicle is in the form of an Individual Savings Account (ISA), a tax-free corporate savings plan through which the money is invested in the stock market. There are numerous ISAs available and because of their complexity, it is worth taking professional advice on which to choose.

Advantages

➤ Particularly tax efficient for those in a high tax bracket.

➤ If it performs well, you will be able to pay off your mortgage at the end of the repayment period and may even receive an additional bonus.

➤ An ISA can be selected according to the level of risk you wish to take. The higher the risk, the higher the potential gain.

➤ ISAs are cheaper than endowment mortgages, and are tax free.

Disadvantages

➤ If the ISA does not perform well, there is no guarantee you will be able to pay off your mortgage when the repayment period is up.

➤ Limitations on the maximum investment may limit your confidence in paying off the loan when the term is up.

Pension mortgages

The repayment vehicle takes the form of a pension plan. This is a stock market investment benefitting from tax relief and tax-free growth. Life insurance cover is provided. When the term is up, the tax-free sum is used to pay off the mortgage and you can then draw a pension from the balance.

Advantages

➤ Frequently used by self-employed or older borrowers.

➤ High rate tax relief (up to 40%) for those in high tax bracket.

Disadvantages

➤ There is no guarantee you will receive enough to pay off the mortgage at the end of the repayment period.

➤ You must use the lump sum to pay off the mortgage. It may be necessary to take out a second pension policy as a safety net.

➤ Because the lump sum is only available on retirement, it may mean that younger investors may have a mortgage term of longer than twenty-five years.

INTEREST RATES

Having chosen the type of mortgage that will best suit your circumstances, it is time to look at the various ways that interest can be paid on the different schemes.

Variable rate mortgages

Monthly payments are made at the lender's standard variable rate (SVR). Depending on the lender, the SVR can be between 1% and 4% above the Bank of England's base rate of interest. As the base rate moves up and down, so does the SVR.

Advantages

➤ There are no penalties incurred if you decide to change your mortgage arrangements.

➤ If the Bank's base rate falls, so will your monthly repayments.

Disadvantages

➤ If the Bank's base rate rises, so will your monthly repayments.

➤ The SVR does not necessarily exactly mirror any fall in the Bank's base rates.

➤ Because your repayments will vary with any changes in the interest rate, it will be harder for you to budget accurately.

Fixed rate mortgages

Monthly payments are made at a fixed interest rate (ie the payments do not vary) over an agreed period. This is commonly somewhere between two and five years. After that the rate usually reverts to the lender's standard variable rate (SVR).

Lenders frequently charge an application fee and apply an Early

Redemption Charge (ERC) to fixed rate mortgages. This effectively locks you into the agreement, meaning that if you cash in your mortgage within a certain number of years, you will be liable to heavy charges. Beware – the ERC can run beyond the fixed rate period. Different lenders levy different charges so it is worth shopping around to see who is the most flexible.

Advantages

➤ Knowing what your repayments will be over the first few years makes it easy to budget.

➤ Protection if the lender's SVR rises.

➤ A lower interest rate may free up some cash for necessary furnishings or redecoration.

Disadvantages

➤ Payment of application fee.

➤ ERC means you will not be able to change your mortgage early on without paying a hefty penalty.

➤ If the lender's SVR goes down, you may be paying an uncompetitive rate of interest.

➤ May also have overhang (ie the ERC runs beyond the fixed rate period).

Discounted rate mortgages

For a certain period, anything from six months to several years, a discount is applied to the SVR. If the SVR fluctuates, so will your discounted rate with the differential between the two remaining the same.

Advantages

➤ Low interest over a period of time may give you room to spend money on other things such as furnishings.

➤ You will benefit if the Bank of England's base rate falls, and the SVR with it.

➤ The competitive initial rates are useful if you need some extra cash.

Disadvantages

➤ Application fees and early redemption penalties will almost certainly apply.

➤ If you take a substantial discount, the increase in payments when the rate reverts to the SVR may come as a nasty shock.

➤ There is no control over how high the rate can go.

Capped rate mortgages

Capped rate mortgages guarantee that for a specific period the interest rate on your loan does not go above a fixed ceiling or capped rate. This means that if the SVR falls below the ceiling, your repayments will be based on the lower rate. However, you are protected if it rises beyond the capped rate. When the period is over, interest will normally revert to the SVR. This arrangement can be combined with a discounted rate mortgage.

Advantages

➤ A fall in the Bank of England's base rate that leads to a fall in your lender's SVR means you will benefit.

➤ Knowing that the interest rate cannot go above a certain point allows you to budget more easily.

Disadvantages

➤ Application fees and early redemption penalties are common. They may extend beyond the period of the capped rate.

➤ Once the interest reverts to the SVR, you may find yourself

trapped in an uncompetitive rate, unable to change your mortgage without paying heavy penalties.

➤ The rate will be higher than a comparative fixed rate.

Cap and collar rate

Similar to a capped rate mortgage except that the interest rate does not
only have a ceiling (cap) but it also has a floor (collar) below which it
cannot fall.

Advantages

➤ A fall in the Bank of England's base rate that leads to a fall in
your lender's SVR means you may benefit.

➤ Knowing the interest rate is fixed between two points makes for
easier budgeting.

Disadvantages

➤ Application fees and early redemption penalties are common.
They may extend beyond the period of the cap and collar rate.

➤ You will be paying an uncompetitive rate if interest rates drop
below the collar.

Index tracker mortgage

The index tracker rate moves up and down with the Bank of England's base
rate. It is usually lower than the lender's SRV and the differential between it
and the base rate is constant for a specified period, after which it reverts to
the SRV. It is possible to find tracker mortgages that continue for the dura-
tion of the mortgage. Tracker mortgages can also be discounted for a
certain period before rising to an agreed rate for a further agreed period,
and then reverting to the SRV. Different rates are available, so again it is
worth shopping round to find the best deal for your circumstances.

Advantages

➤ The rate is usually lower than the lender's SRV.

➤ You will benefit from any drop in the Bank's base rate – not always the case if your mortgage is linked to the lender's SRV.

Disadvantages

➤ Other rates will be more competitive.

➤ Early redemption penalties frequently apply.

➤ You are subject to the unpredictability of the Bank's base rate which may fluctuate swiftly, in which case you may see a startling increase in your repayments.

Buy-to-let mortgages

A buy-to-let mortgage is very similar to a standard mortgage used by an owner-occupier. The lender will carry out the same checks on the borrower and property. Loans can be arranged for terms from five to forty-five years, and for up to 80% of the property value. The rental income will be taken into account, often with the proviso that the property is let by a letting agent and that it will be an assured shorthold tenancy (see Chapter 7 for more information about letting your property).

ADDITIONAL INCENTIVES

When deciding which of the myriad mortgage deals to choose from, there are other benefits that lenders offer to tempt you their way. Just when you thought your head was about to stop spinning...

Flexible mortgages

Imported from Australia, these mortgages are designed to let you overpay and underpay without the threat of penalties. You control how much and when you pay, although you cannot underpay until you have built up a reserve through your overpayments. It is important to manage it carefully because if you consistently underpay, the period of the mortgage will have to be extended and you will find yourself paying more interest. Lenders can impose restrictions, limiting the amount by which you over- or underpay and sometimes prohibiting any borrowing against repaid capital. Check out the terms thoroughly before committing to anything.

Advantages

> ➤ No early redemption penalties.
> ➤ You can pay off your mortgage early.
> ➤ You can frequently borrow against your overpayments.
> ➤ If there is a fall in your lender's SRV, you will benefit.

Disadvantages

> ➤ The mortgage term could be extended if you make too many underpayments.
> ➤ You are subject to rises in the SRV, which could result in an increase in your payments.
> ➤ Variations in the interest rate make it hard to budget.

Current account mortgage (CAM)

This is a flexible mortgage whereby the outstanding balance of your current account is offset against the outstanding balance of the mortgage. The interest is paid on the resulting figure. So, if you have a mortgage of £40,000 and have £2,750 in your bank account, the interest will be paid on £37,250.

Advantage

> ➤ Some lenders will also link savings accounts, credit cards and personal loans.

➤ The outstanding balance of your mortgage is calculated daily, so even if the amount in your current account varies, depending on your incomings and outgoings, there is the potential for saving a considerable sum over the term of the mortgage.

Disadvantages

➤ All your finances need to be in one place.

Cashback mortgages

Some lenders offer a lump sum of money to be given to the buyer when they complete on the purchase. The amount given varies according to the lender. Some give a percentage of the purchase price while others give a flat fee.

Advantages

➤ The money may be useful at a time when you have various bills to pay – solicitor's fees, redecoration, furnishings.

Disadvantages

➤ Application fees may be payable.
➤ These arrangements inevitably involve early redemption charges that will lock you into the deal for a number of years.
➤ As a result, you may be cornered into paying high interest rates.

Contribution to legal costs

Some lenders use this as an incentive to get your business, but you will almost certainly have to use a solicitor of their choice. Check them out before you agree. Some deals will cover your legal costs entirely.

Free valuation

In the event of the purchase not going through because of a poor valuation, you will not be charged for that valuation.

OTHER COSTS

Mortgage indemnity charges

For protection against any losses incurred on a loan above 75% of the purchase price, the lender takes out a form of insurance. This charge is passed on to the borrower to be paid before they begin their mortgage repayments. This charge can be fairly substantial and protects the lender, *not* you. Should your payments fall into arrears, the insurance company can and will come after you for any sums still owed.

Early redemption charges

If you choose any low-cost mortgage, the lender will almost certainly lock you into the arrangement by inflicting punitive charges should you either move your mortgage or pay it off. You may have to pay them the equivalent of six months' interest, or return the cashback or the discounted interest.

It is possible to select a 'No Redemption' or 'No Overhang' option. 'No Redemption' means that while taking advantage of a special rate, you can sell before the fixed period is over without incurring a redemption fee. 'No Overhang' means that you can move your mortgage or pay it off as soon as the period of the special rate has ended. However, opting for either of these does mean that you will not be offered the most competitive rates on your mortgage.

Booking and arrangement fees

You may be liable to pay a booking fee when applying for some mortgages. It may not be refundable. Arrangement fees are sometimes charged on fixed and capped rate mortgages. They can be absorbed into the mortgage repayments.

Valuation fees

The lender will insist that the property is valued so that they know their loan is safeguarded. They may have their own surveyor, but you will then be expected to pick up the tab.

Insurance

You will have to take out a Buildings Insurance Policy to cover the property against damage. The lender will insist on this because it provides security against the loan. You should also take out a policy to cover the contents. It may be worthwhile investing in accident, sickness and unemployment insurance (or a private mortgage payment protection plan) to cover your mortgage repayments should any such circumstances prevent you paying. However, insurance can be expensive and may include restrictive conditions. Read the small print very carefully so you know exactly what is covered and, more importantly, what is not.

WHICH LOAN TO CHOOSE?

The most important thing is to investigate thoroughly a number of different mortgage possibilities, questioning the fees, penalty clauses, costs and insurance clauses before you commit yourself. If you are tempted by a fixed or discounted rate, consider whether you will be able to afford the repayments once the discounted period is over. Do not be smooth-talked by a salesman into taking an endowment policy unless you have good independent reason to believe it is the right one for you. The salesman will almost certainly be getting commission on the loan – not the case with other arrangements. If you are truly bewildered, ask your mortgage broker for objective independent advice. There are a vast range of rates and repayment options on the market, so examine the pros and cons of each of them until you find the one that suits you and your financial situation. The questions you should ask are detailed on page 77. Use Checklist 1 on page 264 to record the answers.

IF YOU ARE REFUSED

Do not immediately despair. If you are viewed by one mortgage company as a bad risk because you are self-employed or have a poor credit rating, another may take a different view. Ask the advice of a mortgage broker who may know of companies who lend to people in your position, provided you have proof of your income. It is possible that a credit refer-ence agency used by the mortgage company to check your credit worthiness may have inadvertently provided incorrect information. Ask the lender why they will not loan you the money – they are legally obliged to tell you. It is possible that they will have seen records of a debt that you have cleared years earlier which should have been amended. If you can prove their information is incorrect, then you can reapply for a loan.

If the lender refuses you a mortgage thanks to the results of their valuation, you have no choice but to try another source or back out of the deal altogether.

CHERRY BEESLEY AND MARK BROWN, IPSWICH

Wanted: 'Our ideal home would be somewhere out in the country – a large house, lots of land. It would be nice if it had some outbuildings in a bit of a ramshackle state. We could put our own signature on it, spend some money and turn it into our dream house. Our budget is between £200,000 and £300,000 although if something came up that was spectacular, we would be flexible about going over £300,000.'

There is nothing like the imminent birth of a first baby to make a couple think about finding a bigger, more permanent home. Mark Brown, who jointly owns and runs a corporate gifts company, and Cherry Beesley were expecting theirs in a month so things were reaching desperation point. Their search was based around their home town of Ipswich, the capital of Suffolk since medieval times. The county is widely regarded as one of the most attractive in the south of England, dotted with picturesque historic villages that have changed little since the wool trading boom of the sixteenth century.

The first house they viewed was thirteen miles west of Ipswich in the village of Great Bricett. A two-storey, fifteenth-century, half-timbered house was set in stunning gardens. The central part of the property was built as a hall house with just one large room with a hole in the roof to let out the smoke. The family would have once lived, cooked, eaten and slept in there. The reeding on the beams and the egg-and-dart mouldings demonstrated the wealth of the original owners. The beams may have had wood rot but almost certainly only in the outside inch where the sap had suffered – something for a surveyor to check. Over the years, the property had developed into something of a rabbit warren with ten rooms arranged over both floors with two staircases joining them. The rooms were not joined by a corridor but ran into one another – a feature that could be changed. The bathroom was long and very dated but had the potential for division into two bathrooms, each easily accessed by its own door. 'It's just fantastic, idyllic. Our only reservation is that it's near the top end of our budget and it needs a lot of money spent on it.'

Eighteen miles north of Ipswich in the village of Wickham Skeith stood an even older property that dated, in part, back to the four-teenth century. Once a Tudor pub, this white-rendered five-bedroom house offered five reception rooms, a great office and several outbuildings. Cherry and Mark were put off by the kitchen almost immediately. 'It looks like it's a great working kitchen but it's more modern than I was expecting.' Yet going into the rest of the house was like stepping back through time with an ancient timber arch and beams. Adjoining it was a good-size office in a converted barn. Flanked on both sides by garden, the property backed onto farmland. It would be important to check who owned it and what degree of development the council would allow should it be bought for development. The verdict? Mark: 'It's got one or two fantastic features. I love the office and I love the fact that outbuildings need to be extended but I don't think it's for us.' Cherry: 'I think it's got a lot of character and I'm sure it would be somebody's dream home, but I don't think it's ours.'

> **TIP: Always find out who owns nearby open land and what their plans are for it. Ask the local council what degree of development would be allowed.**

United in their view, they travelled on to Haughley, fourteen miles west of Ipswich, where they saw a large family farmhouse on the market for £245,000. The front door led straight into the living room, part of the Victorian extension added to the original sixteenth-century house. The ground-floor layout had the potential for change, possibly by removing a wall in the living room to enlarge it and give it a garden view through the French windows, and by blocking one of the entrances so some of the kitchen units could be moved, allowing more space for storage in the kitchen. Unlike the first two properties, this one was not listed so there should be fewer problems changing interior or exterior features. Outside there was a granary that would convert into an office. The property was a possibility until they realised the two strikes against it: the A14 was audible from inside the house; and there was a sewage works over the hedge.

It was on to Kettlebaston, where a thatched four-bedroom house was being sold off from the farm it backed onto. The asking price was £300,000. First impressions were magnificent, although the patterned décor was somewhat overwhelming. Stripping the heavily glossed timber beams would be a time-consuming job, let alone the different patterned wallpapers. Two staircases led to the upper floor with its uneven floors and panoramic views. The only way to even up the floors would be to add another one on top. Cherry and Mark liked the place. 'Lots of potential, lots of charm, lots to think about.' One thing that needed consideration was the pig farm behind the property. The herd was about to be sold off but the future of the farm unit was unclear. 'I think it's almost a necessity that one purchases it with the house to prevent future development of houses there.' Research showed it was not for sale.

> **TIP: Painted timber beams can be sand-blasted clean, but in listed buildings they should be hand-stripped.**

The last property on their list was a forty-minute drive west of Ipswich near Cuckfield. Apart from the four-bedroom house there were eight or nine outbuildings, a pond and seven acres of land – all on the market for £350,000. The living room was a modern extension with a large hatch in its ceiling so furniture could be moved upstairs without having recourse to the original cottage stairs. Outside, among the outbuildings was a huge barn with a high timber roof. 'This is exactly what I was wanting when I said outbuildings. It would make a perfect house, perfect office, even a house for us.' If they did convert it, they would benefit from the spectacular view and seven acres of land lead-ing down to the river.

> **TIP: Always look beyond the surface. Despite appearances, you might find authentic or surprising features. Investigate behind bath panels, under carpets, behind fireplace surrounds.**

After a night's sleep, they decided to give the house at Great Bricett and the farm at Cuckfield a second viewing. One ground floor room at the hall house needed a new floor, but they needed the advice of medieval expert John Berry on the deteriorating wall at the end of the property. The fact that the house was Grade II listed meant they could only carry out repairs within strict guidelines and at times might need specialist craftsmen. John felt the threat to the wall could be removed by rendering it for under £1,000. Back at Cuckfield, they called the local planning department to find them enthusiastic about encouraging employment in rural areas. This meant they would be keener to see the barn converted as commercial premises initially, although a future application for residential use might be viewed more favourably. The house was in good condition with new radiators and electrics, although the kitchen would need some work.

> TIP: Before making an offer, check the local planning department policy on barn converssions

Finally, they decided to put low offers in on both: £275,000 for Great Bricett and £315,000 for Cuckfield. The first was rejected and they withdrew the second because they realised it meant being too far from Ipswich. Then operations came to a temporary halt with the birth of Amelia Lucy, so they decided to move into rented accommodation, ready to move on when they eventually found their dream home.

CONSERVATION AREAS AND LISTED BUILDINGS

Despite the advances in modern technology and design, a huge number of British home buyers want to live in a period property. The more original features it boasts the better for the value of the house.

Conservation areas

To safeguard the historical areas in towns and villages throughout the UK, local planning authorities have designated particular districts of historical or architectural interest 'conservation areas'. This means there are strict rules governing what can and cannot be done to the houses in them. Unless you are making an alteration that will restore a property's original features, such as removing uPVC or aluminium window frames and reinstating wooden ones, no kind of development or demolition is allowed. For a buyer, this is reassuring because he knows the surrounding environment is protected from change. It may be a drawback if it means that he is unable to add an extension or make an alteration that would make the living space more congenial. Any such change would be subject to both listed building consent and planning permission – both difficult to obtain. However, if almost every house in the street added a back extension before the area was designated for conservation, it is likely you would receive permission. What is harder is to set the precedent. When planning your garden, remember that trees have conservation orders on them too. You will need planning permission to chop one down, or you may incur a heavy fine.

Listed buildings

Listed buildings are held on statutory lists of properties chosen for their architectural and historic interest. They may be architecturally interesting because of their design, decoration or craftsmanship. They may be of historic interest in that they illustrate aspects of the nation's social, cultural or military history. Equally, they may have some group value so that a number are notable as an architectural or historical entity, eg model villages, terraces or squares. Once a building is listed, it means that any alterations to either its interior or exterior must not affect its character. Frequently, any internal changes must leave a room showing its original use.

All buildings built before 1700 that are close to their original condition are listed, as are most of those built between 1700 and 1840. With the arrival of the Industrial Revolution many more buildings were built, so tighter criteria are used to list them. Few buildings are listed after 1945 unless they are of exceptional importance. There are three grades of listed buildings:

➤ Grade I – these are buildings of exceptional interest. They cannot be extended or altered, and all repairs must be kept in the original style of the property. English Heritage grants are available for this kind of work.

➤ Grade II* – these comprise buildings of particular importance. They cannot be altered in any way, and it may be possible to receive an English Heritage grant to help with repairs.

➤ Grade II – these are buildings of special interest. If you wanted to make any changes that affected the character inside or out – changing the existing windows or doors or adding new ones, adding satellite dishes/TV aerials, making alterations to the internal layout, changing the surface finishes including the roofing materials, adding an extension or demolishing it altogether – listed building consent is a must. It is a legal requirement so heavy penalties are enforced if it is breached, including a fine or imprisonment and the possibility that the council will ask you to return the building to its original state. If in any doubt, consult your local planning office. If you apply to your local council, the conservation officer should be able to tell you the probability of your plans being passed. It is a good idea to use an architect who understands the nature of your project and knows the whims of the local planning department.

If the local authority decides a listed building is not being maintained to a sufficiently high level, it can serve a repairs notice.

The fact that a building is listed should help in the selling of a property because its associations will undoubtedly attract buyers. As far as buyers are concerned, you will find that its status may increase its value and make it more intrinsically interesting to you. However, you may well have trouble making any alterations that you think might benefit your lifestyle. To find out about available grants, contact English Heritage or visit www.english-heritage.org.uk.

CAZ GRAHAM AND RIGBY JERRAM, KENDAL

Wanted: 'We both work from home so we need to have two offices in any house so that we don't kill each other. We need to have plenty of space and ideally a big garden with an open outlook. We really like the feeling that we are in the country. We have a ceiling of £185,000 and that really is it.'

A couple who want different things in a house can be hard to please. Caz Graham, a freelance radio producer, and Rigby Jerram, a freelance ecologist, live fifty miles apart but had decided to join forces in buying a home of their own. Rigby enjoyed his lifestyle. 'At the moment I live in the middle of a town. I don't have to get into a car to get a paper, go to the pub or go shopping. I don't see many people through my work so to be stuck in the middle of nowhere and then not see anyone during the day might just drive me round the bend.' But Caz had other ideas. 'At the moment I live in a field and I really like living in the middle of a field. I don't want to live on a street where you can see people walking past the whole time.' Would they be able to find a perfect compromise somewhere near Kendal?

Kendal is a historic market town on the doorstep of the Lake

District National Park. The area offers the best of both worlds, idyllic rural living combined with excellent transport links to the major towns of the north. There is a wealth of properties to choose from, from the limestone terraces of the towns, to cottages and farm buildings out in the countryside. The first property they saw was a three-bedroom farm conversion near Old Hutton, on the market for £177,500. It was in a rural location but within easy cycling distance of Kendal. It boasted a good-sized living room with original beams, although the chimney seemed obtrusively monolithic. The kitchen was on the small side and the three bedrooms provided scope for the two offices, although Rigby felt the master bedroom was too small. A three-year-old conversion, the property was in excellent condition and had many attractive features – the fireplace, the beams, the light fittings. Caz liked the location but Rigby was anxious about the shared courtyard. 'If you don't get on with your neighbours, you're really going to know about it.' And neither of them was convinced that the house was right. 'It's too small inside. There's not enough working space. We would kill each other.'

> **TIP: Check what is staying and what is going. Some deals fall through in fights over this. Do not lose sight of the issue. It is the house you want. You can always buy more fittings.**

For £145,000, Fern Cottage in Hincaster offered different possibilities. A two-bedroom property full of traditional features, it had two outbuildings beside the house that might make fantastic offices if re-roofed, properly insulated and with the introduction of more light. The money spent would be likely to increase the value of the property and make it a more saleable asset. The house had been well looked after and was in good condition. It had two good-sized bedrooms but the ceilings were too low, making Caz and Rigby feel claustrophobic. The verdict? 'It's really lovely but it just feels too small.'

> **TIP: More and more people are working from home. The addition of a home office is likely to add value to a property.**

They found more space in a recently refurbished house on Nakeland village green, just three miles from Kendal. Built in 1923, it had a much more contemporary feel at the expense of the traditional features that the couple liked. On the market for £185,000, it had three double bedrooms and bathroom on the first floor with a fourth master bedroom and *en suite* bathroom in the attic. Caz immediately reacted against it. 'There's a staircase in the middle of the bedroom. It might suit someone but I don't like it at all. I wouldn't even want it as my office really.' Overall they felt it lacked the character they were looking for in a home and they could not see a way to transform it into something they would like.

> **TIP: Just because you do not like the modernisation of a property, do not assume that any changes you make will not add to the value of the property.**

Still unable to agree, they looked at a £175,000 Georgian townhouse in the heart of Kendal – just where Rigby wanted to be. With only two bedrooms, it did have a living room and separate dining room so two offices were a possibility. However, more imaginatively, the current kitchen could be turned into an office with the wall between the sitting room and dining room knocked through to make a fantastic open-plan kitchen/dining/sitting room. Although such a conversion would not add value to the house it would make a more practical living arrangement for them. The main bedroom was superb with an unbeatable 180-degree view but, and for Caz it was a big 'but', the garden was too small and facing the wrong direction. Otherwise, she would have been won over.

Finally, they looked in the village of Orton, home to a prize-winning teashop and a chocolate factory. Two ruined barns, one of them an old slaughterhouse, were on the market for £115,000. Planning permission had been granted for their conversion into two houses. One was projected as a three-bedroom house with an office, big kitchen, separate dining room and a large living room. The cost of the conversion was estimated at £80,000 but if Caz and Rigby were prepared to roll up their sleeves, it could be a lot cheaper. Rigby loved the location and Caz was smitten. 'I love it. That's exactly the kind of project I'd really like to do.' But they both agreed that it was a bit too far from Kendal.

The only contender was the townhouse, so they returned for a second viewing. Caz was concerned about its size and the light in the garden. It was obvious that it would only get the sun in the morning and early afternoon, not in the evening. She also wanted to look at the existing kitchen to see if it would be too dark for her office but was reassured when she realised leaving the door open (as she inevitably would) made the difference. Upstairs, Rigby was checking the same thing in the second bedroom but, although a north-facing room, it was very light. What would they decide? 'It's a beautiful house. We loved it. The interior was fantastic and the views were to die for. But it was £175,000 and we need more space for that. We want more garden, two offices and room for us.' But the houses they had seen that were big enough and in the right location were too expensive.

They had no alternative but to continue their search, aware that to get the size they wanted, they would have to be prepared to buy something that needed work – much of which would have to be done themselves. Caz had learned that she could live in Kendal if she had to, and Rigby now knew he was not prepared to live far outside the town even if they found an ideal ruin in an ideal village. It would not be easy to find the right solution.

RESTORING ORIGINAL FEATURES

When buying a period home, there are a number of things you can do to bring the past back to life. There are many features that give a house its particular character. Look behind bath panelling, boarded-up chimney breasts and doors, and under floor coverings. There may be a treasure trove waiting to be discovered. Here are a few starting points to get you going:

Windows
➤ uPVC windows must be replaced with wooden ones in the original style.
➤ Sash windows. Replace broken sash cords and treat wet rot. Ease sticking windows by breaking any paint seals, repositioning misplaced stop beads, oiling the pulley or repairing any faulty woodwork.
➤ Casement windows. Repair faulty woodwork and hinges. Metal casements may need to be treated for corrosion, weather seals replaced and bent parts straightened. Whether or not you need a professional will depend on the degree of neglect.
➤ Glass. The imperfections in horticultural glass make it the closest match to old glass. Remove disintegrating putty from round any loose pieces of stained glass and push in new putty to hold them in place. More damaged stained glass will need the attention of an expert. If you want to reinstate a stained glass panel where it has

long been lost, look in a salvage yard or, having examined the designs in neighbouring houses, commission a suitable new panel.

➤ Repairs to leaded lights will need the skill of a professional.

➤ Buy original or reproduction fasteners and handles.

Shutters

➤ Wide painted window boards may be hiding original internal panelled shutters.

Doors

➤ Separate double reception rooms by reinstating large, folding double doors. The salvage yard may come up trumps. If not, ask a local carpenter.

➤ Replace damaged glass in glazed doors.

➤ If the doors are flush, find out whether this is because a sheet of hardboard has been pinned over the original (flush doors were very fashionable in the 1950s and 1960s).

➤ Strip old paint, repair wood where necessary and oil or wax it.

➤ Use appropriate reclaimed or reproduction handles, hinges, locks and finger-plates.

➤ Polish up existing metalwork.

Plasterwork

➤ Strip layers of paint from decorative cornices and ceiling roses to reveal the detail before repainting.

➤ If a piece is missing, make a mould of an existing section and have a replacement cast in plaster.

Woodwork

➤ Strip paint from original woodwork, especially panelling, and decide whether to return it to its original state.

➤ If parts of the original skirting board, dado rails or picture rails still exist, fill the gaps by taking a mould from the original and have a replacement strip made by a carpenter. Otherwise buy off-the-shelf mouldings appropriate to the period of the house.

➤ Use wood panelling or anaglypta paper under a dado rail for extra wall protection.

Floors

➤ Look under existing floor coverings to see if the original tiles/flags are still there.

➤ Stone can be cleaned using a bucket of water and two tablespoons of washing soda for light stains. Seal if required.

➤ Replace cracked or damaged ceramic tiles.

➤ For encaustic tiles, remove loose pieces, clean and glue back in. Clean with household detergent and water. If really grimy, use a proprietory cleaner.

➤ Wooden floors can be brought back to life by sanding then varnishing.

➤ Floorboards can also be painted, patterned or stencilled.

Staircase

➤ Replace broken or missing bannisters.

➤ Use traditional carpet runner up the centre of the stairs, with stair rods or clips.

ANNE RAWSTHORNE AND TOM PRIESTLEY, LEEDS

Wanted: 'A two- or three-bedroom house with a garden which will give us more space than we have at the moment. If we saw a nice house that needed some work doing to it, we wouldn't be afraid to get our hands dirty. We've looked at up-and-coming areas so I think we may have to pay a touch over £100,000.'

Buying your first home can be a nerve-wracking business, especially when the property market is flourishing and demand is outstripping supply. Anne Rawsthorne, who works for a radio station, and Tom Priestley, who works for a marketing company, were first-time buyers in Leeds. They wanted to move out of their cramped rental accommodation into a house of their own at a time when interest rates were at their lowest for forty years. A good time to take the plunge, but a stressful one since decisions had to made fast.

Leeds is a buzzing metropolis and university town. 150 years ago the woollen mill trades brought wealth to the area, whereas now e-commerce and international finance is bringing demand back to the heart of the city. Tom and Anne already lived on the edge of Headingly and had set their heart on buying in the same area. It has a vibrant village atmosphere, only a mile from the city centre and with plenty of bars, funky shops and café culture making it in demand. The property market was extremely buoyant, with houses demanding high prices and moving quickly. The couple's budget would buy a flat but not a house, so they looked in Hyde Park, only a mile from Headingly but where a lot more could be bought for the money. A three-bedroom, semi-detached house was on the market for £105,000. It offered plenty of space and had a rustic feel thanks to the stripped wood floors, gas stove and comfortable kitchen/dining room. The interior decoration was bright, so it was important to close the eyes, feel the space and imagine how it could be different.

> **TIP:** As a first-time viewer, ignore the colour and furniture in a room. Close your eyes for a second, feel the space and try to imagine it furnished to your taste.

There was a patio outside, but the grass beyond belonged to a nearby building. If something were to be built on it, it would damage the view and the value of this house severely. Secondly, the neighbouring house had a right of access over the patio – something for a solicitor to check out. Tom and Anne were unsure and decided to investigate the area more thoroughly before making a decision.

> **TIP:** If rights of access are claimed through a garden, do not be immediately put off but insist early in the negotiations that the exact wording in the proposed contract is sent through to your solicitor.

It was time for a reality check in Headingly itself, where a two-bedroom flat, only minutes from the shops and bars, was being sold for £95,000. It did not take long to look round the small rooms and galley kitchen. In fact Tom and Anne's minds were made up the minute they walked in. There simply wasn't enough space.

Horsforth is one of Leeds' new property hotspots, about ten minutes further from the centre. A traditional semi-detached house with two spacious bedrooms was priced at £95,000. Owned by a joiner who had not quite finished making improvements, the house seemed structurally sound, though the colour schemes were not to their taste. Despite the potential, Anne seemed put off by the work she thought needed doing, although in the bathroom, for example, there was already a new boiler, new fittings and tiling – all that was missing there was flooring, which would only cost around £150 to rectify.

> **TIP: Look beyond the clutter and check whether the structure is sound and if any work that needs doing is significant or merely cosmetic.**

To make the £100,000 go further, they looked further afield in Cookridge, where there was a spacious modern semi on the market for £98,950 in the quiet cul-de-sac of Haven Rise. It was another house crying out for some TLC, but it had a good open feel to it, with plenty of room for dinner parties in the kitchen/dining room. A new lease of life could be easily given by replacing the cupboard doors, the drawer fronts and adding a new worktop, and would cost little more than £400. Outside, there was a lovely garden, a patio and garage.

The couple had thought they could not afford to buy in Chapel Allerton, a popular area adjacent to Headingly. But they saw a property that was right on budget at £99,950, if they were prepared to take on the work. The kitchen was too small, but could be enlarged by knocking it through into the second reception room to give them a sun-filled room that would even have space for a sofa and TV, leaving them with a more formal living room. Upstairs there were three decent bedrooms, with a substantial garden outside. 'When we walked in, it had a grand feeling to it with the big hall, high ceilings and lots of room upstairs.' But the trade-off for the space and grandeur was that it was a little frayed at the edges. Would Anne overcome her dread of DIY to be in an area she liked?

> TIP: Houses with fewer but larger rooms are increasingly popular. Knocking a wall through can pay dividends.

After a night's sleep, they resolved to view the houses at Haven Rise and Chapel Allerton for a second time. Haven Rise lived up to their memories, but as they looked closer, potential problems raised their heads. The built-in breakfast bar that divided the kitchen and small dining area would only sit six people, so a sensible plan would be to knock it out and make a bigger dining space, perhaps even adding a window seat to confirm the room as the hub of the house. The beige bathroom suite and yellow walls were not ideal, and Anne already had thoughts of eventually getting a white suite with white tiles and a laminate floor. Outside, they noticed that the ramp to the garage was extremely steep, before establishing that the vendors had never actually driven their car down it. However, their reactions generally were positive. 'We could move in and we wouldn't have to do much to it and what there is to do wouldn't be overly expensive.'

They agreed that Chapel Allerton was an attractive quiet area that would look even better during the summer. Anne had reservations about the white stone-effect cladding on the house, but it would be potentially too damaging to the underlying brickwork to remove it although the plain glass could be put in the leaded windows to simplify the look of the exterior. Looking round the back of the house, they discovered a path running right by the back fence – a potential security risk. On their previous visit they had spotted damp in the bathroom. From the outside it was clear that a ledge across the top of an upper window would be enough to prevent any rain dripping into the wall, down onto the window ledge and seeping back through the window. Inside, they still had no doubts about the house's potential and decided there and then to put in an offer. Although it was on the market at £99,950, the couple were advised that an offer of £95,000 would be reasonable given their status as first-time buyers, chain free, ready to move and with a mortgage organised. But there were two more viewings booked for the following day and the vendor was reluctant to lower his price after having only just dropped it from £107,000. Ultimately the offer of £95,000 was rejected so Tom and Anne added another £2,000 and it was accepted. 'Tomorrow we find out the results of the survey, so fingers crossed. We're very excited because we've redecorated every room in the house already and redesigned the kitchen, spent the money already! We just want to get in there.'

FINDING THE NEXT PROPERTY HOTSPOT

Almost everybody buying a property dreams of finding that rundown derelict wreck for next-to-nothing, then doing it up and selling it for a fortune. To do that, you have to have a good knowledge of the property market, a degree of courage and some luck. All these things are also especially important if you have an eye on the resale value of the house, or if you have limited funds. If you are looking in an urban area, you need to spot the right place before anyone else if you are to find the property that will become a thoroughly good investment.

Finding an up-and-coming area involves looking for specific signs. It might not look much at the moment, but if it is next to a property hotspot where prices have been rising and buildings have been redeveloped, you can almost bet that the effect will spill over into the neighbouring streets. The fringes of these areas inevitably benefit as those who have come along later will buy up property in the surrounding streets.

Find out where developers have large-scale projects. Warehouses and commercial properties have provided massive opportunities over the last few years. Once converted, their presence revitalises the surrounding area. Look in the neighbouring back streets for rundown properties that might be worth renovating.

Investigate whether any transport links are planned to improve the commuter possibilities in a badly serviced area. Being able to get to work easily is a big incentive to bring people into an area. Talk to the local planning department to see if you can find out whether there are any new residential developments being proposed along with schools or shops.

Watch out for the tell-tale signs, for example, a discreet but chic restaurant or café or two hiding on the high street. Walk round the nearby streets to see whether other properties are being done up or if there are streets where some houses are being better looked after than the rest.

Tramp the streets to see if you can spot the next area for gentrification. If there are rundown but structurally sound period properties languishing quietly not far from a fashionable area, it will probably not be long before they are bought up for renovation. This may be the time to get in first, before the prices sky-rocket. If they are close to a rundown council estate, contact the council to see what plans they have for the area. They may be on the point of injecting a huge amount of cash into the estate, regenerating it in a way that will rub off on the street in which you are interested.

Buying away from the crowd is a risk, but if you have done your homework and thought through the budgetary implications of your purchase carefully, your investment could more than pay off within a few short years.

4   MOVING HOUSE

At last, you have exchanged contracts, after all the emotional upheaval of negotiation, speeding things along or slowing them down and the anxiety of worrying about whether the property would slip from your grasp at the last moment. It is now almost yours – bar the most extraordinary turn of fate. However, this is not the time to sit back and relax. There is plenty to be done as you prepare for completion, possibly both for the sale of your old property and for the purchase of the new, and for what can be just as big a nightmare if not properly planned – the move itself.

BETWEEN EXCHANGE AND COMPLETION

Buildings insurance

Now is the moment to check who is responsible for insuring the property. If the vendor's solicitor has used the TransAction Protocol, then the seller is responsible for insurance until the completion date. If not, the buyer assumes responsibility from the date of exchange. Your mortgage company will insist on it. Make sure the insurance covers the reinstatement cost, ie what it would cost to rebuild if destroyed. The mortgage valuation should tell you the correct amount. If you think it may be wrong, you could ask your surveyor to provide their figure. Premiums for buildings insurance vary depending on the building itself and on whether it is in a high or low risk area.

If you are buying a leasehold property, it is important to check with the freeholder whether or not they cover the insurance for the property. You do not want either to double up (making a subsequent claim might be difficult) or for the property to remain uninsured. Similarly, if you are buying a new property direct from the developer it is also usual for them to assume responsibility for the insurance until completion.

If you are liable for continuing to insure the house you are selling, make sure your premiums continue in case your buyer drops out.

Many mortgage companies offer insurance policies. You are under no obligation to buy one from them unless it is a condition of your mortgage deal, and you are almost certain to make a saving by shopping around. Some insurance companies will pay the fee some mortgage companies charge if you do choose to take out insurance elsewhere. An insurance broker will help you find the best deals.

Contents insurance

Tell your insurance company that you are moving, making sure that your possessions are insured properly over the period of the move. If you decide to buy new things for the house, or are downsizing and getting rid of much of what you own, you may need to adjust the amount. If you are moving to an area with a higher or lower crime rate and from a five-bedroom Georgian house to a two-bedroom bungalow or vice versa, your premiums will in all likelihood change. As a rule of thumb, the higher they are, the more comprehensively you will be insured. If necessary, you can add cover for accidental damage or for theft away from home. If the premiums are prohibitively high, there are ways of cutting costs, so shop around to see the different deals that are on offer. It helps if you have an approved security system and/or smoke alarm, a person is in the house most of the time (perhaps retired or self-employed), if you buy more than one policy from the same insurer or if you agree to a higher excess (ie you pay a higher sum before claiming from the policy).

Motor insurance

Inform your insurer of your change of address and whether there is a change in your parking arrangements. If your car's new home is a garage not the street or vice versa, your premiums may change.

Life insurance/insurance broker/travel insurance

Notify all insurers of your change of address and the date of your move.

Council tax

Notify your new local authority to register for council tax, water charges and to be put on the electoral roll. Notify the one you are leaving too.

Telephone

Liaise with the vendor to see whether or not he is taking the handsets with him. If he is, you will need to know how many to buy and decide whether you want built-in answerphone and fax services.

Contact the relevant telephone company to let them know that you will be taking over the existing line. If you are, ask the seller not to have the line disconnected but to be billed on the day of completion so that you can take it over from that moment. If there is even a day's break in connection, you will be liable for connection fees. If you are moving within the same area, you may be able to transfer your old number to your new home, although there will be a charge.

If you need to connect a new line, shop around for the best deal, whether it be from British Telecom or the local cable company, who may have special offers that would help you. Similarly, if you need new sockets (particularly if you are going to be working from home and need a separate fax line, business telephone line or internet access in an office), shop around for the best offers and arrange a day for them to be installed after completion.

Do not forget to give your existing telephone company a minimum of one week's notice before your move. Ask them to close your account and provide your new address so they can send you your final bill. Inform them whether or not the new owner will be taking over the line, or whether it should be disconnected.

Electricity and gas

Apply to the local electricity and gas companies with plenty of time to make the necessary arrangements to take over the supply. You will be sent an application form to complete and will need to arrange to have the meters in the new house read on the day you move there. The previous owners should have done this, but it is better to cover yourself just in case they overlooked it. Also arrange for an engineer to connect any appliances that you will be bringing with you on the day of your move, or as soon as possible afterwards. Confirm the appointments a few days before the move.

Contact your existing electricity and gas companies, asking them to read your meter on the day you move out of the property. Leave them your new address so the bills can be sent to you there. If you need an engineer to disconnect any appliances, remember to book him with enough notice so he can come on the morning of your move.

Appliances

Ask the vendors if they can leave any instruction manuals, guarantees and service agreements that will help you master unfamiliar appliances. Make sure you know where the mains switches are.

In your old property, leave all the instruction manuals, guarantees and service agreements that you can lay your hands on that will be useful to your buyer. Give them any tips as to how to get the best out of a difficult appliance and make sure they know where the mains switches are.

Rental companies

If you have a rental television, video or digital recorder, check whether or not you can take them with you, transferring your account to another branch. If not, arrange to have them taken away, take out a new contract with a company local to your new home and arrange for delivery of the new items when you have moved in.

Notice of change of address

Have a checklist of all those whom you need to notify (see Checklist 6 on page 275). When you have worked out how many you will need, buy the appropriate number of change of address cards or economise by designing and printing one yourself on a PC.

Bank accounts

Contact your bank and the holders of any other savings accounts etc with notification of your change of address. If you are moving to another part of the country or somewhere where it would be more convenient to move to another branch of the bank, or indeed a different bank altogether, you will need to apply for a transfer. Notify your current manager in writing and make the appropriate arrangements with the new bank, selecting the appropriate account and signing a transfer letter authorising the change.

Make sure that the arrangements are such that any deposit accounts are closed and opened on the same day so that you do not lose any interest.

Notify the recipients of any direct debits from your account or anyone regularly crediting your account of your change of address, your new account number and the bank's sort code and address.

If you are moving away from an area and hold any charging accounts with local retailers, arrange to have the account closed and the final bill sent to you. If you want to keep the account going, notify them of your change of address.

Mail

However many change of address cards you send out, there is bound to be someone you leave out. Rather than impose on your buyer by asking them to forward everything to you, take advantage of the Post Office's redirection service. They will forward your mail for a period of one month to a year, depending how much you pay. Everyone in the house who needs to have mail forwarded will have to sign the form. You must give five working days' notice for the service to start.

It is also wise to leave your new address and other contact details with your buyer, so that you have all eventualities covered.

Furnishings

If you have not already done so, ask the vendor if he will allow you to measure up for curtains and floor coverings where necessary. Work out which appliances you will need for the kitchen and check the ones you want will fit. There is no point in ordering a huge American-style fridge if you have no room for it. Arrange for delivery as close to the day you move in as possible.

Locks

You have no way of knowing who has keys to your new house. The vendor may have forgotten himself. It makes sense to arrange for a lock-smith to change the locks as soon as possible after your arrival, as a security measure.

Storage

It is possible that you may complete on the sale of your house before you complete on your purchase. This may be because the chain ahead of you has broken, or because you have decided to press ahead so that you can move swiftly when need be. In this instance, if nobody comes up with an empty spare room or garage, you may have to put your belongings into storage.

Find a storage company through the *Yellow Pages*. The costs involved will cover the cost of packing your belongings and transporting them to the depository, how much cubic space you have to rent and for how long, insurance, removing them from storage and delivering them to your new home. It is important that you make an inventory, valuing the items and recording which container they are stored in, so you know immediately if anything is missing.

You can get insurance cover through the storage company or through your insurance company. Shop around, comparing premiums, excess clauses and small print. Check the sum for which they are valuing your possessions is enough and that the insurance covers 'all risks'. Check the premises to see the conditions under which your possessions will be stored and what security provisions will be made.

Eventually, when it is finally delivered to you, check everything on your inventory is there in case something has been left behind. It will be much easier to find straight away, than when someone else's things have been moved into your space.

Booking the removal company

Hiring a removal company to move your belongings from one place to another is the most expensive option, but it may also be the one that saves you the most amount of anxiety.

To find the best company for the job, ask friends or your estate agent for a recommendation. Otherwise, the British Association of Removers (BAR) will be able to provide a list of their members in your area. Because prices and degrees of service vary, it is wise to get as many as three quotations if you can. Insist that they come to see exactly the amount of work involved and do not give an estimate over the telephone. If you are moving some distance, it may be cheaper to hire a removal company nearer your new home. Charges vary so make sure you understand whether mealtimes are included in an hourly rate scheme, when overtime kicks in and whether payment rates are according to the time of day or week. Depending on the amount of belongings to be moved and the distance they are going, your move may even develop into more than one day's work. This may be a little more relaxing but it will be heavy on the purse since you will be responsible for any overnight accommodation involved.

When you talk to the removal company, establish exactly how much you want them to do. It will be cheaper if you agree to pack everything yourself, but it will be extremely tiring and neither the removal firm nor their insurers will accept responsibility for objects they have not packed themselves. You will have to arrange appropriate cover with your own insurers. The removal company will be able to deliver enough packing cases or other containers to you. On the other hand, you may prefer them to do the bulk of the packing while you take responsibility for packing just the more valuable or fragile pieces. Again, remember to ensure they are properly covered by insurance. If you decide you want them to take charge of the whole thing, point out the things that you would like to be treated with extreme care, eg pictures, mirrors, ornaments, valuables, computer equipment, antiques, televisions and audio equipment, plants, the fridge/freezer, a fish tank and so on. Discuss how they are going to transport your clothes. If it saves you packing them all into cases, so much the better. Remember to include any curtains and carpets that you are taking and establish whether they will re-lay them for you or whether you need a carpet layer on hand soon after your arrival. If any pieces of furniture such as wardrobes, beds or tables need dismantling, ask whether they will reassemble them after the move.

It is also important to establish how much they are going to do for you at the other end. The cheapest option would be for them to dump the stuff, leaving you to unpack, then returning for the chests and boxes at a later date. A more expensive option would be for them to unpack it all for you. This will need some forward planning, with you marking your belongings so they go into the right boxes and get unpacked in the right room. Another possibility is to draw a diagram of the house, marking were you would like all the stickered pieces of furniture to go. If you do decide to go this route, take into account how tiring it will be after a long day of travelling as the unpacking goes on into the night.

Try to anticipate any difficulties the removal men might have and mention it at this early stage, so there are not any shock expenses when you find they have to take out an upstairs window to get your four-poster bed in. They would need special equipment for something like this, so better they have it with them and are prepared. Removal men are experienced in manoeuvring large pieces of furniture through narrow passages, round tight corners and up steep stairways, but it does take time and that time will cost you money. If you are moving somewhere where there is difficulty parking, either reserve a space in the road with dustbins, explaining to your new neighbours what is happening, or contact the local police to have parking restrictions lifted while the van is there. Similarly, warn the removal company if the van will not be able to pull up right outside the house so the men are prepared to lug your furniture down a narrow lane or up a steep driveway.

When you accept an estimate, make sure you have everything you have agreed in writing, including the date and time of their arrival, so there can be no misunderstanding.

Doing it yourself

This is the cheapest way of moving house, although it is only realistic if your possessions will fit into a hired van or in the back of friends' cars, and you are not moving too great a distance. Otherwise you will end up making a number of exhausting journeys. You will need to hire enough boxes or packing cases and stockpile enough newspaper or bubble wrap to protect anything breakable. You will also need a number of able and willing friends.

When you hire the van, make sure that doors open widely enough and that it is big enough to admit any large pieces of furniture, and check whether it has a tailgate or ramp to make the loading easier. Also check the terms of the hire agreement so you know when it has to be returned, what the exact cost of the hire is and what insurance cover is provided. If you have a lot of possessions, load the van carefully so that the weight is evenly distributed with the heavier items at the bottom. Do your best to pack it so that things will not move around too much while you are driving. Do not let your friends disappear once the van is loaded, as you will need them at the other end to help you unload. Make sure you have a few beers ready for when the job is over.

Clearing out

Moving house is a great opportunity to put your life in order. Now is the time to get rid of all those things that have been gathering dust for years.

There is absolutely no point moving things you are not going to have use for in your new home. Go through every room systematically, ruthlessly deciding what you do and do not want to keep. Weed out bookshelves, go through your wardrobe (some would say if you have not worn an item of clothing for a year, get rid of it), pile up all the children's games that are no longer played, empty drawers of half-used cosmetics. Go through old paperwork, filing what you need to keep and binning the rest. Ask yourself whether or not you really need the extra dining room chairs that have been replaced, but that you could not bring yourself to throw away. Are there any other items of furniture that will not suit your new home? The more exacting you are with yourself, the clearer your mind will become. and the more pleasure you will feel settling into your new home without all this unnecessary junk.

Before throwing anything away, put it into piles: charity shop; local hospital; Oxfam; auction rooms; car boot sale; the dump. Do not let your emotions cloud your mind so that you send things that are too worn or unsuitable to deserving causes. They do not deserve that. Ask your buyer whether they would be interested in any pieces of furniture that you do not want to move. If you can sell anything, it will give you extra cash to buy something special for your new home.

Reduce the contents of your freezer by as much as you can as you approach moving day. The less there is in it the better because it will make it more difficult for the removal men if they are weighed down by its contents. The day before you move turn the temperature to maximum so everything is frozen solid. Once it is switched off the next day, do not open the door. Freezers are vulnerable to damage if they are tipped or the back is knocked. When it arrives in its new home, leave it to stand for a couple of hours or so, so that the system has a chance to settle before being turned on again.

This is also the perfect moment to get any furniture cleaned or even re-upholstered so that it fits in with a new colour scheme. Carpets could also be removed for cleaning if you are taking them to the new house. If moving locally, the firm should deliver them back to your new address. One thing less for the removal men.

If you are packing yourself, leave yourself enough time to do it calmly. It invariably takes much longer than one anticipates.

ON COMPLETION

On completion day, your solicitor (or you, if you are braving it alone) will have completed the conveyancing and organised the transfer of money to the vendor (and from your buyer). As soon as that is done, the keys are released to you either by your solicitor or, more usually, by the estate agent.

Pack

Whether or not you are packing yourself, it is sensible to mark your belongings so that they go into appropriate packing cases. It is also a good idea to mark larger pieces of furniture with coloured sticky labels so the removal men know where to take them on arrival at your new home, especially if they arrive before you.

Whether the removal men are packing all or part of your belongings, make sure you have any essential things travelling with you that you or they might need before anything is unpacked:

➤ Kettle
➤ Mugs
➤ Teabags
➤ Coffee
➤ Sugar
➤ Teaspoons

- Knife
- Plastic plates
- Bottle opener
- Tin opener
- Sandwiches/snacks
- Light bulbs
- Matches
- Soap
- Towels
- First aid kit
- Cleaning agents and cloths
- Vacuum cleaner
- Bedding and towels
- Lavatory paper
- Pet food
- Food and water bowls for pets
- Nappies
- Baby food
- Favourite small toys
- Clean clothes
- Plugs/adaptors
- Basic tool kit
- Champagne

Also carry with you all your important documents, including:

- Cheque book, credit cards
- Passport
- Driving licence
- Motor insurance certificate
- Removal contract

Not forgetting:

➤ Cash

➤ Any valuables

➤ Your new keys

MOVING DAY

If you are not moving too far, it is probably the most sensible thing to arrange for your children and pets to be looked after elsewhere for the day. If you can take them to stay with friends the night before as the real upheaval begins, then pick them up and take them straight to their new home where their things are already unpacked, it will minimise any upset. If you are moving further away, see if they can be looked after elsewhere at least while the packing and loading is being done. Pick them up when you are ready to put them straight into the car and drive off with the minimum of fuss. Some children may be excited by the prospect of moving to a new home but others may find it disturbing, as will most pets. If you can minimise the trauma for them, you will also minimise it for yourself.

Make sure the removal men are aware of any special requests you made to the estimator, then leave them to it. The best thing you can do is to provide regular cups of tea and biscuits. It is an idea to cover a hall carpet with a dustsheet to protect it from any mud or dirt being traipsed across it. When everything is loaded, have a last look round, making sure that everything has been taken, checking in all drawers and cupboards. Do not forget any carpets and curtains that should be going with you.

As you leave the house, remember to turn off the gas, electricity and water if that is what you have agreed with the new owner. Close and lock every window and door and leave a set of clearly labelled keys for him.

Before you speed away, remember to make sure the removal men have the address where they are going, directions and a mobile telephone number in case of emergencies. You should try to arrive at the house first so that you can supervise the unloading.

On arrival

Put any dogs or cats in a locked room with a bowl of water, their basket and a litter tray. You do not want them tripping up the removal men or running away while the front door is constantly open as the van is unloaded.

Retrieve the dustsheet and cover your new hall carpet. Direct the men carrying the labelled boxes and furniture. Either tell them as you go or give them the explanatory diagram you so thoughtfully drew a week earlier. When they have finally unpacked the last box, check the van to make sure nothing has been left, sign the discharge form (marking it 'unexamined' if you have not checked over all your belongings to see if they are in one piece), tip them and wave goodbye.

Release the dog from its room but, before letting it into the garden, check that it cannot escape. The cat should be left to get used to the house for a few days before it is let out so there is less chance of it getting lost.

Tempting as it may be to rush to unpack everything, take it easy. Get your sleeping arrangements sorted out first, so collapse is possible whenever necessary. Turn the hot water on, so a hot bath or shower is a possibility. Unpack the essentials first. Open that bottle of champagne.

Making a claim

If something gets broken by the removal men during the move, make a note and ask the foreman to sign it. This gives verification for the insurance company when you make your claim. If you do not spot it until after they have left, make a list and present it to the removals company and your insurer.

JOHN MITCHELL AND SARAH NICHOLAS, LIVERPOOL

Wanted: 'Somewhere we can live and relax. The location is definitely important. We'd like to spend about £85,000 but for the perfect home, we would probably stretch to £90,000.'

Sometimes, an important consideration when buying a new home is that it should have enough storage space for all one's possessions. John Mitchell, who works for the NHS, and Sarah Nicholas, a speech therapist, were sharing their rented accommodation in Liverpool with sleeping bags, a mixing deck, two scooters, guitars, scuba gear and more. They loved the vibrancy of the city and were desperate to find somewhere to buy. But it was a sellers' market and it seemed as if there was a queue of people looking for the same thing with the same budget. 'One of the problems we've found looking for properties on the internet is that we'll find them on Sunday night but on Monday morning, when Sarah phones the estate agents, either they'll already have gone or there would be an offer on them. Every time we go to view houses, there's always at least one offer. We're never the first.'

Liverpool owes its growth to the River Mersey, which helped develop a small town into a major trading capital on England's west coast. Today, the old industries have given way to a surge of dockside redevelopment schemes catering to the trend for city-centre living. Despite the boom, there is a wide variety of property available, ranging from contemporary waterside apartments to Victorian terraced houses or elegant and expensive Georgian terraces.

Sarah and John's search began in south Liverpool, about four miles from the centre, where row upon row of terraced housing sprang up in the nineteenth century to house dockers and migrant workers. A Victorian terraced house was for sale in Colebrooke Road, and at £79,950, it was well within their budget. Totally renovated yet still retaining many original features, particularly the floor mosaic in the hall and both fireplaces in the through reception room, the house also boasted four good-sized bedrooms and a well-equipped contemporary kitchen with stainless steel worktops. The bathroom was clean, green and spacious with a white suite and an ideal laundry room next door. 'From the inside, it's absolutely perfect in a way – the design, the layout, the character, the size. It's just the location that might not be quite right for us.' The only other possible fly in the ointment was the playing fields and allotments over the road. Currently a wide open view, it would be dramatically different if they were built on. Definitely a case for checking with the local planning department.

Focusing on location rather than space, they found a conservation centre not far from the city centre. A three-bedroom house in a quiet cul-de-sac had just come onto the market at almost £90,000. A smarter area, closer to work but a more expensive and more compact house. Immediately striking were the uPVC windows. Double-glazed wood-framed windows often look better and can last just as long if properly looked after. In a conservation area, it would be important to ascertain whether or not the vendor had permission to use them, or an unsuspecting buyer might find himself having to find traditional replacements. However, the deciding factor against it was the lack of space. 'This one hasn't got character, but I think the main problem is the room sizes.'

> **TIP: If in a conservation area, check that planning permission has been given to use uPVC windows, or they may have to be replaced.**

Still in south Liverpool, they had to use their imagination to see the potential of a three-bedroom Victorian terraced house lived in by students. The living room was being used as a bedroom but looking beyond the general mess, they could see the original cornicing and picture rail, convincing them that redecorated, the room could look both grand and spacious. Beyond the decoration, the house had great potential. Through the reasonable-sized dining room was a tiny galley kitchen, but it would be possible to make the larger room the kitchen, and change the kitchen into a utility room.

> **TIP: Always look at the layout of the kitchen, checking the ideal work triangle between fridge, sink and cooker.**

Upstairs, Sarah was not keen on the yellow bathroom suite, preferring something more classic.

> **TIP: Bathroom fittings are cheap to replace provided the plumbing remains in the same place.**

There was a lot of work to be done here, though, with all the rooms needing to be taken back to basics before redecorating could begin. It was too daunting a task for Sarah and John.

Over the past five years, Liverpool has seen a sharp rise in a number of warehouse conversions and new dockside apartment complexes. At £98,000, slightly over budget, a two-bedroom flat had come onto the market in Waterloo Quay. Completely different from the previous properties they had seen, Sarah and John would have to think modern and consider different, more contemporary solutions to any design or decorating problems that arose. The investment potential in a flat like this would be very high. It would be easy to maintain and to let out if necessary. A key selling point was the balcony over the water. 'If you had this in any other city in Britain, you'd be paying through the roof for it. If we can get it for a reasonable price in a growing city like Liverpool, should we jump on it now?'

Undecided, they went to look at a property in Bayward Road, Eggburgh, where they were the first viewers through the door. It was a four-bedroom Victorian terraced house with lots of original features and an asking price of £95,000. The pointings and flashings looked sound, and although there was some mortar loose under the gable, it did not look like too much of a problem. Inside, there was plenty of potential. For example, the bedroom might benefit if the cupboards were removed and a walk-in wardrobe and shower room were installed. 'It's an excellent size. Once again, the décor is not exactly as we'd want but there is a lot of scope.'

> **TIP:** Look for signs that a damp-proof course has been installed. Make sure that it is properly guaranteed.

Finally, they went to see a terraced house that was still under construction, with a week's worth of work left to do. It was exactly the size John and Sarah were looking for, with three good-sized bedrooms and a massive kitchen, priced at £76,950. Although finished to a high standard, it lacked all the original features they liked in the other houses. They knew immediately it was not for them.

By the next day they had decided they 'absolutely and definitely' wanted the house in Bayward Road. Having been the first people to view it, they were anxious not to be disappointed, so put in an offer of the asking price straight away on the condition that no one else was to be shown the house. The offer was immediately accepted and they agreed to have the survey carried out in two weeks, with exchange as soon as possible with deferred completion. Another happy ending.

> TIP: Once your offer is accepted, you must push your solicitor and your mortgage lender, liaising with the agency and keeping everyone informed.

TIPS FOR REDECORATING

Whether preparing a property for sale or doing it up for your own benefit, there are a few considerations to bear in mind if you want to get the best results.

Colours
➤ Dark colours and busy or intrusive prints can make a room seem smaller.
➤ Soft neutrals and discreet light patterns can give it a new sense of space.
➤ A monochromatic scheme using different whites or beiges can enlarge a room.
➤ Raise the ceiling by painting it white.
➤ Lower the ceiling by painting it a darker shade and bringing the colour a little way down the top of the wall.

➤ Using vertical stripes will give a room height.

➤ Working with horizontal lines (eg adding a dado, and painting different colours above and below, decorative borders, picture rails, a single stripe) will make it seem wider.

➤ Use a colour scheme inspired by an object in the room – a rug, lampshade or cushion cover.

➤ Buy tester pots and paint large squares of lining paper to hang at different places in the room. Or pin up wallpaper samples. Watch how the changing light alters the effect through the day.

➤ Use the right finish for the right room. Use waterproof, wipeable finishes in kitchens and bathrooms. Matt emulsions provide good background colours in living rooms and bedrooms.

➤ Use off-whites and neutrals rather than brilliant white in period properties.

➤ Colour influences mood, so select your palette appropriately. Red is passionate, whites and pale blues and greens can be cool and calming, yellows are upbeat and life-enhancing. Muted earth colours are warm yet soothing.

➤ If undecided or unconfident, use a soft neutral and add colour through accessories such as rugs, cushions, throws, lampshades, ornaments and pictures.

➤ Protect wood with gloss, eggshell or vinyl paint. They will also reflect varying degrees of light into a room.

Techniques

➤ Complete all wiring and fix any broken fixtures before you start.

➤ Have the essential equipment to hand: assorted clean brushes, rollers, paint pads; assorted sandpapers; filler and filling knife; radiator brush and roller; bucket, rags and sponges; white spirit; dustsheet.

➤ Prepare all surfaces thoroughly. They should be dry and clean, with cracks filled and any chips, blisters or flaking paint sanded down.

➤ Doors may need to be sanded, blow-torched or dipped.

➤ Start with the ceiling, then walls, then woodwork.

➤ Use specialist paints for floorboards, tiles and radiators.

Finishing off

➤ Use mirrors to bring more light into a room and increase the sense of space.

➤ Create and emphasise a focal point in each room. This could be a fireplace, a window with a sensational view or a particular piece of furniture or artwork.

➤ In a monochromatic room, use different textures in the furnishing to add interest.

➤ Use curtains or blinds to play up or down a view outside.

➤ Try to keep curtains back from the windows to admit as much natural light as possible.

➤ Use accessories to complement and highlight your colour scheme.

➤ Do not over-furnish the room.

➤ Pay particular attention to the lighting. It can make all the difference.

NATASHA WARRALL, LONDON

Wanted: 'I love Balham. It's got a really young vibe, and some great bars and restaurants are starting to open. It's next to Clapham and Brixton where there's a lot going on too, and the transport links are great. My ideal property would be a first floor, probably purpose-built, Victorian-style maisonette, if I could get it. It's got to be pretty spacious and I'd love a garden if I could get one. My budget will stretch to £215,000.'

Prices had skyrocketed over the year that Natasha Warrall had been looking for her first home in south London. 'I was first looking for a two-bed flat for about £170,000. A year on, I'm looking for up to about £215,000 and I'll be lucky to get a one-bed for that around Balham now.' Wandsworth, Clapham and Balham were once separate villages but now form neighbouring areas of London, south of the River Thames. Thanks to yuppie money, the first two became pricey and fashionable during the 1980s, and now Balham is following suit with property prices more than doubling over five years. Natasha had seen an incredible one hundred properties over the past year and had made five offers, all of which had fallen through. The time had come to widen her choices.

Property number one was in Ritherton Road, a smart address in a leafy conservation area on the borders of Balham. A bright, spacious, first-floor, one-bedroom flat in a red brick Victorian terrace was on the market for £199,950. Natasha immediately liked the square bay window in the living room and was encouraged by the potential to knock through the wall into the kitchen to make an open-plan living area, although she would have to seek the freeholder's permission first. The impressive master bedroom was down some stairs, but a look through a gap in the floorboards and a window revealed that a large back extension was being built downstairs. What better time to apply for a roof terrace? But Natasha was not convinced it was right for her.

> TIP: In a leasehold property, any structural changes must have the freeholder's permission.

On to Clapham where, in Devereux Road, there was a two-bedroom flat priced at £275,000. It was a bit of a tight squeeze to get through the front door, and overall the flat was less spacious than the last one. However, there was potential to move the bathroom into half of the second bedroom, leaving the remaining half and the current bathroom to become a dining room, thus freeing up the living room. Upstairs, the master bedroom had a great view but felt rather cramped because of the low ceiling, although there was the possibility of extending up into the loft space. 'I think in terms of space, the lounge and the bedroom weren't quite big enough for me. The kitchen was lovely but it's just not quite what I'm looking for.'

> TIP: The cost of extensions and improvements has not risen at the same rate as the cost of the properties themselves. If looking at somewhere that seems small, keep an eye out for the potential to expand.

Further north in Clapham, nearer to the bars and shops Natasha liked, was a first-floor, one-bedroom flat in Grandison Road with an asking price of £199,950. Wondering if she could have exposed floorboards in the living room, she was told that it was unlikely because of sound restrictions. A feasible alternative would be to have a floating floor. Although the kitchen appeared new, a closer look revealed it was a clever revamp. Outside the bedroom was an accessible flat roof, but it was unlikely that it could be made into a roof terrace in this conservation area where no precedent had been set.

TIP: To get planning permission in a conservation area you will almost certainly need a planning precedent to have been set. It is now rare to be the first to do something in a street.

Next stop Battersea, home of the historic landmark Battersea Power Station. Here, a top-floor, one-bedroom flat with a share of the freehold had come on to the market at £215,000. Even though it was pushing Natasha's budget, it did represent good value for money, with a reasonable-sized kitchen and a superb airy living room that had been created by removing a small second bedroom. Swapping the positions of bathroom and kitchen would give more privacy, and although it would cost around £15,000 it should add at least £25,000-£30,000 to the value of the property. An alternative would be to widen the kitchen into the corridor and have the entrance to the bathroom through it. 'A great flat. It's got good potential. It needs some TLC but is very spacious and in a great location.'

TIP: The freeholder must keep the communal areas in good condition but the individual leaseholders foot the bills.

For something a little different, she was shown a ground-floor flat in Tregarvon Road, just off the north side of Clapham Common, on the market for £205,000. A long lease of 101 years, original Victorian features and a small garden with a vine-clad pergola were extremely seductive. Less attractive was the damp patch in the living room. Outside, behind the original cast iron downpipe, the moss on the brick-work showed that water was escaping into the wall so the pipe would have to be replaced.

> **TIP: Always check the length of a lease. Anything under sixty-five years will require a special mortgage.**

Before making up her mind, she went to see a new flat in a modern development – something quite different from the other properties she had viewed. For £195,000, there was allocated parking space, garden and large purpose-built rooms but a small kitchen and little individual character. 'It's a shame that the thing that lets the flat down is the kitchen. I think there's been a real lack of imagination put into it. I'm still a big fan of Victorian properties but it has opened my eyes so I wouldn't write off modern properties in the way I did before.'

Natasha chose to revisit the flats in Battersea and Tregarvon Road with her boyfriend, Darren. The arrangement of the kitchen and bath-room in Battersea was the deciding factor against it, while they delib-erated long and hard over Tregarvon Road. Darren felt that the living room and bedroom were on the small side. They also discussed the possibility of extending the kitchen into the side return although the neighbours would have to be consulted because it would take away some of their light. Natasha was undecided. 'It's tough. I love the flat, it's very sweet, and I love the location. But are we prepared to trade off space for location?'

In the end, she passed on both, but the following week another flat came on the market in Balham. 'I rushed there. It was £189,950. It's a ground-floor flat with great room sizes and a 20-foot (6m) garden. I got Darren round there the next day and put in an offer of the asking price. Before, I didn't want to look at garden flats but now I'm actually buying one!'

FREEHOLD vs. LEASEHOLD

Freehold

If you are buying a freehold property, you are buying the property and the land it stands on within fixed boundaries. You are entirely responsible for its maintenance and repair. However, that does not necessarily mean that you can do anything you like to it. There might be restrictive covenants that may determine the use of the property or prohibit you from building an extension. There may also be rights of access or easements on the property that, for example, may allow people to cross your land or have access to their drainage systems that run under it. These should show in the searches and must not be ignored because they are legally enforceable. Make certain that it is clear who has rights to what.

Leasehold

If you buy a leasehold on a property (as will be the case with most flats and a very few houses), you are buying the property but *not* the ground on which it stands. The property is owned for a certain number of years, after which the ownership reverts to the freeholder. The freeholder owns the site and charges the leaseholder an annual ground rent. The leaseholder will also be bound by the conditions of their lease, which sets out his rights and responsibilities (so read it carefully), and will pay a service charge to the freeholder to cover the maintenance and repair of the building and common parts.

In 1993, the law changed and the Land Reform Housing and Urban Development Act gave tenants satisfying certain qualifications the right to club together and jointly buy the freehold of thier property. A joint freehold means that each flat owner owns a share of the freehold and has a share in the responsibility for the upkeep of the building. If buying a joint freehold flat, it is important to establish whether the flat owners manage the building themselves or whether they employ a managing agent. If the former, be prepared for disagreements – the owner of the top flat will feel the roof repairs have higher priority over the flooding in the basement, but the basement flat owner will disagree. Whoever manages the building, there will be an equivalent of a service charge so that there is a fund to cover all expenses, including repairs and maintenance. Check whether a sinking fund exists to cover one-off major repairs. If not, be prepared to fork out for those extra costs when they occur. A joint freehold also means that there is no ground rent to pay and there is no lease on the flat – an advantage when you come to sell. The act also made it possible for certain leaseholders to extend their lease by ninety years. If the landlord decides to sell the freehold, he is obliged to give the present tenants first right of refusal. If he does not, he is liable to a hefty fine.

For more information, visit The Leasehold Advisory Service www.lease-advice.org, or The Association of Residential Managing Agents at www.arma.org.uk.

SARAH SIMPSON AND PETER MCGLYNN, NEWCASTLE-UPON-TYNE

Wanted: 'We're definitely buying a house that fits our collection of paintings, because we've run out of wall space. We're looking for a property with a lot of wall space, big size rooms and lots of light. It has to be somewhere that makes money, definitely. It's not a house for life, it's a house for five years. We're prepared to spend up to £250,000.'

Forget any idea of the north-east being a depressed area. Newcastle is on the up and house prices are rising with it. During the nineteenth century, shipbuilding and mining flushed the city with wealth and the consequent housing boom gave Newcastle the distinctive look it still has today. Two hundred years later, new industries mean new jobs, new money and new homes. The city is home to Sarah Simpson, an art gallery exhibitions organiser, and Peter McGlynn, creative director of a graphic design company. They were particularly keen to stay in Jesmond, the area where they and many of their friends lived. The only problem being that £250,000 did not buy much there.

Across the 45-acre Jesmond Dene Park, on the opposite side of the village to the one in which they lived, was a five-bedroom Victorian mid-terrace house on three floors, with an asking price of £225,000. The rooms were large and had original features, including door handles, door plates, window catches, cornicing and fire-places. The house could do with redecoration but it offered plenty of space, with the potential to knock through the dining room into the living room. Upstairs there was the possibility of enlarging the bath-room by knocking it through into a smaller bedroom, while combin-ing the two attic rooms could make a perfect art studio for Peter. The snag was that turning a five-bedroom into a three-bedroom house might seriously damage its value.

> **TIP: Reducing the number of bedrooms can significantly reduce the value of your home when it comes to resale.**

With food for thought, they went to Osbourne Road, where a light and airy penthouse was on the market for £225,000. They both liked the contemporary feel and the floor-to-ceiling windows but its greatest selling point, the balcony, was a total turn-off for Sarah whose fear of heights would prevent her from using it.

With that behind them, they travelled to Highbury, on the other side of Jesmond, where an Edwardian terrace boasted a massive four-bedroom house for £275,000. Although over their budget, it might be available for less because the owner had already moved and was anxious for a quick sale. The awkward arrangement of rooms on the ground floor could be remedied by taking down the wall between the dining and living rooms, and the attic had been converted into what would make a superb studio.

> **TIP:** The existence of planning permission for an extension will increase the value of the property even if the vendor has not carried out the work.

Meanwhile outside, the garage was another possibility for Peter to convert into a room for himself, but it was all too close to the busy railway line. 'Although I love it, the fact is that this house is £50,000 more than the first one and I can't see £50,000 of difference.'

> **TIP:** Use your imagination to see how the space might be used if you knocked one room into another.

For something completely different, they agreed to look at a renovated farmhouse in Sunnyside village, fifteen minutes out of town over the Tyne Bridge. Despite the double garage, big garden, three bedrooms and jacuzzi bath, they disliked it on first sight. 'I think it's for people of an older generation, that's all.'

So it was back into town to Brewery Bond in North Shields, to an unfinished riverside loft apartment. They were the first to view the flats, so donning hard hats they picked their way through the building site. The high ceilings would be supported by pillars and huge industrial girders. For £220,000, they could buy two ground floor apartments to give them more floor space than anything they had seen so far. The cost would include kitchen, bathroom and a designer so Sarah and Peter could create an interior to suit their lifestyle and, as importantly, their art. The developers had created a show flat in a previous conversion to give a feel for the height, space and quality of fittings buyers could expect. Peter was immediately won over. 'It's my ideal kind of flat really, the kind I read about in magazines.' But Sarah was unsure. Open-plan living meant that there would not be a studio for Peter unless they made one, and lost the sense of height and space they both enjoyed.

To clear their minds they looked at a completed waterfront development at Mariners' Wharf, where £285,000 was being asked for a three-bedroom apartment. It offered plenty of living and wall space but, 'It's too plain. It's a box.' Despite the attractions of a modern home with river views, their hearts were set on Jesmond Dene. 'The more I think about it, the more I like it and I can't think of anything I can fault it on.'

Sarah was keen to go back to see how far it was from her work – an extra fifteen minutes. Walking into the house, they still felt enthusiastic, recognising that it would look better without the woodchip paper and painted white. They could add value to the house by restoring the original features. All the windows were painted shut, but the sound of the weight banging when the sash cord was pulled meant they were working and just needed stripping. Having seen the Brewery Bond apartment, the idea for a more dramatic solution for the ground floor arose. Removing both dining room walls, leaving a supporting pillar, would give them one massive room with stairs in the corner at a cost of about £6,000. Checking the outside of the house, they noticed some work above the window bay. Although it did not seem to be a problem, it would be worth asking the surveyor what happened and what was done about it.

> **TIP:** Take time to check the condition of the roof tiles, the guttering and the walls. Note any queries for your surveyor.

They agreed that this was the house for them and decided to offer immediately, in the knowledge that two other couples were viewing it for a second time that evening and aware that properties in the area were being snapped up within hours of going on the market. Despite Peter's willingness to pay up to £230,000 to secure it and his anxiety that they might lose it, they were advised to make an opening offer of £215,000 that was turned down but after three days of haggling, they ended up as the proud possessors of their new home for £220,000.

> TIP: When making an offer, do not be panicked into overbidding. Calculate what is reasonable and begin there, knowing you may have to go higher, particularly in a booming market.

TYPICAL PERIOD FEATURES

Original period features are often highly prized and may increase the value of a property. It is useful to know the possibilities and recognise them when you are viewing.

Georgian 1780–1830
- Flat-fronted, built of brick or brick and stucco
- Large sash windows with multiple panes in plain window openings
- Fanlight above exterior doors
- Terraced with half-basement and steps to raised ground floor
- Parapet hiding servants' rooms and roof
- Entablatures, pediments, consoles and either pilasters or columns round doors and windows
- High ceilings
- Wood panelling
- Internal shutters
- Marble, scagliola (coloured stone and plaster), plaster and painted pine or cast iron fireplaces

➤ Stone staircases

➤ Delftware fire surrounds

Victorian 1810–1901

➤ Bay windows

➤ Sash windows with single panes

➤ Carved stonework

➤ Stone dressed window and door openings

➤ Porches

➤ Back extensions

➤ Well-proportioned rooms

➤ Internal boxed window shutters

➤ Ornate plasterwork on cornicing and ceiling roses

➤ Encaustic, geometric tiles on pathway and in hall

➤ Decorative tiles in cast Iron fire surrounds

➤ Skirting, dado rail, picture rail and frieze

Gothic 1855–1875

➤ Steep pitched roof

➤ Terracotta ridge tiles and cast iron finials topping slate roof tiles

➤ Diamond and fish-scale patterns in roof tiles

➤ Coloured/patterned brickwork

➤ Medieval details

➤ Spires and turrets

Edwardian 1901–1910

➤ Similar to Victorian

➤ Mock Tudor with rough cast walls, magpie work, small leaded window panes and rustic bricks

- Jacobean details, eg mullioned windows, gargoyles, Dutch gables, studded doors
- Neo-Georgian with sash windows, bays, columns and pilasters
- Stained glass in front doors and windows
- Larger windows
- Large halls
- Porches and inglenook windows
- Decorative tiled floors and kitchens
- Wooden fire surrounds
- Skirting, dado rail, picture rail and frieze
- Scullery off kitchen

Art Deco 1930s
- Pantile roof, half-timbering
- Flat roof, white-rendered exterior walls
- Crittall's metal window frames with horizontal lines and sometimes curved corners
- Decorative wrought ironwork
- Plain tiled fire surrounds
- Larder

Country cottage
- Beams
- Inglenook fireplace
- Thatch
- Small wood-framed windows
- Timber-framed walls
- Tiles, flagstones
- Downstairs bathrooms

5   SELLING YOUR PROPERTY

Once you have decided to sell your property, it is not just a question of putting it in the hands of an estate agent and sitting back and waiting. Achieving a quick sale at the highest price with the least amount of aggravation needs careful planning. If your move is work-related, you may not have much choice about when you sell your house, or have much time to prepare it for the market. However, if you are moving because your current home is too big or too small or because you would like to move to another area, try to leave yourself enough time to prepare your house for sale. Not every property gets snapped up the moment it goes on the market, so be prepared to wait until the right buyer comes along with the right offer. Once he has, there is no guarantee that everything will go smoothly. There will inevitably be frustrating hold-ups that will add to the general stress of moving house. When your property is looking its best, you will need to decide the best way to handle the sale – using an estate agent or selling it privately. You need the advice of a solicitor, and will need to keep in touch throughout the process until the day the contracts are signed and the keys handed over.

WHEN TO SELL

Before putting your property on the market, check your mortgage agreement to make sure that selling at this time is not going to incur any early redemption penalties. These may be a crippling addition to the general costs of buying, selling and moving. If you cannot delay your move, it may be more sensible to rent your property out until you can sell it without such punitive restrictions coming into force.

The best time to sell is when the market is active and demand outstrips supply, as that is when property prices will be at their most buoyant. The busiest time in the property market tends to be between March and July – as people emerge from their winter hibernation and before they disappear on holiday. Of course, there is another key factor – the level of interest rates. If interest rates are low, borrowers are ready to latch on to new mortgage deals that put them in a financially advantageous position.

Conversely, the worse time to sell is when there are fewest buyers around. If interest rates are high, there will be fewer, as there will be during the winter months. These are the times when prices remain sluggish or even fall. Keep an eye on the market through the property pages in local and national newspapers, or through talking to estate agents.

When planning to move, it is advisable to put your house on the market before you begin looking for a new home. If you have an offer on your house in place when you find a property you want to buy, it will put you in an advantageous position in the eyes of the seller. It will also help you to budget better if you know how much you are getting from your sale.

PREPARING THE PROPERTY

Before putting your property on the market, it is essential to get it looking its best in order to snare a buyer. You may love it the way it is and turn a blind eye to the old-fashioned kitchen, the odd patch of damp, the garden-cum-football pitch or the crowded shelves, but potential buyers will not. You must make it easy for them to see the potential of the property and to imagine themselves living in it.

Take a good long look at the place and be as objective as you can be. This property should immediately stand out from the others on the market. As soon as a buyer draws up outside, it should be inviting them to the front door, not suggesting they drive straight past.

Make sure the approach to the property is inviting:
- Fix a broken gate.
- Remove any broken-down vehicles.
- Prune hedges and trees.
- Mow the grass.
- Tidy the flowerbeds.
- Clear up the side alley.
- Remove the dustbins from view.
- Tidy up any mess.

Now look at the house itself:
- Clean the windows.
- Remove any junk from the window ledges.
- Wash any net/lace curtains.
- Make sure the curtains/blinds are clean and straight.
- Touch up the window frames with a lick of paint if necessary.
- Repaint the front door.

➤ Polish the door furniture.

➤ Mend any broken guttering or drainpipes.

➤ Replant window boxes and hanging baskets.

Right. Now you have interested your buyer. If the place looks this good on the outside, it must be impressive on the inside too. Make sure he comes to the front door and not to the side or in through the kitchen because that is the entrance you always use. If you introduce him into the house the wrong way, he will not get a proper sense of its flow and it will be more difficult for him to remember it accurately.

It is time to carry out all those running repairs that you have begun and never finished, or meant to attend to but have never quite had the time. All these things will catch the buyer's eye and he may assume that if you have not bothered with them, there may be other more major problems left unattended.

➤ Finish all incomplete DIY jobs.

➤ Replace missing banisters.

➤ Fix broken door knobs.

➤ Mend broken hinges.

➤ Replace missing/cracked tiles.

➤ Replace the broken washer on the dripping tap.

➤ Replace broken light bulbs and switches.

➤ Attend to damp patches.

➤ Fill cracks.

➤ Box in gas and electricity meters.

Now look at your colour schemes. Be honest. Are they a bit too daring for the average person? They buyer will get a clearer idea of the house if he is not distracted by your taste. Are the colours flattering the rooms, or making them appear smaller or darker than they really are? Consider repainting in soft neutral colours that will maximise the space and available light. See Maximising Space and Light on page 227. Going to this trouble may transform your house and achieve a much faster sale. You are going to have to pack up the room eventually, so why not do much of it now, getting rid of the distracting clutter.

Floors are an aspect of a property that can easily be overlooked. On reflection, would a new floor covering create a better impression? Worn kitchen and bathroom flooring looks unhygienic and is off-putting. It may be worth the expense of replacing them with a durable, waterproof flooring that is easy to clean. If your living room and bedroom carpets have seen better days, at least have them professionally cleaned if you prefer not to go to the trouble and expense of replacing them. The hall is the area that gets the greatest amount of wear and tear, so it may be worth replacing that carpet altogether to give that vital good first impression.

Two rooms that are major selling points in your home are the kitchen and bathroom. It is vital that they look clean, hygienic and welcoming. If a buyer walks in and immediately feels he will have to replace the fittings, he will see thousands of pounds added to his costs. It is absurd to suggest that you should invest in a brand new kitchen or bathroom suite at this point, but there are things you can do to transform their appearance at a fraction of the cost. You probably will not have to do all these things, but one or two of them may improve the appearance of the room no end.

Kitchen

➤ Replace flooring.
➤ Paint the walls.
➤ Change the unit doors and drawer fronts.
➤ Change the handles on the units.

➤ Replace any chipped/cracked tiles.

➤ Replace the work surface.

➤ Buy a new hob/oven if yours is irreparably stained.

➤ Clear surfaces of everything inessential.

➤ Make sure work surfaces are adequately lit.

➤ Clear out cupboards and fridge.

➤ Clean thoroughly.

Bathroom

➤ Replace flooring.

➤ New toilet seat.

➤ Repair chips in the bath/basin with enamel paint.

➤ New shower curtain.

➤ New blind.

➤ Clear surfaces of everything inessential.

➤ Clean thoroughly.

➤ New towels/bathmat.

All the other rooms should be thoroughly tidied, with all clutter removed. Remove all traces of pets and children – some buyers may not be as keen on them as you and if they are, they will be distracted from the purpose of their visit. Shelves should not be so crowded with possessions that it looks as if the house is too small for them all. Thin them out and the room will immediately look larger. Make the most of any focal points such as a beautiful fireplace or a view, thereby taking attention from the less attractive features. Do not let too much or badly positioned furniture block the flow of the room.

Cleaning the windows and opening the curtains fully will admit as much natural light as possible. The clever use of mirrors can add more light and create an impression of more space. You may be able to use the lighting to your advantage. It can highlight the good features in a room and disguise the bad.

Do not forget to clear out cupboards, lofts and cellars as well. No buyer wants to be buried in an avalanche of clothes or saucepans when he opens a cupboard. If he can see the potential for development in the loft or cellar space, it may help your sale.

Finally, the garden. If you can transform a playground into an inviting outdoor space where people can imagine themselves relaxing or entertaining, then you have added to the value of the house.

PREPARING YOURSELF

If you can, unearth the last year's worth of relevant bills. Any potential buyer will appreciate knowing how much the property costs in terms of heating, electricity, gas, council tax, ground rent or service charges. Any guarantees and warranties for major work or items you are leaving behind should be made available.

After all that preparation, you are ready to sell.

BUDGET

It is as important to budget for the sale of your property as it is for the purchase of a new one. Firstly, there will be the redecoration costs. They will depend on however much work you decide is worthwhile doing to present the property at its best. If you spend up to 1% of the asking price getting the property up to scratch, you will almost certainly recoup it in the sale. Most estate agents charge a commission of between 2% and $3^{1}/_{2}$% of the sale price depending on whether they are the sole agent or one of several. If you sell at auction, there will be a commission of approximately $2^{1}/_{2}$% of the sale price and occasionally additional minor costs to cover any advertising. If you sell privately, there will be the cost of advertising the property. Finally, there will be your solicitor's fees and associated legal costs – usually only the land registry charge.

HOW TO SELL

Estate agents

When selling a property, there are three routes from which to choose. By far the most common is to instruct an estate agent to sell your property for you. But which one? In most areas of the country you will be spoiled for choice, so there are a number of points it is wise to bear in mind.

Estate agents need no qualifications, nor do they have to belong to a recognised professional body, so you should always be wary. It is important that you choose one with membership of a professional organisation that will at least give you some protection against malpractice. The largest is the National Association of Estate Agents (NAEA), although some agents belong to the Royal Institute of Chartered Surveyors (RICS), the Association of Building Engineers (ABE) or the Architecture and Surveying Institute (ASI). Take into account any personal recommendations.

Investigate how and where they market the properties on their books. Those reaching the largest number of potential customers may stand more chance of selling your property quickly. Look at the sort of properties they sell successfully and make sure yours will fit in with them. Watch out for 'Sold' notices in the area (although they may not all be genuine). Do they use press advertising, their own website, mailing lists and/or brochures?

When you have narrowed the field down to the two or three most suitable, invite them all to value your house. Their valuations should be based on their knowledge of the marketplace, the condition of the property, interest rates and economic trends. Doubtless their valuations will differ. It may be tempting to go with the highest, but that is not always the wisest move. If the property is overpriced, potential buyers may be frightened off and it will languish on the market unsold until you lower your expectations. Once you lower the price, buyers may feel there may be something wrong with the property. Valuations are free.

Ask the agent about his terms and conditions. If acting as sole agency, the estate agent should work hard on your behalf knowing he will earn the full commission. Make sure you do not give him sole selling rights, which entitle him to a percentage even if you sell the house privately after all. Check the length of the term of employment. If eight weeks go by without a bite, you may want to change agents and not be locked into a longer deal. The disadvantage of sole agency is that you are reliant on that agent's customer base, but it does reduce the risk of gazumping and encourages buyers. An alternative is to have joint sole agency where two agents combine in your interest, possibly a small locally based one and another with a national reach. This arrangement may necessitate a slightly higher commission than a sole agency. Equally, under a multiple agency agreement, you can instruct a number of agencies to compete against one another to sell the property. This will cost more in commission but may sell the property faster. When appointing an agent to act for you, haggle over the commission if need be. There is no harm in telling the agent with whom you want to work that his commission is too high and you are tempted to go with one of his rivals who is offering better terms. Discuss with them how they will arrange viewings. Will they have a key to the property and show people round, or should they make appointments for you?

Private sale

If cost is a priority, then you may want to sell privately. Get a clear idea of what similar properties in the area are fetching. If in doubt, ask a couple of estate agents to value your property – you are under no obligation to sell through them. Pitch the price above what you will ultimately be prepared to accept, but not so high that it scares buyers off. The more interest you can generate the better, so decide how you are going to market it. A home-made 'For Sale' board outside will not attract many buyers. You can use word-of-mouth and advertise in local libraries, newsagents and on your work notice board. Some classified papers such as *Loot* and *Dalton's Property* will run ads for free, while the local newspaper will charge a small fee. More expensive, but with a far wider reach, are the national newspapers.

Internet

More and more people are turning to the internet to advertise their property. There are a huge number of sites that allow you to advertise, some are free and some charge depending on the facilities on offer. At best, they can provide video tours of the house, giving a clear visual picture of the property alongside the description, a floor plan and the seller's details.

Auction

If you are in a hurry to sell but have the problem of sitting tenants, an unusual property that is hard to value, in bad condition or equally in great demand, the fastest route might be through an auction. It may cost you more than an estate agent and, beyond setting a reserve, you have no control over the price you eventually receive, but it is quick. It is essential that the auctioneer should be a member of the Incorporated Society of Valuers and Auctioneers (ISVA). Research the sort of properties sold by the auction house. If yours is very different, it will be more unlikely you will find a suitable buyer there or therefore the optimum price. Settle on a reserve price after discussion with an estate agent or the auctioneer. Instruct your solicitor to prepare a contract plus information on any special conditions of the sale. Some auctioneers ask for a seller's information pack to be prepared (see page 170). The downside of the process is that you must make the property available for open viewing, ie to anyone who might be interested, and subsequently to their surveyors, so there is a greater invasion of your privacy. If you specify at the outset that you would be open to taking it off the market before the auction subject to the right offer, you may sell it before the big day. If not, you must wait until the hammer falls. From that moment, there is a binding agreement between buyer and seller, the buyer must pay a 10% deposit on the spot with the balance due within twenty-eight days.

VIEWINGS

If you are conducting the viewings yourself, it is worth taking the security precaution of having someone in the house with you. If you are not using an estate agent, only let people in who have made an appointment, not a casual passer-by who has seen the board. Otherwise, there are a number of key things to remember:

- ➤ Once you have tidied up, keep it that way.
- ➤ Fresh flowers and the smell of coffee helps the place feel more homely.
- ➤ Light a fire in the winter.
- ➤ Put away anything of great value.
- ➤ Switch off the television.
- ➤ Leave the children and pets with the next door neighbour.

➤ Do not give the impression you are desperate to sell.

➤ Remain calm – do not get worked up when someone criticises your home.

➤ Let the buyer enter a room first – they will see it more clearly and it will feel less crowded.

➤ Do not refer to neighbours from hell, the smell from the pig farm or the noise of the twice daily deliveries next door unless asked.

➤ Be truthful when replying to a question.

➤ Do not volunteer information that may put the buyer off.

➤ Emphasise the strongest features of the property and the area.

➤ Have any relevant information (bills, warranties etc) to hand.

➤ Be clear about whether carpets, curtains etc are included in the asking price.

➤ Be specific about when you want to move.

➤ If you have an estate agent, leave him to talk about money.

The buyers will doubtless have numerous questions to fire at you, but you should have your own armoury ready. Remember to establish their position. It will be relevant if they make you an offer:

➤ Are they selling a property?

➤ Have they had an offer?

➤ Do they know how long a chain they are in?

➤ Do they have a mortgage approved in principle?

➤ When do they want to move?

➤ Have they been looking long?

Make a note of their name and contact details as well as the answers to the questions.

If you are using an estate agent he will act as the middleman when it comes to negotiating the deal. If you are acting for yourself, keep your head. The negotiation should be conducted reasonably with some give and take on either side. If it is a booming market you may be offered the asking price or even more. You may even have more than one offer. All you have to do is to decide which to accept, taking into account the strength of the buyer's position and his ability to move fast, your own financial requirements, whether or not you have found a house you want to buy and the condition of the market. If prices are steady or falling you may not be offered more. Normally a buyer will offer something up to 20% lower than the asking price. If you are in a hurry to move and they are in a position to move fast you may want to suggest a compromise figure. Remember, no one can force you to accept an offer, but weigh up the pros and cons carefully before turning one down. If you receive two or three equal bids from buyers in similar positions, you may want to ask for sealed bids or invite them to take part In a contract race. The latter may result in them all withdrawing, so judge your response carefully.

After you have accepted an offer, your buyer will want to have the house surveyed as well as having it valued by his mortgage company. As a result of his findings, he may try to negotiate the price down if there is a substantial amount of unaccounted work to be done. Ask for his estimates and weigh up whether you can afford to lower the price. If you can, some compromise may be reached. If you cannot, you will have to assess the seriousness of the buyer's complaint and the state of the market, then decide whether to risk putting the property back up for sale.

THE SALE

Once you have accepted an offer, it should be confirmed in writing by you or by your agent. You should inform your solicitor that you have a sale and provide him with the buyer's details.

Your solicitor will immediately contact your mortgage lender, requesting the title deeds to the property. He will also prepare a standard property information form plus a draft contract. If he decides to use the Law Society TransAction Protocol, he will include a 'Fixtures, Fittings and Contents' form, copies of the entries if registered with the Land Registry or copies of earlier title deeds (if unregistered) and a property information form. He will respond to the preliminary inquiries sent to him by the buyer's solicitor and, once he has received the title deeds, prepare a draft contract specifying the Particulars and Conditions of Sale to send in return. Eventually, once the buyer has conducted his checks and both solicitors have negotiated the terms of the contract and formally acknowledged that they are ready to proceed, the draft will be sent to you for approval. Once both parties are entirely happy, a copy of the contract is sent to each for their signatures. Then the contracts are exchanged and the buyer's deposit paid. After this point neither side can back out of the deal without incurring severe financial penalties.

Your solicitor will find out from the mortgage company exactly how much you owe them, taking into account any additional charges including early redemption penalties. Having approved the transfer deed, he will ask you to sign it ready for completion. He will receive the balance of the purchase price from the buyer's mortgage company or his bank by electronic transfer. Then he will release the title deeds to the buyer and the sale is complete. Before he hands over your money, your solicitor will take his and the estate agent's fee, pay off the mortgage company and finally transfer any surplus to you.

SELLER'S INFORMATION PACK

The UK's system for buying and selling property is one of the slowest in Europe, made particularly stressful by the fact that there is no legally binding deal until contracts have been exchanged. The government is pressing for reforms to speed up the process with all the parties involved being encouraged to reach more efficient levels of service. Although a few estate agents do currently use seller's information packs, the aim is that they should become compulsory.

In future, the seller would prepare the pack, making it available to all prospective buyers. Under current proposals, it would include:

- A draft contract
- A surveyor's report
- Ownership documents
- Local authority searches
- Relevant guarantees and warranties
- Relevant planning or listed building regulations.

Leasehold properties would also require:
- Details of the lease
- Buildings insurance policy
- Details of the service charge
- Freeholder's regulations.

THINGS THAT CAN GO WRONG

Breakdown of the chain

If someone drops out of the chain ahead of you and the purchase of your new home is delayed, the delay may force your buyer to look elsewhere. If the chain behind your buyer breaks, he may be forced to drop out or at best delay.

Survey

If your buyer's survey reveals some horror that needs extensive repair, he may drop out or try to renegotiate the purchase price.

Gazundering

The buyer reduces his offer just before contracts are due to be exchanged.

SCOTLAND

The seller contacts his solicitor before putting his property on the market. This gives the solicitor the opportunity to check the title deeds, the amount of the outstanding loan to the mortgage company and carry out the local searches. He needs to do this early in the process because a binding deal is entered once an offer is accepted.

The most common ways of selling a house are through a solicitor or an estate agent, or by doing it yourself.

If you choose to use a solicitor, discuss his commission beforehand and negotiate where necessary. It is common for them to charge between 1% and $1^1/_2$% commission on the sale, plus legal fees for conveyancing, plus VAT. A solicitor will register the property with a property centre for a fee. The details of the property are displayed there and any potential buyer will contact you directly. If using an estate agent or selling privately, the process is the same as for the rest of the UK. However, it is essential you notify your solicitor so the initial paperwork is prepared and tell your prospective buyers to whom their written offers should be addressed.

When advertising the property, an 'offers over', or minimum price, must be stated and offers invited to come in above it. Your solicitor or estate agent will advise you on the right level but if selling privately, look at similar properties in the area and take a lead from them. You will also need to specify a date when all offers are to be received. This may be done at the outset or when you have received a number of expressions of interest.

By this time the property will be prepared for sale (see above) and prospective viewers will make appointments to be shown around. If they like the property, they will doubtless revisit for a second viewing and then make an appointment for their surveyor.

On the due date, the offers are received from the buyers' respective solicitors. You are not bound to accept the highest, or indeed any of them at all if they fall short of your expectations. You can go back to all of them to ask them to improve their offers or, if an offer is acceptable but the accompanying conditions are not, it is possible to negotiate these before reaching agreement. When any adjustments have been made between the solicitors as they finalise the finer points of the deal, they exchange letters – a process known as 'concluding missives'. At this point, the deal becomes legally binding and the buyer assumes responsibility for the building's insurance. The missives set a formal entry date to the property, usually about a month later.

When the missives have been concluded, your solicitor must send the title deeds to the buyer's who will check them and prepare the disposition. The disposition is a document that legally transfers the property to the new owner. He will inform your mortgage company that missives have been concluded and arrange for the amount of the loan to be repaid on completion of the sale. Your solicitor will also institute a search of the Registers to ensure there are no untoward entries against you or the property.

All that remains is for you to arrange how the keys to the property will be transferred to the buyer. The disposition will be handed over in return for the purchase price. Out of it, your solicitor will deduct his own fee and pay your outstanding mortgage and any bridging loan. Anything over will be transferred into your account.

ANTOINETTE THOMPSON, NOTTINGHAM

Wanted: 'I'm looking for something with lots and lots of space. I do woodwork and aromatherapy massage so I'd like somewhere big enough to incorporate both those things. I'm probably going to have a lodger so I'd need space for that. What I'm looking forward most to having is a large kitchen/diner and I'm absolutely happy to take a sledgehammer to a few walls. My maximum budget is £90,000.'

There are two ways of getting more for your money when buying a property – move to a cheap area, or buy something that needs a lot of work. Social worker Antoinette Thompson had lived in London for twenty years but decided to move back to her home town of Nottingham. Lower property prices there meant that her dream home was at last within her reach.

Lace-making and textiles brought money into Nottingham two hundred years ago, but now this thriving university town is back on the style map with its retail and café culture. The housing boom of the late Victorian period means there are a wealth of red-brick terraced homes on the market that might be right up Antoinette's street. She was keen to live as close to the city centre as possible, so her search began in New Basford, just fifteen minutes away. A three-bedroom Victorian mid-terraced house in Mandalay Street was on the market for £70,000. The front door led straight into the living room – a typical feature of many of these houses but not one Antoinette was keen on. The room looked deceptively small due to the owner's poor use of the space, and the kitchen was not big enough. Upstairs, the generous *en suite* orange bathroom was the making of the master bedroom. Throughout the house the wall colours were confidently bright, particularly in the vivid pink attic room that would be ideal for a lodger. There was also a cellar – perfect for her woodwork – and the advantage of Nottingham's new tram link planned to pass at the end of the road, strengthening the property's investment potential. 'It's much bigger than I would have thought. There is a feeling of space but the downstairs layout wasn't what I was expecting. I'd like a slightly bigger kitchen/dining area.'

> TIP: Any work done on a cellar may affect the support structure of the house. Always use a specialist firm.

The next property she saw was a mile from the centre in the fashionable area of Sherwood, where prices were soaring. Above her budget at £92,000 was a three-bedroom terraced house offering a narrow hallway, and a kitchen and dining room that could be opened up by knocking down most of the wall between them. There might be potential to widen the kitchen by extending it across into the garden return as the neighbour had done. Upstairs, three sizeable bedrooms and a bathroom would give Antoinette enough space for everything she wanted. 'I like the house. It has some amazingly good rooms. The top room and the one below are both very big. I don't think you could ask for more space.'

TIP: If adding a ground-floor extension, in order not to block the light entering the internal rooms, add a light well or glass roof.

On to Sneinton, where a very different terraced house provided a real investment opportunity, with three bedrooms and an asking price of just £49,000. The house was in a very basic state, but the back of the work had been broken with all the wiring, plumbing and heating installed. The largely cosmetic work that was needed would cost in the region of £10,000. Antoinette was not put off by the amount that needed doing and was drawn to the possibility of living in the area where she grew up, but she was not convinced that the layout of the rooms would give her the space she wanted.

TIP: If the property needs renovating, take a builder around the property to get a quote before you make an offer. Find out how much each job will add to the value of the property so you do not waste resources on unprofitable work.

A large Victorian semi in Basford Road was on the market for £99,950. It was over budget but it did have many original features, three reception rooms, a large kitchen diner and a cellar for her woodwork. The reception rooms were well proportioned, one with a beautiful fireplace and another with the original tiled floor and corner cupboard. The kitchen appliances were not included in the asking price so they would form part of a separate negotiation unless Antoinette wanted to splash out on new ones. There was also the possibility of extending the house into the attic and the cellar to provide space for her hobbies and a lodger.

TIP: If the appliances are not included on the estate agent's details, negotiate for them as part of the purchase price.

Finally, across the road was a detached double-fronted family home with three generous bedrooms, priced at £79,000. The interior was a riot of patterned wallpaper and carpet in homage to the 1960s. The living room ceiling had been lowered, probably hiding the original cornicing. There was plenty of space for a huge kitchen, laundry room, study, sitting room and downstairs bathroom but it would involve a huge amount of work – wiring, plumbing, roofing and more. Antoinette was not sure. 'Obviously there's a lot of space but the layout isn't quite as good as the last house.'

The first house in Basford Road had won her heart but she decided to revisit the house in Sherwood as well, so she had a point of comparison. In Sherwood, a local surveyor confirmed that it would be possible to extend the kitchen by taking out the existing ground floor wall if a steel or concrete beam was first put in to support the floor above. The work would take about a month and cost between £5,000 and £7,000. 'It's a fair amount of hassle. I think perhaps it's better to spend that money on a house that's all ready and has the dimensions I need.' Back to the Victorian semi where Antoinette still felt as positive as she had on the first visit. Looking at the exterior of the house, she saw that the brickwork at the side and back was dated. Many of the bricks were blown where moisture and frost had got behind and pushed off the front. In three to five years, those areas would need repointing for roughly £2,500. Despite that her mind was made up. 'I am absolutely crystal clear that the over-budget house is the house for me. I don't want to move again and there's so much potential and flexibility in it that I think it will meet all my needs, so I'm prepared to stretch.'

Her offer of £96,000 plus £2,000 for all the white goods was made with the proviso that all marketing of the house had to cease for three weeks. After some negotiation both parties agreed to a deal of £98,250. But the celebrations came too soon. 'Unfortunately, the survey revealed a whole host of problems I was completely unprepared for and it didn't make economic sense for me continue with the purchase. It will make a fantastic house for someone else who's got a lot of money and time but sadly not for me.'

RENOVATING YOUR PROPERTY

If you are buying a property that is rundown and needs renovation, think about where you are going to stay while the work is being done. Depending on the amount of work necessary, it may be intolerable or impossible to live there. You may be able to delay the sale of your previous home until after the worst of the work has been done. If not, factor into your budget the cost of renting temporary accommodation. When planning the renovation, take into account the location of your property and local property prices. There may be a ceiling to the value of the property, so do not spend more than you know you will get in return.

If rebuilding is extensive then you may need the advice of an architect who, if briefed thoroughly, will be able to conceptualise your ideas and possibly develop them further. Find one through personal recommendation, the Royal Institute of British Architects (RIBA) or the *Yellow Pages*. Always talk to two or three and familiarise yourself with their previous work, talking to the owners where possible. Check they have sufficient insurance. Having chosen one and agreed on the plans, he will submit them to the local authority for planning permission and building regulations approval. You cannot proceed without these. To apply for planning permission, either you or your architect will need a planning permission application form, a description of the proposed works and detailed floor plans, elevations of the exterior and details of materials to be used, plus the fee. In theory, it takes up to two months for permission to be granted but it may take longer. The building regulations application is made the same way, but will include more detailed structural drawings. The building inspector is concerned with the structure of the house. He will inspect the building works at various stages to check they comply with the approved plans. Do not go ahead without his approval – he has the power to make you dig up foundations to make sure they are laid soundly. If you are changing a listed building, you will also need listed building consent and the approval of your mortgage lender.

Once planning permission is granted, the architect will put the work out to tender with a number of builders and ask for their estimates.

If you are not using an architect, then choose a builder in the same way, using recommendations wherever possible. Then, when drawing up a contract with one of them, make sure it includes the start and finish date, any financial penalties if the work overruns, what happens if you change your mind about an aspect of the work, the retention fee to be withheld until the work is completed to your satisfaction and the stages at which payment is to be made. Whether using an architect or working with builders, make sure you budget in a 10% contingency fee in case things go wrong – unfortunately, they almost certainly will.

If the work is less radical but consists of remedial and repair work, then a building surveyor should be able to advise. A timetable will be necessary working out which contractor will be needed when. For instance, the wiring must be done before the plastering; plumbing must be done before the floors go down; the kitchen units must arrive before the fitters do. Allow for illness and late delivery etc.

Even if you are an ardent DIY fan and the renovation is more superficial, take care to employ professionals when necessary, particularly when it involves gas or electricity.

Old houses will almost certainly need rewiring, so plan the lighting well. Good lighting can transform a room so ensure you have the right number of wall and ceiling fittings, power points and switches. Plan the position of all your kitchen appliances. An approved electrical contractor must carry out all the work. If you are altering the plumbing, work must comply with the water regulations. If nobody can recommend a plumber, contact the Institute of Plumbing. During extensive renovation, have the telephone system updated so the wires can be hidden beneath the new plaster.

If you are clear about what you are doing, plan ahead and prepare for delays, you will almost certainly find that your wreck will be transformed into a desirable property and a first-rate investment.

HOUSEHUNTERS

STELLA BURTON AND ADRIAN BARRITT, OXFORD

Wanted: 'We are looking for something much like the place where we are now, but it is rented and unfortunately we can't buy it. We're looking for something spacious, light and airy in a rural location. I have a ridiculously large television with very large speakers and the new home will need somewhere to house it. Our budget is £300,000 but we could stretch to £400,000 for the perfect place.'

Having a particularly large item to find house room for can be problematic, as games designer Adrian Barritt and jewellery designer Stella Burton found when they were searching near Oxford for their first home together. They had met nine months earlier through an online dating agency, had got engaged and were planning to move out of their perfect rented home into somewhere of their own. They had a very clear idea of what they were looking for and one thing was certain – there had to be room for Adrian's home cinema.

Oxford is one of the most famous university towns in the world. Some of its colleges date back to the twelfth century and its dreaming spires have nurtured some of the world's most prominent artists, politicians, scientists and philosophers. An easy commute to London has tempted many to move to the Oxfordshire countryside, making the surrounding villages extremely popular with home-buyers. Stella and Adrian wanted to find their perfect home in one of them.

The first property they saw was on an exclusive estate, fifteen miles from Oxford. With twenty acres of private parkland shared among the twelve owners, the house itself was a converted stable for sale with a guide price of £325,000 to £350,000. The property extended over three floors with a large entrance hall big enough to house an office, a first-floor open-plan kitchen and living room and two good-sized bedrooms above. With the drawback of losing the second split-level bedroom, it could be converted into a cinema with an elevated seating area. They loved the setting but felt the house was too much like a flat, and one bedroom was not enough.

A former manse in Long Hanborough, fifteen miles from the centre of Oxford, was entered through a walled garden. In fact, the garden had once been the school house but when the roof fell in it was never replaced, leaving the walls and arched window frames to shelter a courtyard garden. Of course, the possibility existed of converting it back into an additional room. The house was on the market for £290,000. It had a large modern kitchen with views over the garden, wood flooring from the turn of the century running through the dining room, study and downstairs bathroom, while the attractive sitting room led into the courtyard through French windows. There was a generosity of space all round, with four large bedrooms and space in the sitting room for the cinema, but the house was on the main road.

TIP: If you are sent details of a house near a road, check it out. You do not know what noise levels will be like until you are in the house.

'There's a lot of space and it's got lots of character but it would be such a compromise with the location on the road. It's not really rural which is what we are looking for.'

Deep in the Oxfordshire countryside, forty minutes from the town, lay the sleepy village of Adderbury. A modern four-bedroom house built in the local Horton stone to give it the period look was for sale at £375,000. By contrast with the last house, the silence was certainly impressive, only broken by the sound of the odd bird. Inside, the combination of rural and contemporary worked well. The large hall doubled as a dining room and led into the fully fitted rustic-style kitchen on one side and the spacious living room with exposed stone wall on the other. The benefit of the new build was the size of the windows – much larger than tradition demanded. Upstairs there was plenty of storage space, and a large master bedroom with an arch through to a dressing area. Already unimpressed, Stella disliked the first-floor glass extension although was reassured to think it could be largely bricked over. They also noticed that a flower bed abutted one of the external walls above the height of the damp-proof course. That would have to be rectified unless the room inside had been tanked. A question for both surveyor and solicitor. Overall it was a thumbs down. 'It feels quite modern and towny. It doesn't feel rural and cottagey.'

The fourth property they saw was in Buckland – a stable conversion being sold privately for £400,000.

> TIP: When there is no estate agent, it is important to do your own research to make sure the right price is being asked. Also, you will have to do your own negotiating.

A stunning dining hall did have space down one wall for the cinema, although it would slightly interfere with access to the staircase. The standard of craftsmanship in the country kitchen was superb and the large, attractive living room led straight into the garden. Upstairs there was one particularly low-slung beam that had resulted in the section of floor beneath it (part of the living room ceiling) being lowered. The beamed bedroom had an unusually high ceiling for a conversion of this kind lending both it and the blue-and-white bathroom a good sense of space. 'There's an awful lot about it that's nice. We think the kitchen's great and the location's fantastic.'

> TIP: Barn conversions were not originally built for human habitation, so look carefully at the uneven floors and location of windows. Are they charming or inconvenient?

Finally, they viewed a semi-detached, four-bedroom stone barn conversion in a private development shared with ten other conversions, with a guide price of £345,000. The beamed wooden kitchen and diner were slightly on the small side for Adrian and Stella, though its size was compensated for by the view to the garden. The living room boasted a brick fireplace and plenty of attention to detail, for instance allowing the plaster to reveal the original stonework around the window. The attic could be converted into a splendid cinema, but none of it grabbed them as much as the house in Buckland. On revisiting Buckland, however, they decided its negative points outweighed the positive.

They were despairing until they heard another house had come on the market in the estate they first visited. This time it was the old coach house, at an asking price of £425,000. The sitting room was elegant and spacious, with tongue-and-groove panelling made from the original kickboards from the stables. There was plenty of room for the cinema here. There was a large fitted country kitchen with a table in the centre. Upstairs was as impressive, again with lots of character.

Although there was plenty of storage, Adrian was left almost speechless when Stella even volunteered to sacrifice some of her wardrobe to live here. 'The interior is superb and I think after a lot of searching, we've actually found somewhere with a nicer interior than our current place.' After a second visit to confirm their feelings, they made an offer. 'Obviously they wouldn't accept £385,000 to start off and they asked us if we would go somewhere halfway between that and £400,000. We're playing hardball at the moment, so we are up to £390,000 and we'll see where we go from there.'

But in the end, they pulled out. At nearly £400,000, it was just too expensive and they had to return to the hunt for something cheaper.

BARN CONVERSIONS

With the change in the rural economy over recent years, many redundant barns have been effectively re-employed for domestic use. Converted sympathetically, they can make exceptional homes with character, history, space and light. The value of a barn conversion lies in the quality of its design and the materials used, so it is vital you find an architect or specialist whose work is both imaginative and reliable. Before appointing one, ask if you can see some of their previous conversions to assure yourself of the calibre of their work. When making plans, remember that they should have minimum impact on your neighbours, highway safety and the green belt.

Before making an offer for a barn, check with the local planning office how open they are likely to be to plans for a change of use. If planning permission has already been granted in principle then draw up plans with your architect or specialist and submit them to the planning office, bearing in mind any restrictions they may have in force. You should also have a structural surveyor's or engineer's report.

Remember that undertaking this sort of conversion may be more expensive than building a house from scratch, because major structural alterations may be needed. You will also need to bear in mind the cost of connecting the property to the mains services and building any access routes if it is particularly remote, across a field or away from the main road. The building will also need insulation, and probably damp-proofing. Timbers will have to be checked and possibly treated for wood-boring insects and rot.

All local authorities will insist that the character of the original building is retained as far as possible. Some specify that any plans should avoid raising the roof, altering its pitch or adding dormer windows. If it is sound, the roof will almost certainly have to be kept. Because barns were not built for human habitation, the existing windows may be oddly positioned. The openings, arches or lintels may have to be retained. In some cases, new windows may not be allowed at all. External pipework will almost certainly have to be kept to a minimum. Modern materials may have to be avoided in favour of reclaimed ones and, in some cases, exact materials for doors or blocking windows will be specified. Extensions may not be acceptable so you may have to rely on adapting any neighbouring outbuildings into a garage, study or playroom. There may also be restrictions as to what you can do to the land immediately around the building.

It can be difficult to reconcile the barn's form with your demands. An imposing open interior with few windows may be difficult to divide into a comfortable living space, particularly if the local authority is strict about making new external openings. A successful conversion will invariably depend on getting expert advice.

There are a number of listed barns throughout the country. If you do get permission to convert one, it will undoubtedly require extra sensitivity. There will be more restrictions to observe and it is likely that the internal features, such as roof trusses and framing, will have to be left visible. You will also have to make a separate application for listed building consent.

If nothing else, the building may have been the home to barn owls and bats. Both of these are in decline in rural areas, and barn conversions have been partly to blame. It is your responsibility to secure their well-being if clearing them out. The local planning department should be able to advise you.

GEORGIE ALLEN AND GRAHAM LASLETT, SHEFFIELD

Wanted: 'We want a bigger house than the one we have. Something unique with a bit of character and three bedrooms. May be a bigger garden but still close to the Peak District so we can go walking, climbing, and just spend some more time outside. The maximum we can spend is £150,000.'

Location and more space are often prime considerations for people moving house. Georgie Allen, an analyst programmer, and Graham Laslett, a computer programmer, had lived in the centre of Sheffield for long enough and wanted to move further out, where they hoped to get more for their money. Sheffield is the largest city in Yorkshire and is surrounded by the countryside of the Peak District National Park. A thriving industrial town, known for its steel and cutlery production, it has been transformed by the popularity of its university, two new sports stadiums, a film school, leisure parks and an airport. This regeneration has turned Sheffield into a commercial and progressive success, yet it remains the most wooded city in England thanks to a twelfth-century law that prevented its woodlands being developed. There are many residential areas convenient for the centre, with particularly sought-after areas in the south, south-west and south-east of the city. Georgie and Graham had their heart set on the south-west. Close to city and country, it is the perfect location, but its convenience makes it more expensive.

The first property they looked at was a four-bedroom Edwardian house boasting many original features. It was in a stunning street opposite the botanical gardens and priced at the top end of their budget at £49,950. They were not keen on the original features, including the striking tiled fireplace in the living room, although the magnificent claw-footed, roll-top bath did strike a chord. There was no point paying for features that they were going to remove so they decided to look elsewhere.

> **TIP: If you want to remove an original fireplace, do not agree to your builder taking it away as a favour. There is a big market for reclamation fireplaces and surrounds.**

Ten minutes further from the town centre, they viewed a three-bedroom Victorian semi in another desirable address, among the tree-lined streets of Eccleshare. It was well under their budget at £124,950 but the seventies décor might be off-putting. There was an attic space but it looked as though the floor joists were too weak to support an extension. A new bathroom and a more up-to-the-minute kitchen were needed. Their joint view was that even if they were prepared to do the necessary work, it was not the house for them.

> **TIP: Check the strength of the floor joists before embarking on alterations in an attic space.**

On to the wooded suburb of Totley, only fifteen minutes from the city centre, where an unusual modern house was on the market for £150,000. Positioned on a hill, the three-storey layout was upside down, with the living rooms at the entrance level on top and the bedrooms downstairs. It sported a balcony on the living room and had plenty of *al fresco* appeal, with a garden leading from the large master bedroom down to a council wood. The boundary to the property was unclear and the public access to the wood meant that security might be an issue. Graham was not convinced. 'It wouldn't have been the first house I'd have come to see. It's nice but it feels like it's lacking in something, but I don't know what.'

> **TIP: If boundaries are unclear, check the title deeds to see where they lie.**

Property four had a bit of everything. It was a modernised eighteenth-century, four-bedroom house by a stream priced at £145,000. The kitchen retained some original features such as the chimney breast, but incorporated contemporary units and appliances. The beamed living room was a seventies extension that blended perfectly with the rest of the house. An enclosed cottage staircase led up to an airy master bedroom with lots of cupboard space and an *en suite* shower room. Looking at the outside of the house they noticed a number of cracks in the wall, particularly near a window. They could be caused by weather erosion, settlement, subsidence, sloping ground or the extension. A surveyor's opinion was crucial.

> **TIP: Do not be embarrassed to assess the water pressure and temperature by turning the shower on.**

Next it was back to their favourite district of Totley, where a three-bedroom Victorian semi was on the market for £134,950. Again, it offered a pleasing blend of old and new, with a big kitchen featuring a large range and coloured tiles. The attic conversion had potential as a master bedroom with a fantastic view. Outside, there was a long garden with possibilities for a covered barbecue area (or a parking spot for Graham's prized motor bike) with outbuildings that would add £15,000 to the value if converted. Graham and Georgie gave it an eight and a nine out of ten.

TIP: Outbuildings can offer a great chance to increase the value of a property.

Lastly, they left the city and went twenty miles to the seventeenth-century village of Litton in the Peak District. Two seventeenth-century workers' cottages had been knocked together to make a three-bedroom property with a modern interior including a new kitchen extension. The asking price was £154,950. A number of original features had been left, including the tremendously thick walls, the small windows, a fireplace and the exposed beams. The kitchen looked great, although the layout was poor and could be tiring to use. Georgie and Graham loved the place but in the end its distance from their current friends, life and work back in the city turned them against it.

The two houses they decided to take a second look at were the second house in Totley and the house by the stream. The major issue with Totley was its size. It did have a big kitchen, but no dining room, while the attic had quite a lot of unusable space under the eaves. On the other hand the bedrooms were big and there was scope for an extension. Neighbouring houses had had the same idea, so it was unlikely there would be any problem with planning permission. 'I'm not convinced enough on the rest of the house to warrant the disruption building an extension would cause. Viewing it for a second time, I can see that we're not finding the things we want here.' Returning to the house by the stream during the rush hour, they discovered the road past it was very busy although inside, things were as good as they remembered, with the bonus of a basement that could be used as a utility room or a den. A surveyor deemed the cracks cosmetic, and in need of £1,500 worth of repairs.

Their decision? 'The house by the stream is what we originally wanted but it is right next to a busy road and we're trying to decide whether we can sit out in the garden and cope with that.' But they deliberated too long. By the time they decided to make an offer of £140,000 they had been pipped at the post by someone who wanted it more than them. They had no alternative but to go back and restart their search.

CRACKS IN WALLS

If you spot a crack in an interior wall or ceiling when viewing a prospective property, do not automatically assume the worst. Cracks appear for a number of reasons, not all of them property-threatening.

Hairline cracks frequently appear in the plasterwork of walls and ceilings, both old and new. They rarely mean the worst. They are more than likely due to routine changes in temperature or humidity. It will usually be enough to fill them and paint over them. Where the ceiling and wall meet is a weak point where cracks often occur, usually due to the slightest natural structural movement of the property. If that is the cause, the cracks can be hidden under cove cornicing. Look to see if you can see any signs of patching, and try to find out why it was necessary.

If you suspect something more serious, make sure you draw your surveyor's attention to it. Cracks in the brickwork may have more serious implications of shrinkage, subsidence, land movement on a slope, vibrations caused by passing trains or traffic, intrusive tree roots or faulty foundations. Equally, they may just be a result of leaking drains that can soften the ground leading to slight movement, or to shallow foundations under a bay window that may lead to cracks at the join with the house.

You may be alerted to them by a patch of damp on the inside of the house where water has been let through. Look at the correspond-ing part of the outside wall. In any case, you should keep an eye out when examining the exterior of the house. Check particularly around doors and windows, chimney flues, any exposed concrete at the base of the house and look to see where the nearest tree is. It should be as far away from the house as it is tall (when mature) to be safe. Any signs of cracking must be checked by a surveyor or structural engineer to ensure they are not symptomatic of any serious structural fault. If they are, it may involve horrendous expense and upheaval to put them right.

The most important thing is to get sound advice from a surveyor, who should be able to advise you as to the cause of any cracks and recommend where to turn if there is any cause for concern.

6 MAKING MONEY FROM YOUR PROPERTY

Buying property is a big investment, and a homeowner can usually assume that their capital will grow over the period of ownership. If the bare minimum is done to maintain the structure of the place, it is unlikely to lose value in the long term, but by planning more carefully, it is possible to increase your profit beyond the level of natural inflation when you come to sell. Before going ahead with any radical renovation, ask yourself – why? Is this something that you or your family will benefit from and enjoy, or is it because you want to make money on the house? If the first, do not expect the second to follow automatically. If the second, then remember you are creating something that should appeal to the taste of as many potential purchasers as possible – not necessarily the same thing as pleasing yourself. The fact is that the value of the property resides largely in the eyes of the prospective buyer.

RENOVATING YOUR PROPERTY

If you are renovating the property so that you and your family will benefit from it, and plan to live there for a number of years, the changes you make may or may not increase the long-term value of the house. The most important thing is that you are adapting it so that it gives you enjoyment. Nonetheless, as you make changes, it is always worth bearing in mind the resale value – will you recoup your expenditure in the long term?

In the first instance, there are a number of ways in which you can improve your house so that it actually saves you money. The government is phasing in new building regulations to make our homes more energy efficient. The aim is to reduce the amount of heat being lost from houses by insisting on double glazing on all replacement windows, energy efficient boilers, low-voltage lighting and better-insulated conservatories and extensions. All these improvements mean heating and electricity bills will be lower. In conservation areas and listed buildings it may be more problematic to introduce such measures, but every property should be looked at to see if there is a way that new works could improve its efficiency.

If you are tempted to make structural alterations to your home, the rule of thumb is that the only way of substantially increasing the value of your property is to add rooms. The most valuable commodity you have is space, so, where you can and within reason, enclose it and make it habitable, bearing in mind the costs involved. When planning the addition of extra rooms, do not extend beyond the basic amenities of the house. For example, one bathroom is not enough for a house with five bedrooms, Equally, if it has five bedrooms and no dining area, you have just built yourself a problem. Also, consider the style of the property, its location and the effect your alterations may have on the neighbours. There is no point applying for planning permission when it is obviously not going to be granted. Sympathetic extensions and conversions that do not block light from the adjoining properties or overlook them are likely to be regarded more favourably. Remember too that value is found in the quality of the design and workmanship, so it may be worth paying a little bit extra for something that will last and look appealing.

If you need the professional help of an architect or builder, turn to the feature on renovating your property on page 179.

Generally speaking, the things likely to increase the value of your property substantially are: a one- or two-storey extension, a new kitchen, a garage and central heating – it is rare to find a home without it in the UK these days.

Extensions

An extension provides extra living space on the ground floor, whether a substantial kitchen/dining room, a living room or garden room, with perhaps a bedroom and bathroom above it. If you have the space and finances to stretch to the extra floor, do so. It may only be a few years before you decide you need it after all and then it will be much more expensive and you may not get planning permission. Unlike a roof conversion, its exterior is not integral to the existing structure of the house so it is particularly important that it is designed to suit the style of the property and is in proportion with it. Look to see what neighbouring properties have done and what works best on similar buildings. If there is an extension you particularly like, the owners may even recommend their architect.

Make sure that the extension does not block any light from existing rooms, particularly if it spans the back of the house across external windows. In a one-storey extension, a light well may be the answer, and in a two-storey extension you and your architect will have to look care-fully at the design to see if anything can be done to help. Always check with the local authorities to see if you need planning permission and building regulations approval. If you do, talk to your neighbour before you apply, explaining everything to them. Show them the plans so they can see exactly what you are proposing and how you have minimised the effect it may have on them. If you do not consult them, they may react negatively when they get the first notification from the council. Their objections can hold up the process and may lead to your having to attend an appeal. If you can avoid this by consultation, your life will be much easier.

Kitchens

The kitchen is the hub of the household, where families gather to eat, chat and pass time. Creating a spacious environment that works efficiently but has a friendly atmosphere is a must in any family home. Even in a bachelor flat, where cooking may be kept to a minimum, it is important to have a kitchen that looks good and functions well. Size does not matter as much as the design and finish.

There are a plethora of kitchen designs available, from rustic country with tiled floors, Aga and a large pine table to unadorned Shaker wooden units, and from stream-lined urban minimalism with pale wood units, granite worktops, metal handles, glass doors and splash-backs to industrial chic with functional stainless steel or zinc predominant. The look you choose must depend on personal taste and the style of the rest of the property.

When possible, the design should evolve round the work triangle of fridge, oven and sink. These are the key areas in the workspace so they should not be too far apart for things to work efficiently. If designing a galley kitchen, the oven and the sink should be on the same side. Your worktops should be durable and easy to clean, at a comfortable height and with as much room to manoeuvre as possible. There should be workspace available on either side of oven/hob. Allow for plenty of storage space that is easy to reach.

Pay attention to lighting. The worktops should be well lit so that the cook can see what he or she is doing. Recessed ceiling lights on a dimmer are an ideal way of lighting a kitchen that doubles as a dining room. If the lights are on different circuits, you will be able to highlight the area of the room you are using. For example, at the end of the evening, the seating or dining area can be lit softly while the washing-up is hidden.

Flooring should be hard-wearing and easy to clean. Floorboards are not always a good solution because crumbs and dirt will collect between them unless all gaps are refilled and they are thoroughly sealed. Tiles, vinyl or wood laminate offer more practical solutions.

Garage

A garage saves the risk and inconvenience of parking in the street, and should cut down on your insurance premiums. Depending on its size and position, it may fall within permitted development. Apply to the local planning authorities to find out.

Other improvements may increase the value but by how much can depend on the location of the property, the workmanship involved and the state of the housing market.

Bathrooms

Bathrooms can be a major selling point in a property. The right bathroom in the right place can add value to a property, and there is no doubt that a sparkling clean one will at least encourage a buyer to look more favourably on it, so installing a new one will not be on their list of anxieties. You cannot go wrong replacing a dated coloured suite with a white one. If you are starting from scratch, read the design tips below. They will apply wherever you are installing it. *En suite* bathrooms are increasingly popular. If you have the space to add one to your master bedroom, perhaps by converting an old dressing room, adjoining small bedroom or office, then it is definitely worthwhile. Older properties sometimes have their bathrooms on the ground floor, beside or through the kitchen. It is much more practical and comfortable to have at least one on the same level as the bedrooms. It might be possible to squeeze one into a landing space or install an *en suite* into a large master bedroom. Alternatively, if you have more bedrooms than you need it may be feasible to convert one into a bathroom.

Before embarking on the work, you will need to get approval from the local building regulations officer and, if altering the water supply, notify the local water company. If converting an internal room, a macerator will be needed to grind the waste and pump it to the outside of the house. These can be noisy, expensive and worse, can get blocked, so think carefully about your decision.

Plan the room carefully. Measure up to see how big a bath you can accommodate. There should be enough room for you to get out of it and towel yourself down comfortably. Allow enough room to stand straight in front of the basin and to sit comfortably on the toilet or bidet. If the room is under the eaves, this will need particular attention. Try to arrange the layout so that the toilet is hidden behind the door when it is opened. Depending on the size of room, consider the possibility of having a separate shower cubicle. Whether there is a window or not, there should also be some sort of ventilation built in to prevent condensation. Include storage systems where you can, perhaps allowing for a unit below the basin or behind the toilet. If space is tight, a wall-mounted radiator can double as a towel rail.

When choosing the fittings, remember that any colour will do as long as it is white. They should be in keeping with one another and with the style of the house. Introduce colour into the room through your eventual choice of floor or wall coverings. If choosing a roll-top cast iron bath, double check the floor joists are robust enough to support it.

Employ a plumber who will run the waste and water pipes and

connect the fittings. You will also need an electrician to rewire the room. It is illegal to have light switches and power sockets, apart from shaving sockets and cord pull switches. This is your opportunity to create atmosphere with a new lighting scheme on an external dimmer switch.

Walls and floors should have a waterproof covering. Tiles come in myriad materials, shapes and sizes to give a durable, easy-to-clean finish. If you use paint or wallpaper, they should have vinyl finishes. Floorboards are extremely difficult to make watertight. Every join, knot and crack should be sealed before either varnish or specialist floor paint is applied.

Conservatories

A conservatory is a versatile space that lends itself to all sorts of uses. It can be anything from a quiet study or a rowdy playroom, to a sophisticated dining room or comfortable sitting room. Its use may depend on the direction it faces and when it receives most sun. South-facing means it will get the sun all day, all year round, so is ideal for a general living area. West-facing gets sunlight on summer afternoons and evenings, and is ideal for after-work relaxation or entertaining. East-facing is best for a breakfast room while north-facing is the chilliest option of all – deliciously cool in summer, it may need extra heating in winter. The mood is infinitely variable depending on the style and the choice of flooring and accessories.

The addition of a conservatory can be a spectacular improvement provided its proportions fit with the rest of the house and the style belongs to the appropriate period. Whether you will need planning permission depends on its proposed size and siting and the local planning regulations. Ask your local authority or the National Conservatory Advisory Service (NCAS) for advice. When designing the conservatory, do not let it hide any particularly attractive features of the property or take up too much of the garden space. Have a professional contractor check that the site is suitable. Proper foundations should prevent damp problems.

Proper insulation, ventilation and light will ensure it can be used throughout the year. Underfloor heating, double glazing and efficient blinds will keep it warm in the winter. Proper ventilation involves more than just opening a window. Air should be able to enter at a low level and circulate before leaving via the roof. Fans in the highest point of the roof will aid this. Plan how you will light the conservatory in the evenings. The key thing to remember is not to shine lights at the ceiling or walls because they will shine right back. In fact, the most important lights are outside in the garden, whereas inside, candles give the best light for relaxing or eating, with the odd task light for any particular activity such as reading or sewing. Always choose the best conservatory you can afford. Cheap, badly designed, poor quality conservatories will not add value to your home.

The best conservatory companies will pay a site visit, design the structure to suit the property, deal with necessary planning permission and building regulations and advise on every aspect of the building including insulation, ventilation, heating and sometimes even plants and furniture. They may offer a free design service and supply plans and drawings after the initial visit and discussions. Further modifications may need to be included before drawing up final plans. It is important to be clear as to what exactly is included in the package and what extras may need to be paid for.

The structural work should be guaranteed for a fixed number of years. Keep the guarantees in case of problems and to pass on to any future buyer. A conservatory is not guaranteed to recoup its value when you come to sell, though if it is sympathetically designed, well-built and fulfils the other criteria above, you may make back 50% or more.

Loft conversions

Buying a property at a reasonable price knowing that one day you can use the loft to add another room is usually a sound investment. Loft extensions are a way of expanding your home at a fraction of the cost of moving to a bigger one. An architect or specialist loft conversion company should be able to advise you on the various key points to be considered as well as the design of the interior.

Planning permission may be required for the external work. Generally, dormer windows are not permitted on the side of the house facing a public road. In an urban conservation area, permission is needed for any dormers at all, and the loft extension may have to be situated so it is hidden from the street. Permission often depends on guidelines such as: the roof ridge of the roof must not be broken by the extension; two small dormers instead of one; no box windows; any tiles must match those on the existing roof; the roof should be pitched to match the existing one and so on. An architect or professional loft designer will be aware of the local stipulations and how to comply with them. Some loft extensions fall within permitted development so check with your local authority.

Questions to ask:
> Is there enough headroom?
> Is the floor area big enough?
> Will the house support the structure?
> How do I get a staircase up there?

The ideal height of the room would be 8 feet (2.5m). If your roof is made with standard roof trusses, there may be no alternative but to take the roof off and replace it.

The floor joists may not have the strength to carry the load required in a habitable room. If so, new joists can be placed between them to support the new floor. Alternatively, a new floor could be installed above the existing one. Take into account the reduction in floor-to-ceiling height. If there is any danger to the structure of the house, reinforced steel joists may be needed. All these details must comply with building regulations. Again, your architect/loft designer will apply to the local Building Inspector. If you are having work done on the floor, now is the time to install any new ceiling lights in the room below.

Building regulations will also stipulate the measurements and position of the staircase. Retracting steps and loft ladders are not allowed. If you do choose a spiral staircase, work out the practical aspects of moving furniture up and down it.

The conversion must also comply with strict fire safety regulations. The stairway must be of 30-minute fire-resisting construction, and smoke detectors should be installed. The dimensions of an escape window will be determined by building regulations.

The space should be properly ventilated, insulated and heated. Windows can be at the gable ends, or dormers can be built (according to planning permission) to give added floor space. Skylights are another possibility. Proper insulation should ensure it is cool in summer and warm in winter. Make sure there are enough power points and switches. If your central heating system cannot be extended, add electric wall heaters.

Whether adding a master bedroom and *en suite* bathroom, a children's bedroom and bathroom, an office or playroom, make sure it is designed to maximise the available space. Like everything, the worth of your conversion will depend on the quality of the design and workmanship. Done well and in the right location, it can add as much as double its cost in value to your home.

Windows

Replacing wooden sash or casement windows in a period house with uPVC substitutes will not add value. Looked after properly, wooden frames last as long and add a character to your home that uPVC never will. Ask advice for window replacement and care from the NWRAS (National Window Replacement Advisory Service). In a new house, it is worth looking for good quality uPVC windows that come with a guarantee and need little or no maintenance.

Garden

Spending money on landscaping your garden will be worth it for the pleasure it gives you. But a well-maintained, mature garden will certainly encourage buyers to see the property in a more favourable light, and therefore add value to it. If you do not have a conventional garden, it might be possible to establish a patio garden or a roof terrace as an outdoor room. Remember that potted plants need constant attention and regular watering in the summer.

Tennis courts

These can add value to a property and are usually straightforward to maintain. When not being used for tennis they can double for other outdoor activities – badminton, basketball, roller skating. If you have the space and can site it at a discreet distance from the house, they can make a sound investment.

Swimming pool

However attractive the idea of a pool, do not make the mistake of thinking it will add to the value of the property. In some cases it can even lower it. Pools can be dangerous to unsupervised children and pets and are expensive to install and to run. Some future buyers may be actively put off by the thought of having to maintain it, particularly during our less balmy summers. The running costs will include chemicals, filters, parts and heating and call-out charges when things go wrong. The rubber liners used for outdoor pools usually have to be replaced about every ten years. However, if you do decide the benefits to your family are worth it, check with the local authority whether you need to apply for planning permission. This will depend on the pool's position and size.

Off-road parking

If parking is a problem and there is a way to provide off-road space, this will be considered a big plus point by any buyer. If you have a large garden and a drive, it may be easy to create a parking space. In an urban environment it is more likely to mean sacrificing your front garden or, if it is accessible from behind, a section of your back garden. However, for the added convenience, extra degree of peace of mind and the possible saving on your insurance premium, it may be worth it. If you can secure the area with a gate, so much the better.

BUYING TO SELL

Buying a rundown property cheaply, doing it up and selling it on fast can be an extremely shrewd way of investing your money. It can also be a way of climbing the property ladder more rapidly, taking you closer to the sort of home to which you aspire but cannot, at the outset, afford. To do this effectively and efficiently there are a number of guidelines you should follow.

Target market

In the first place, you should keep your buyers in mind throughout, improving the property in a way that will appeal to the greatest spread of them, making it more likely that you will achieve a quick sale when you need to. You must be very clear in your mind who they are likely to be – students, young professionals, first-time buyers wanting to start a family, an elderly couple. Each of these target markets will have very different demands and expectations. Be aware of them.

Your target market will depend to a large extent on the area in which you buy. Study it thoroughly, looking at the facilities and at who uses them. For example, if close to parks, schools, shops, think family; if there are new office developments nearby or good transport links to a business centre, think young professionals.

Location

The location of your property is a key factor in your investment. If it is in the wrong position, no amount of work will help. If you can buy into a good residential area, so much the better, but if your budget is more limited, the smart move is to find an up-and-coming area where property has only just begun to be developed (see Finding the Next Property Hotspot on page 118). The chances are you will be able to buy reasonably and then a combination of your improvements with the changing housing market will considerably increase the value of the property. Look on the fringes of fashionable areas. Find out where new office and residential developments are planned – often in rundown industrial areas. Watch for the tell-tale signs of coffee bars, new estate agencies, restaurants, bars and new shops beginning to spring up, and surrounding houses being renovated.

Layout

Once you have found your property and decided on the target market, look at the space it offers and decide whether it can be used more effectively. How does the layout work? Could it be better? Does the space suit the function of the room? If the only bathroom is on the ground floor, would it be more convenient if it was upstairs? Could the resulting down- stairs space be better used as an extension of the kitchen, or as a study? Could you utilise the loft by converting it into one or two bedrooms and an *en suite* bathroom? Similarly, a cellar might offer potential for more living space. Would the kitchen be better situated in the larger dining room? Or could the rooms be knocked through into one another to create a large family kitchen/dining room? Knocking through rooms does not only appear to create space, it can make the whole area seem much lighter. However, it is important to remember that knocking walls down may not be what your potential buyer will want.

When considering how best to use the space, always keep the ques- tion, 'Will it add value?' in the forefront of your mind. If the answer is, 'No,' then do not do it. For instance, converting a bedroom into a bathroom may make practical sense but ideally you should then be able to use the old bathroom or another room as a bedroom. The number of bedrooms is key to an estate agent's valuation of a house. Getting rid of one may improve the look of the house, but it may well diminish its worth.

Budget

Before starting on any work, be clear about whether there is a ceiling to property values in the region. Talk to local estate agents who should be able to give you a view. Only compare like with like. If there is a ceiling to the sale prices of similar renovated properties, work out your budget accordingly. It is pointless spending more on improvements than you can hope to recoup in a sale when your goals are to sell quickly and to make a profit. The size of your budget is less important than what you do with it. Work out what will add value and what will not, then set your priorities before beginning work.

Sticking to your budget is going to be the most important factor in making the enterprise successful. Plan out what work is needed to achieve the best possible sale, list the various projects involved in the renovation and allocate your money between them. This makes it much easier to keep track of where it is all going. It is also possible to compensate for additional unforeseen expenses in one area by tightening the reins in another.

DIY

If your budget is limited, enormous economies can be made if you can do much of the work yourself. However, make no mistake, if you are an enthusiastic but hopeless DIY fanatic, do not bother. The quality of the work is crucial to the additional value you will be putting on your house. If potential buyers feel that they are going to have to do it all over again when they move in, they will not be persuaded to part with their money. You will have to be prepared to put in an enormous amount of time and energy into getting everything right. If in any doubt, employ professionals. It will probably save you money in the long run. Another consideration for anyone embarking on DIY is time. It is important to be realistic about the amount of time you will have to spend on the project, and things inevitably take longer than imagined. If you go over your deadline, you will end up making more mortgage repayments than you had allowed for. From that point on, you will be making a loss every month until the property is sold.

Organisation

The other consideration is organisation. Everything must be meticulously planned so that the materials you require arrive when you need them and not too soon before or afterwards. If you are organising the project and buying materials, but using professional labourers, you should have a timetable of the order of works so you know when to book them in and when to order the materials. If the project is more ambitious than you can manage alone, the answer is to employ an architect.

Design

The quality of the design is as important as the standard of work. It is advisable to keep things simple, however stylish. Looking good does not always require a great deal of money. To appeal to the widest group of potential buyers, you should be providing them with the most perfect blank canvas on which they can imprint their own personality. You must remain emotionally detached from the design at all times. There is no point paying a little extra here and there on details that you particularly like. This personalises the property and, although some buyers may like the touches, others may be put off. Make it easy for the buyers to imagine the property is theirs. Your job is to give them the opportunity to buy into a certain lifestyle. Kitchens and bathrooms should be both smart and functional. They do not have to be brand new but can be revitalised beyond recognition.

Bathroom and kitchen

These rooms are of key importance in selling your home. They must be spotless and inviting. If there is any suggestion that the buyer may have to replace them, your quick sale may founder. Replacement bathroom suites and kitchen units do not have to be expensive, but they do have to look good. Keep them simple for the best effect.

If there is an existing kitchen or bathroom suite that is basically sound, do not automatically rip it out. See if it can be given a new lease of life with some judicious styling. (See Chapter 4 Selling Your Property for some ideas.) Remember your target market and provide what they need.

Decoration

When it comes to decorating, keep colours neutral. This maximises the sense of space and light and will not disturb a buyer's concentration. You want them to look at the room, not at the décor. If you are selling a flat and are tempted to strip and sand the floorboards, check your lease to see whether it is allowed. It is frequently stipulated against because the noise of footsteps will be an intrusion into the flat below. If you are not living in the property, you might be advised to stage the property for the sale. Use appropriate pieces from your own home or beg, borrow and steal them from friends. It can even be worth hiring some for the short length of time it will take to sell the property. Make sure to add in the vital accessories that give the place character without being overwhelming.

Garden

Do not forget the garden. A well-tended garden can increase your selling price. If you have bought a building site, start work on the garden early so that it has a chance to mature a little before the property goes on the market. Think about your prospective buyer when planning the garden. You may like to spend hours outside, mowing the lawn, planting, nurturing and pruning but your ideal buyer may not. A family may be more interested in having a play area or football pitch, with a terrace where they can eat. Young professionals with an active social life will want a low-maintenance garden where they might sit out or entertain occasionally. Think of your target market and design it for them. Think of the space as an extra room and present it as such, adding garden furniture so that the buyer can see how it could be enjoyed at its best.

Your changes do not always need to be expensive. If things are kept clean, simple and impersonal and you have researched your market and its demands thoroughly, stuck to your budget and remained organised, it will not be long before you have a buyer.

BUYING TO LET

The prospective landlord should think of buying to let as a medium to long-term investment. The buy-to-let market has boomed over recent years since mortgage lenders introduced specific buy-to-let mortgages and interest rates reached an all-time low.

Investing in property to let aims for capital growth and a regular income that will cover the mortgage and relevant expenses with some left over for the investor. To achieve this, you must be as focussed and organised as a professional property developer. The location of your property is as critical as your definition of a target market. A city slicker is not going to be interested in living in a student area nor vice versa. Your criteria should be as if you were buying to sell, but with a few added considerations. Having decided on your market, you must cater for its demands. Emotional detachment is paramount. You are not buying and preparing the place for your pleasure, but to provide a congenial home for someone else who you hope will stay put or who will be easily replaceable. Do not buy a property that needs a lot of maintenance. Steer clear of large gardens or a substantial amount of woodwork. They may look great, but you are buying hard work for yourself and not adding to the value of the rental.

Be very clear about what you will be expected to supply. If you are aiming at the top end of the market, the corporate let, you will find you are expected to provide innumerable luxuries such as cable television, a DVD player, power shower, top-of-the-range finishes, bed linens, parking facilities, a share in the concierge and more. You cannot afford to scrimp and save in the corporate lettings market. At a more modest level of a young professional who burns the candle at both ends, a smaller kitchen, larger bathroom and larger wardrobe might be the major considerations. A family will want a good-sized kitchen, enough bedrooms and bathrooms and a low-maintenance garden. At the other end of the market, the demands of a student flat will be considerably lower.

Safety

Taking on the role of a landlord involves the assumption of certain responsibilities. The first is your tenants' safety. The electric wiring, sockets and appliances must be thoroughly and regularly checked. Any gas pipes and appliances should be certified as safe and inspected annually, with records kept. Smoke detectors and fire extinguishers should be fitted. As of 1997, Fire Safety regulations apply to the furniture you use. Sofas, chairs and padded headboards must all carry a government-approved label. Mattresses, pillows, loose covers and cushions must all comply with the regulations. If you are at all unclear, ask your local trading standards office or the letting agent, if you are using one.

Materials

With those provisoes in mind, make the appropriate alterations to the property. Bear in mind that the finishes you choose may have to take some wear and tear, so they need to be easily and cheaply replaceable. However nice your tenants seem, however thoroughly you have checked their references, accidents and worse do happen. Even if not, just day-to-day use may necessitate replacements and redecoration in between tenants. You need to cut the time taken for this as much as possible. Every day you or the decorator are in your flat is a day without rent. Be practical.

Floor coverings should be resilient and neutral. Pale varnished wood is a hundred times better than pale pile carpet. If you insist on carpet, and you may be forced to in a leasehold flat, you will have to have it cleaned before every new tenant moves in.

Walls should be kept neutral to make the space feel light and airy. Steer clear of wallpaper. It is more expensive than paint and will take longer to replace. Keep a note of the BS numbers of any distinctive paint colours, although the most straightforward thing to do is stick to white or off-white. In any event, avoid vivid statements. They will put off as many people as they attract. Do not skimp on buying the paint because it will show. The more rooms you paint the same colour, the less paint you will waste in leftovers. Keep leftover pots for touching up. Redecorate in the same colours so that you will only need to use one coat, unless you have been very unlucky with tenants.

Furnishings

Furnishings should be kept to a basic minimum. The tenants may want to add their own. If they need an extra chair or table, they can always ask you to supply it. Try not to buy furniture that only fits in certain places. Tenants may well want to move it around. Living room sofas and chairs should be covered in loose covers that are machine washable. When buying them, it is a good idea to buy two sets of covers, so you can change them the minute one tenant leaves. Dark coloured covers work well because they will look better for longer and may not show the odd red wine stain so noticeably. Cream may look elegant to begin with but it will show every stain and soon look tired and dirty. Similarly, do not go overboard on the pictures and ornaments. Most tenants will want to personalise the place while they are living there and will bring their own. When you first prepare the place for tenants you may be tempted to buy second-hand furniture. This is a mistake. New furnishings may be more expensive but they will come with guarantees or warranties, operating instructions (keep all these for the next tenants), readily available spare parts and, even better, delivery to your door. Stick to recognised brand names. Keep an extra kettle, toaster and other small items so that you can replace them immediately. Buy mattresses that can be turned between tenants and replaced inexpensively.

Remember that you are responsible for repairing or replacing everything you supply. The easier and more cost-effective you can keep the maintenance, the better.

Follow that principle through to the garden, and keep to low maintenance there too. One tenant may share your love of gardening but the next may not. Keep flowerbeds to a minimum and have grass, flagged or brick paths and patios and terraces, even decking. If you insist on a garden, be prepared to provide a gardener to keep it flourishing.

Presentation

The more pleasing the environment you present, the sooner your potential tenant will snap it up. If you are letting a furnished flat, make beds neatly (even if you are not providing the linen with the flat), hang towels and add flowers. Before letting the property, decide whether it is to be let furnished or unfurnished. The benefits of furnished lets are that they achieve a higher rental income, but the furnishings have to be bought, have to comply with safety standards and be replaced when damaged. The insurance premium will be higher too. Once you have prepared the property for let, you are ready for your first tenant. How to let your property successfully is looked at in the next chapter.

JO JOHNSTONE, SOUTHAMPTON

Wanted: 'I'm a solicitor working really hideous hours so I need to be able to come and go with reasonable ease. I want to find somewhere light and airy where the rooms are big and I can see out and not feel hemmed in. I must have a minimum of two bedrooms, a sitting room, a separate dining room and lots of period features, especially open fireplaces and wooden floorboards. I also have to have a decent size garden. My budget is about £110,000 at the bottom and £150,000-ish at the top end.'

Southampton is the busiest port on England's south coast. Originally a medieval trading centre, a fair amount of the old city still exists. During the nineteenth century, the coming of the docks and the railway meant the city flourished and it has never looked back, finding particular popularity as a Georgian spa town. Heavy bombing during the Second World War meant many of its more recent period properties were lost, and since then it has been subject to major redevelopment.

Jo Johnstone was brought up in a village in the Lake District, where she was used to lots of space. She bought her first home, a flat in

Southampton, after she graduated but seven years later was looking for a change of scene. She was extremely clear about what she was looking for. So much so that she had already viewed and rejected dozens of places before appearing on the show.

The first property was in leafy Lyndhurst, a dream location in the heart of the New Forest. The prestigious address predictably carried a high price tag, but otherwise it met Jo's criteria. At just under £170,000, the period two-bedroom cottage had two reception rooms, plenty of original features and a 38-foot (11.5m) garden. Jo immediately liked its country feel. The low ceilings, wooden beams and exposed brickwork fireplace in one of the bedrooms all added to the appeal. The bathroom, though charming, lacked a bath. But if the toilet and sink were reorganised, enough space would be freed for a roll-top bath. The other strikes against the property were its lack of working fireplaces – surmountable if there was still a chimney that could be made to work – and its size. There was no doubt that Jo could find more for her money closer to town.

> **TIP: Check which way gardens face. For all-day sun, the ideal position is south-facing.**

The suburb of Shirley is only ten minutes from the city centre. A three-bedroom Victorian terraced house was on the market there for £112,950. It boasted huge rooms, including a 27-foot (8m) living room, and a 75-foot (23m) garden. Although there was not an existing fireplace in the living room, there was a chimney breast in the bedroom directly above. One option would be to rebuild the chimney breast on the ground floor and connect it to the existing one above. Alternatively, a cheaper solution would be to install a wood-burning stove with a pipe connecting to the chimney breast in the bedroom. Jo did not like the way the bathroom led off the kitchen. 'One thing I really hate is people in my kitchen when I'm entertaining.' A possible solution would be to convert one of the upstairs bedrooms – how expensive that would be would depend on the complexity of the plumbing involved. However, most importantly, the house did not have the period features she so wanted.

> TIP: If you are thinking about reinstalling fireplaces, check whether or not there is a working chimney. Also budget for the cost of installation.

Three miles north of the city is the green, sought-after area of Bassett. At just under £160,000, a Victorian terraced house offered plenty of period features with a fireplace in almost every room. A bedroom had been converted into a big bathroom and there was more space in the converted attic above. Downstairs was a good-sized living room, a separate dining room and a long modern kitchen with a dining area at one end. Although the garden seemed short, it could be extended by knocking down the 22-foot (6.5m) garage at the end.

> TIP: Garages add value to a property. Think carefully before deciding to remove one.

With plenty to think about, Jo went on to see two more properties. The first was only ten minutes from the city centre in the up-and-coming suburb of St Denys. Priced at just under £112,000, a late-Victorian mid-terrace house boasted huge rooms with lots of potential and a 90-foot (27.5m) garden. The potential fly in the ointment was the busy main road and railway line that ran past the end of the garden.

Last to be considered was a detached, two-bedroom Victorian villa stood in a quiet cul-de-sac back in Shirley. The house, priced at £152,500, was full of character and the owners had carefully researched the right historical colours for the walls. The kitchen was on the small side but the free-standing units could go, allowing for space-saving, custom-made units. Jo liked it, particularly the light master bedroom with its fireplace and the superb mature cottage garden.

The time had come for Jo to make up her mind. She decided to return for a second look at the last three properties. On consideration she realised that removing the garage at the end of the garden in Bassett was probably not on. A quote for four days labour and removing three skips of rubbish came in at £1,200. But she also had to weigh up the fact that a garage always adds value to a property – in this case about £5,000. Did she really want to pay to devalue her property? When she returned to the long garden in St Denys, it was rush hour on Monday. It only took a moment for her to realise that she would not be able to live with the traffic and train noise day in, day out. Finally, it was back to the Victorian villa in Shirley in the knowledge that other viewers were booked to see it in the afternoon and the vendor wanted a quick sale. Stylishly maintained with a major selling point in the mature garden, the only minuses as far as Jo was concerned were the price and the possibility that the neighbouring playing fields might be developed.

> **TIP: Do not assume neighbouring plots of land will stay empty. Check with the local council to see if there are any development plans.**

Finally she plumped for the house with the garage. It was in great condition inside, and outside she had the option to create a bigger garden. Currently on the market at £159,950, it was judged to be worth around £150,000, making the right starting offer £145,000. But as the bid was made, someone else offered more. It looked as if Jo had lost the property, but the story did not end there. Two weeks later, the other deal fell through and Jo's revised offer of £152,000 was accepted.

INSTALLING AND RESTORING FIREPLACES

A fireplace is one of the most rewarding features to reinstate in a period home. It immediately adds character and value to the property. Many fireplaces were bricked up or boarded over in the 1950s and 1960s, so it is well worth looking behind the wallpaper on a boarded-up chimney breast. Occasionally, the surround is left and the original grate replaced with an electric or gas fire.

Before reinstalling the fireplace, the chimney should be cleaned by a professional chimney sweep to ensure the removal of any blockages and to check the chimney has not been capped. A smoke pellet will demonstrate whether the flue is drawing properly. If it is not, it may be because the room is not sufficiently well ventilated or because there are cracks in the flue. At worst, you may need a specialist to replace the lining of the chimney and even the chimney itself. Any alterations must comply with building regulations.

If only a section of a fireplace remains, obtain the rest from a salvage yard or from a fireplace supplier who will be able to advise on exactly what you need. To be sure the fireplace is appropriate to the period of your property, see if you can find an original in one of your neighbours' houses or ask a specialist supplier's advice. The latter will probably provide a fitting service and be able to replace any cracked parts that still exist. To ensure you buy one that fits properly and is not out of proportion with the rest of the room, measure the chimney breast and the opening first. Many excellent reproductions are available if an original is hard to find or too expensive.

If you have inherited an old fireplace from the previous owner, simple restoration may be enough. Cracked firebricks may need replacing or, if the cracks are minimal they can be repaired with fire cement. Remove any rust with a wire brush, then a rust-remover and coat with an anti-rust agent. If a cast iron surround has been painted, it can be sand-blasted or chemically stripped before being painted with a black graphite polish. Any cracks in the iron must be welded or, if not in range of the heat, they can be glued with epoxy resin. Grate bars may need replacing – ask a blacksmith or specialist fire supplier to weld them for you.

Either remove a wooden surround for stripping or set to with some paint stripper. The decorative detail may be gesso, in which case great care needs to be taken with the stripping. A warm soapy solution may be enough to clean a marble surround. If not, try one of the proprietary marble cleaners. A word of warning: a marbled paint finish on a slate or wood surround can look like the real thing and is best left to a professional cleaner. Check which it is before you begin the treatment. Ceramic tiles should be wiped clean with soapy water. If they have been painted over, use water-washable paint stripper. If any of them are cracked, the fireplace will have to be removed so that they can be replaced from the back.

DIONNE BOATMAN AND EWAN MARSHALL, SOUTHEND

Wanted: 'The most important criterion is location because I have to commute to London. We want something light, airy and spacious with big windows. We're first time buyers, our finances are in place – we've got about £100,000.'

Sunny Southend has been a magnet for holiday-makers since the turn of the century. A hundred years later, the Edwardian houses and weatherboard cottages are still in great demand. Just a fifty-minute train ride to London, Southend offers a relaxing home life to those young professionals with high-flying jobs in the city. Getting on the property ladder is tough, and the rediscovered charms of seaside living has sent the prices rocketing by an extraordinary 60% in the last five years. Dionne Boatman is one of those commuters. She wanted to move out of her parents' home in London and to buy a first home with boyfriend Ewan Marshall, a local primary school teacher. They hoped to live in Leigh-on-Sea, the fashionable part of Southend, but the competition for property was fierce, explained Ewan. 'We've been blown out of appointments an hour or so beforehand or even half an hour because they've been snapped up so quickly. I don't think we're going to get anything where we can put in an offer under the asking price.' On the other hand, as first-time buyers without a home to sell, they were in a strong bargaining position.

The first house they saw in the popular area of Leigh-on-Sea was in Oakley Park Drive. A balcony flat with two bedrooms was on the market for £94,995. Ideal for a young couple, it was a stone's throw from the chic cafés of Leigh Broadway and the station was only a mile away. It was an Edwardian house conversion spread over two floors, with its own front door. The living room was bright and well proportioned, but a modern fireplace was hiding the original. The kitchen was far too small for Dionne, and there was no room for a table. A possible solution would be to swap the kitchen with the small second bedroom that had originally been the kitchen when the flat was converted. The master bedroom in the roof was the best feature, although there was a patch of damp that probably was traceable back to the flashings. If it was going to cost much to repair, it would be wise to subtract the amount from the purchase price. 'I like the idea of using the current kitchen as the spare room and vice versa. I also like the fact that it's quite neutrally decorated so we wouldn't have to do that immediately.'

> **TIP: If there are a number of B&Bs and hotels in a street, think about how much increased noise there will be, and about any possible parking problems.**

Five minutes away was another two-bedroom conversion at the same price, in Dawlish Drive. The immediate impression was of space and light, again helped by the neutral colours. The one thing that needed changing was the fixed and louvred windows in the spare bedroom – out of character with the house and, in a fire, nobody could get out of them. The living room was very big, with lots of windows and plenty of scope. Outside there was the bonus of a garage and garden. Dionne was quick to spot another plus. 'Location is good. We're close to the Broadway, within walking distance of the station and I've just spotted the church spire which means we're close to the pub.'

The third property was in Pall Mall, a little closer to the station. The flat had the traditional Edwardian layout that meant the rooms were on the small side. The plus point was that it had lots of period features – original fireplace, picture rail, cornice, bay window, original stained glass. The kitchen had room for a small table. Both it and the bathroom needed a revamp but, at £84,950, the flat was below budget and £2,500 spent on the kitchen could increase the value by £5,000. However, Ewan was concerned by the fact it was on a busy road and there was no parking.

The next property on their list was further from the seafront where prices were lower. For £106,950 they could buy a three-bedroom detached house. It had heaps of potential with room for a conservatory at the back, space for a loft conversion and to extend the kitchen into the dining room. With such neutral décor, it was easy to see that all the rooms were light and airy, with large windows. The verdict? 'It's not an area we know or are familiar with. I don't think it's really where we see ourselves.'

It was on to a two-bedroom Victorian conversion in Wilson Road in Southend's conservation area near the sea. It was a ground-floor flat that had been stylishly modernised, with wooden floors in the living room and two reasonably sized bedrooms and was on the market for £79,000. Dionne particularly liked the exposed brick fireplace in the living room. Because it was on the ground floor with no one below, the lease would probably allow Ewan to have his dreamed-of wooden kitchen floor. The garden was very overlooked by a number of high-rise blocks – the deciding factor against the place.

> TIP: In conservation areas, significant grants are usually available to repair sash windows and old iron railings.

Finally, they viewed a ground-floor flat in a converted Edwardian house in Westcliffe Avenue. It had two double bedrooms, lots of space and fell well within their budget at £82,950. The huge, light bedroom was positioned so that the occupant would hear everyone coming and going through the front door of the house, which was a drawback. Otherwise the rooms were all large and bright, but it was on the corner of two busy main roads.

> TIP: If the property has a leasehold, check who is responsible for which parts of the building. Speak to neighbours to find out about how helpful and reliable the freeholder is.

They decided the only one they wanted to see again was in Dawlish Avenue. Looking more closely, they found evidence of damp in the living room, but it seemed that the guttering was responsible so could easily be fixed – something to ask their surveyor about. They marked out different bed sizes on the floor to help them imagine how they would fit in.

> TIP: If you have important pieces of furniture that you will be bringing with you, take their measurements and a tape measure with you on viewings.

The neighbour they spoke to was very helpful and recommended the freeholder wholeheartedly. After staying for a long time to get a good feel of the place and its proportions, they decided to put in an offer of £93,000, remembering to point out the strength of their position and the speed with which they would be able to move. The agent came back quickly to say it was not enough. They countered by offering £94,000 on the condition it was taken off the market immediately for three weeks, during which they could get all their paperwork done. It was accepted. The survey was fine, as was the mortgage valuation, so Dionne and Ewan had found their first home together.

MAXIMISING SPACE AND LIGHT

Many potential home buyers want to find a property that offers them as much space and light as possible. When looking around a property that seems on the cramped and dark side, do not automatically strike it off your list. Ask yourself whether the seller is presenting it at its best and whether, if you moved in, you could do better.

The obvious way of introducing more space and light is to take out walls and add more windows. Of course, this depends on the layout of the house. Certainly, many dismal Georgian and Victorian basement rooms have been transformed by being knocked through into one large airy kitchen/dining/living room. However, when wielding a sledgehammer is not desirable or practical, there are a number of tried and tested tricks that will help in each room.

Colour scheme

Use monochromatic schemes in pale neutral shades to make the rooms feel larger. Keep ceilings the same colour or slightly paler to make them seem higher. Keep soft furnishings within the same palette, adding interest through the use of different fabric textures rather than colours or patterns. If you do want to liven things up, the judicious use of one or two brightly coloured accessories – scatter cushions, rugs, pictures, flowers – will be enough.

Floor coverings

Follow the neutral theme – think pale carpet, blonde wood or seagrass matting. Use the same covering across one floor of the property, or even throughout the house. The kitchen and bathrooms will need a more practical finish, but again stick to the same palette. A large expanse of the same shade and texture unifies the space and makes it seem larger, as one room flows into another. Steer clear of patterns unless they are extremely subtle.

Windows and doors

Hang curtains so that they pull back to expose all the window, letting in the maximum amount of light possible. Make sure windows are kept sparkling. If you are uneasy about being so exposed to your neighbours' gaze, use soft muslin or voile curtains, or slatted Venetian blinds that can be angled to let light through while retaining privacy. Instead of blocking light from a bathroom with a solid roller blind, use a slatted blind, or frosted or etched glass. A less expensive measure is to use spray etch or frosted film. Use half glazed or fully glazed doors to let light enter one room from another or to brighten up a dark hall.

Furniture

Keep furniture to a minimum. A crowded room will always look like a small room. Try not to arrange the furniture around the edge of the room but around a focal point. Every piece should be in proportion with the room and should not block the flow of traffic nor hide an important feature. The trick is to show as much of the floor and walls as possible so the dimensions of the room are obvious. Surfaces and shelves should not be overcrowded. Let the back of a shelf be visible behind ornaments, books or storage jars. Some kitchen units are fitted with legs, making the space seem larger, although it makes extra work to clean underneath. If you can put appliances into a utility room, space will be freed up. Similarly, bathroom basins, toilets and bidets can be off the floor, attached to the wall. A high cistern means the toilet can be further back against the wall. Provide efficient storage systems so every room is free of clutter.

Reflection

One way to introduce more light is by using reflective surfaces to bounce it back into the room. The most obvious choice are mirrors. Hung where they catch the incoming light, they can make an enormous difference. They also enhance the sense of space, whether hung at the end of a hall, over a mantelpiece or fixed to a wall in a small garden. Use your imagination to find the best place. But mirrors are not the only reflective surface: gloss woodwork, wall paints with a slight sheen, glass or metal finishes and even glazed fabrics will all help.

Lighting

Lighting can make or break a room at night. Use up or down lighters to give a gentle wash of background light, then accent the features or key areas in a room. Take care to illuminate work surfaces, dark stairways, halls and corners properly. Steer clear of pendant lights, and use wall lights and dimmers to create mood and space.

LUCY COX AND GRAHAM JOHNSTON, STOURBRIDGE

Wanted: 'A two or three-bedroom property with a garden. We'd prefer something with a bit of character, probably a period property. At the moment we're thinking about a budget of £110,000 but we would go higher if it was something very special.'

After ten months, the appeal of renting a flat above a funeral parlour in London's Finsbury Park was wearing a little thin for occupational therapist Lucy Cox and her boyfriend Graham Johnston, a physiotherapist. They had decided to relocate to the Black Country, to the town of Stourbridge, where Lucy was born and bred and where her family still live. They planned to marry the following year, so were hoping to find a house with room for a family of their own.

Stourbridge is in the West Midlands and sits on the edge of the Black Country – so called because of the smoke that belched from the chimneys of the industrial revolution. The heavy industry of the region may have declined somewhat, but there is still plenty of Victorian housing stock around.

Lucy and Graham began their search in Woolaston village, just a few minutes west of the centre of Stourbridge. Falling well within their budget at £96,500 was a two-bedroom, mid-terrace house typical of the area. The entrance was directly into the living room. An outside porch was unlikely to be permitted by the council because the house was in a conservation area. The kitchen extension was through the dining room, with a bathroom extension beyond that. Lucy was not keen. 'In the night, you'd have to come all the way downstairs. It would be nice to have a toilet upstairs.' The final black mark against the property was that the back alley leading to the garden ran across the neighbour's land. It would be essential for their solicitor to double check that the right of access still legally existed. But no need. Lucy and Graham had already decided against the house on grounds of size and the position of the bathroom.

> TIP: Ask your solicitor to check whether you have rights to cross a neighbour's land or they yours.

The next property was in the Quadrant, right in the heart of Stourbridge. Its popularity means prices are high and there was a three-bedroom terraced house in Western Road on the market for £104,950. A long hall-way with stairs off it led to the comfortable living room, complete with wood-burning stove. The bathroom was downstairs again but this time there was a solution: knocking through the smallest bedroom into a cupboard in the master bedroom could provide an *en suite* bathroom to both remaining bedrooms. Other plusses were the large cellar and a private back garden.

Round the corner was a bigger three-bedroom mid-terrace house on the market for £92,000. It had been rented out for a number of years and allowed to go to seed. There was a wider variety of carpet and wallpaper in every room than one would have thought possible, but there were still some stunning original features such as the living room fireplace and the original wood windows. The living room itself was big enough to have an indoor porch built in. Again, the third bedroom could convert into an upstairs bathroom, while downstairs there was scope for knocking down the extension and building a conservatory to overlook the garden. But Lucy was unsure. 'It feels like an upside down house, completely out of balance.' The potential was good but the amount of work was daunting.

> **TIP: Would one room work better if used for another purpose? Use your imagination when viewing a property.**

By going twenty minutes out of town to Kidderminster, Lucy and Graham could get much more for their money. A Victorian terraced house priced at £84,950 seemed to offer everything, including an upstairs bathroom, but neither Lucy nor Graham were convinced. 'As we've moved up the house, we've started to notice bits and pieces. The gut feeling is that it's just not the one for us.' Although the snags of exposed pipes, loose electric sockets, slipped roof tiles and an unfinished fireplace were all minor, if their hearts were not in it, it was time to move on.

> **TIP: Unfinished DIY jobs can signify other more important repairs have been overlooked.**

Location was one of the key issues in Lucy and Graham's search, so they returned to the outskirts of Stourbridge, to Kinver, where they viewed an eighteenth-century brick and timber-frame house with an asking price of £118,950. There was an open-plan living/dining room, and a large modern kitchen with a dining area at one end. A down pipe delivered water directly on to the flat roof, but a few hundred pounds would put that right. Lucy and Graham were not convinced. 'You can't really fault it on the way it's been done up, but it is little. Also there's the main road going through Kinver so it looks as if it will be quite busy and have implications for the parking. It's a great area with great schools but I don't know if that's enough to make us want this house.'

TIP: **Flat roofs are particularly vulnerable to the elements. Check their condition thoroughly.**

Finally, staying in Kinver, they viewed a modern, semi-detached, two-bedroom house with its own drive and parking space, on the market for £94,950. Lucy's immediate reaction was against the laminate flooring but as they looked round, they could see the house did have its charms. An ex-local authority property, it represented very good value for money with a bright and spacious living room, a big kitchen that needed a little alteration to flank the cooker with work tops, generous bedrooms and an opportunity for a loft extension. But even on a second viewing Lucy still felt that it lacked the necessary x-factor.

They decided to take another look at the second house they had seen, in Western Road. Outside, parking did not look as if it would be a problem. Inside, they still appreciated the hall and the welcoming living room. They got a plumber's quote of £2,100 for parts and labour excluding the building work necessary to create the upstairs bathroom. Downstairs in the cellar there was a damp problem, but they were recommended to use a cavity membrane damp-proof system and were quoted £7,000 to make the room entirely useable, including plastering, painting, electrics and flooring.

TIP: **If you see evidence of damp, find the source and get an estimate for its repair.**

This time they were 100% convinced it was the house for them and decided to put in an offer of £100,000. Even when they upped it to £102,000, the vendor remained adamant that he wanted the asking price. Graham's reaction? 'I'd be sick as a dog if someone snuck in ahead of us.' And Lucy's? 'I'd kick myself if someone else got it.' Their final offer of £105,000, the asking price, was accepted, the house was taken off the market and they could look forward to starting their married life in their new home.

DAMP – DOES IT MATTER?

The answer is of course that it *might*. Left alone, it can cause rot and dry rot, and weaken the structure of the house. If you find evidence of damp, you need to know whether it can be prevented and how much it will cost to do so before you buy the property.

When viewing a prospective property, keep a wary eye out for stains on the walls, bubbling plaster or paintwork and soft, rotten wood that you can stick a knife in easily. If you spot any of these signs, investigate the cause to see whether or not it can be remedied easily, or ask your surveyor for advice. In fact, if you see little evidence thanks to a quick decorating job, be doubly cautious. Is anything being hidden?

Water can cross any porous surface and our houses are full of them. In a modern property, all it takes is a piece of mortar accidentally dropped on one of the ties connecting the inner and outer cavity walls for water to travel through from the outside.

Modern properties are all built with a damp-proof plastic membrane that runs under a solid ground floor and connects with a damp-proof course (DPC). A DPC is an impervious material used in the lower part of a wall to prevent rising damp or, in a room below ground level, lateral damp. In older buildings, slate was used. If damp is rising up internal walls, it may suggest that the membrane is missing or damaged. This may entail extensive repairs – at worst, taking up the entire floor and putting in a new one. It is important to take expert advice and ask a couple of reputable companies to quote for repairs. Check along the skirtings to see if there is any sign of damp. Look outside to see if you can see evidence of a DPC – either protruding material or plugs where it has been injected. Make sure that any flowerbeds next to the house do not come above the level of the DPC. The owner may have a DPC certificate or guarantee. Before you accept it, check the company is still operating. If it is not, the guarantee is not worth the paper it is written on and you will have to start from scratch. Make sure closed-up chimney breasts have air bricks so they are property ventilated.

If there is damp around the windows, doors or bays, the seals may be faulty or the walls may be cracked or need repointing. Damp often results from nothing more serious than a blocked, overflowing gutter or cracked drainpipe – both easily rectifiable.

Rain can get in through the roof if there are missing, slipped or cracked slates or tiles. Cement or lead flashings can also crack. Once spotted, it is easily mended. Pay special attention to a flat roof. If water is pooling on it or it is covered in moss, it suggests that the fall should be corrected. Felt roofs only last about ten years, and asphalt about thirty. Find out how old they are and whether you might need to replace them. Get roofers' estimates before you make an offer or exchange.

Timbers can be affected by rot. Question any springy ground floors, especially around bay windows. Wet and dry rots can affect any woodwork. Wet rot begins when the timber becomes saturated with water and it breaks apart. It can usually be simply remedied by treating the cause and replacing the rotted timber. Dry rot is much nastier. It is a fungus that takes up in a piece of damp timber and dries it out until it crumbles to the touch. It can spread rapidly and is often not noticed until in an advanced state. Watch for it in damp, smelly, airless corners. If rot is caught early, it need not be an expensive operation to put it right. Obtain an expert opinion and quotes for treating it from timber specialists.

7   LETTING YOUR PROPERTY

Becoming a landlord requires a number of qualities: responsibility, organisational skills, good communication skills, patience and fore-thought. Having prepared a property for let, as the landlord you must assume responsibility for both your asset and the welfare of the tenant, having observed the relevant fire and safety precautions. The arrange-ment will generate a considerable amount of paperwork whether a letting agent (see below) is used or not. It is important that the landlord remains on top of it and can retrieve relevant information when required. The rela-tionship with the tenant may or may not be close but it should be a professional and amiable one to ensure that each party gets what they want from the arrangement. It is important that the landlord thinks ahead and provides for every eventuality in advance. If you are thinking, more modestly, of letting a room in your own home, look at the feature on Letting a Room on page 64.

RENT

The decision as to how much rent to charge should be taken bearing in mind the competition. If a letting agent is handling the let, they will be able to advise. Otherwise, look in the local papers to see what similar properties are being rented for and take into consideration the fact that yours may be in a better location and in better condition. You cannot change the location, but you can do something about the condition. You should also bear in mind that the rent should cover your borrowings and costs. Allowing for the fact that the property may be empty for some months of the year between tenants, it is cautious but wise to calculate rental income based on forty-five weeks in a year.

DEPOSIT

It is common to take between six and eight weeks' rent as a deposit on a property to be repaid at the end of the tenancy. This is a safeguard against any damage done to the property and subsequent costs. If it is more than one month's rent, the tenant will be less likely to leave without paying the last month's rent. Agree that the deposit should be repaid a couple of weeks after the end of the tenancy so that you have time to check the property and make any necessary deductions.

THE TENANCY AGREEMENT

Before searching for a tenant, it is sensible to prepare a tenancy agreement. This is not a legal requirement, but it is a legally binding document that will protect both the landlord's and the tenant's interests and, if thought through carefully, should avoid or certainly minimise any disagreements between them. Letting without one means that you have no recourse to law when your tenant refuses to leave the property; when you want to raise the rent; when you are left with unpaid bills; when your tenant decides to sub-let the property or uses it in ways you would prefer he did not; when he makes alterations to the structure without permission or keeps animals against your wishes and so on. Both you (or the letting agent on your behalf) and the tenant should sign the agreement. If there is more than one tenant jointly and individually liable for the tenancy then they should all sign.

You can draw up a lease yourself, but if inexperienced in such matters, it would be more sensible to ask a solicitor or letting agent to do so for you. Standard leases are obtainable from legal stationers but they may need to be modified depending on your demands on the tenant and the nature of your property. The agreement must comply with the Housing Act 1988 (as amended 1996).

There are two sorts of tenancy. An assured shorthold tenancy guarantees your right to get the property back after six months. The minimum terms and level of rent must be set before the tenancy begins. The term of the let cannot be broken without both sides' agreement. This is most commonly used for domestic lets. An assured tenancy gives the tenant the right to remain in the property until a court of law allows the landlord to take possession. The rent is fixed unless a review date is stipulated in the contract. This tenancy is so weighted in favour of the tenant that it would not be recommended for a private landlord.

There are two types of let. A 'fixed term' letting is when the property is let for a set period of time. This means you can gain repossession of the property at the end of the term without having to provide a reason. However, the tenant must be given two months' written notice or the tenancy will begin another fixed term under the same conditions. A 'periodic' letting is when the property is let from week to week or month to month with an agreed notice period from either side. Again, after the initial six months, you are entitled to repossess your property after giving the tenant two months' notice.

The agreement should specify the landlord, the tenant and the property. It should specify the contents (further detailed in an inventory), the term of the tenancy – specifying a start and finish date, notice period, the amount of rent, when and how it is payable and the date it is first due, and the deposit and the conditions of its repayment. It may also name a guarantor who guarantees payment of rent. This is common if the tenants are young, or students.

Think about how you want your property to be looked after and make sure that every eventuality is covered. There will be a number of clauses detailing the conditions of use, ensuring as far as possible that the tenant will treat the property well. Among other things, it should protect the landlord against damage to the property, specifying that no alterations or redecorations can be made without the landlord's consent, that the property should be kept clean and in good repair, that it must be kept secure, that it should not be left empty for longer than a certain period or used as business premises or for illegal activities. It should also have a policy on pets, noise and anti-social behaviour, and prohibit any sub-letting. If you allow the latter, you will lose control over who is living in your property. It should also be made clear what the tenant's responsibilities are with regard to maintaining the property day to day. This might range from checking drains and gutters to ventilation and smoke detectors.

The landlord should be able to have access to the property for inspection purposes, but he should not be allowed to let himself in unannounced whenever he feels like. He should have certain rights to cover collecting rent arrears.

It will also make clear which of you is responsible for paying council tax, gas, electricity and telephone bills and reconnections when necessary, water charges and TV licence. If the property is self-contained, the tenant usually takes responsibility for paying council tax and service bills.

It should also state what will happen, or what compensation should be made, should the tenant or landlord fail to comply with any of the above.

The agreement may also allocate responsibility for insuring the building (usually the landlord) and the contents (the landlord is usually responsible for the contents he provides, but the tenant should insure his own).

If there is an agreement about the renewal of the tenancy, then it should also be included. Similarly, you may want to include a provision for increasing the rent at that time.

Once the agreement is signed by both parties and witnessed, it should be stamped by the Inland Revenue Stamp Office and stamp duty paid. Many landlords do not bother with this, but if left unstamped it cannot be produced as evidence in a court of law.

INVENTORY

It is sensible to itemise the contents of the property both for insurance purposes and because it is the only proof you have if anything is lost or damaged beyond repair and you want to claim compensation or to deduct it from the deposit. Both parties should sign the list, having checked it through. To be absolutely certain as to the state of repair of the contents at the start of the let, the landlord might take photographs of the relevant pieces and attach them to the inventory. Both tenant and landlord should keep a copy.

INSURANCE

Make sure the property is properly insured. The cover should include the building, the contents that you have supplied (the tenant is responsible for his own) and the rental income should it be interrupted by damage to the building or contents. You might also want to include public liability insurance (in case a claim for injury is made against you by the public or your tenant) and personal accident insurance (should you be injured on the property) if you do not have it under another policy. Shop around for the best policy, read the small print and do not take out unnecessary cover.

BANKING

Open a separate bank account for your property so that you are ready to receive rental payments immediately. Ideally, have them made by standing order straight to your account whether direct from the tenant or the letting agent. Do not rush out to spend the rent immediately. Put some aside for the taxman (see below) and your mortgage lender. Save some for expenses you know will occur but also hang on to some for those that are unexpected. Use the account for paying your monthly insurance premiums.

TAXATION

Working out your tax liability can be a minefield. If you need professional advice, go to your local tax office, bank manager, accountant or a specialist tax adviser.

You will be taxed on your rental income after the deduction of allowable expenses. The profit will be included with the rest of your taxable income in your annual tax return. To be exact about which expenses you personally can deduct from your income, ask your tax adviser, accountant or the local tax office. Generally, you will be allowed to deduct letting agents' fees, advertising costs, financial fees, interest payments, advisory legal fees related to the let, book-keeping fees, council tax, insurance premiums, bills for mains services, repairs to and maintenance of the property (excluding improvements) and contents, renewal costs for soft furnishings and appliances (unless wear and tear is being claimed – see below), any stationery and telephone calls used for matters regarding the property or tenant, travel expenses to and from the property when carrying out inspections and collecting rent. You will not be able to claim capital costs such as the initial outlay for furniture or kitchen appliances, personal expenses such as time spent chasing up repair men or clothes bought for your role as landlord, the legal costs of drawing up the lease or the costs of upgrading the property.

If you are letting a furnished property, you can choose to deduct a wear and tear allowance of 10% from your rental income, less any charges normally borne by the tenant (eg council tax, utility bills etc). This has the advantage of being extremely straightforward to administer.

In the case of joint landlords, the share of the rental income will be taken to be identical to the share of the ownership of the property. If it should be different for some reason, it is up to you to notify them accordingly.

When you come to sell your property, the capital gain or 'chargeable gain' will be liable for capital gains tax (CGT). This capital gain is usually the difference between the figures for which you bought and sold the property minus certain deductible expenses. These include the costs incurred when you bought and sold the property, any costs you have incurred in capital improvements (ie the addition of things that have raised the value of the property, such as central heating, loft conversion, extension, double glazing etc), and costs incurred in defending yourself in any disputes over the property. For every year you own the property after 1998, the less you pay in CGT. This is called Taper Relief. Prior to 1998, indexation relief was allowed on the acquisition costs of the property. This relief was based on the rate of inflation. Check with the Inland Revenue to see by how much you can reduce your gain.

You will only be liable to pay CGT if the gain exceeds your CGT personal allowance for the year in which the property is sold. If you sell to your spouse, you are not liable. If you are going overseas and letting your property the letting agents may be obliged to deduct basic rate tax from the gross rent. To avoid this, contact your professional adviser or the Inland Revenue and complete a form NRL1.

If you have let your main residence, any chargeable gain that arises on disposal of the property is time-apportioned. For example, if you owned the property for ten years, but it was your main residence for only seven years, only three tenths of the gain would be chargeable. However, there are further reliefs available where your main residence has been let as residential property up to the lower of £40,000 or your main resident's exemption. Contact a professional adviser. If you have let part of your property as a self-contained flat (ie it is not part of your main residence), the aforementioned exemptions and reliefs are not applicable.

ESSENTIAL PAPERWORK

To let your property efficiently, initiate a filing system that covers all aspects of the let so that you can find everything you might need as soon as it is required. It may include details of the tenant, any correspondence with him or with the letting agent, correspondence related to the property, insurance details, tenancy agreement, inventory, insurance, receipts, taxation etc. Remember to keep every receipt for any expenditure – such records will be essential for your tax return and will also let you see where your money has gone at the end of the year. Always confirm any agreements with the tenant or letting agent in writing and issue receipts whenever you receive rent.

FINDING A TENANT

The most stress-free way to find a tenant and let your property is through a letting agent. Some are specialised agents while others may be departments within local estate agents or solicitors' practices. Before choosing one, visit a number of them to find out exactly what they will offer you and how much they will charge for their services. Do not necessarily go for the cheapest, they are not always the best. It is wise to choose one who is a member of a professional body such as the Association of Residential Letting Agents (ARLA), because it guarantees a professional code of conduct and gives you somewhere to lodge any complaints.

They usually will provide two kinds of basic package, although non-standard deals should be possible if your demands are not fully met. At most, they will do the following:

> - Prepare and evaluate the property.
> - Ensure it complies with safety regulations.
> - Advertise for a tenant.
> - Conduct viewings of the property.
> - Take references from the tenant and check them thoroughly.
> - Draw up a lease.
> - Prepare the inventory.
> - Collect both deposit and rent (including arrears).
> - Regularly inspect the property.
> - Report on the condition of the property.
> - Deal with the tenant's complaints.
> - Broker any disputes.
> - Maintain the property.
> - Organise repairs.

➤ Deal with any emergencies relating to the property.

➤ Inspect the property when the tenant moves out.

All this will minimise the headaches for you, the landlord, and minimise your contact with your tenant. However, you may have to pay over as much as 15% or even 20% of your rental income for this comprehensive service. Make quite sure that there are no other additional one-off costs to surprise you.

A cheaper alternative would be to use a letting agent to find a tenant and take and retain the deposit for you. From then on, you will be responsible for the management of the property. Depending on your tenant and the quality of work in your flat, this may be preferable. For this you will pay a lump sum to the letting agent, perhaps the equivalent of one month's rent.

Cheaper still would be to take on the whole burden yourself. Obvious ways to find a tenant are by advertising in shop windows or in the local press. Avoid giving out too many personal details such as your name and address, and the address of the property. Suggest times during which you would prefer to be called, give the rent, brief details of the property and the date it is free. If you have picked a particular target market, you may be able to reach them more directly by advertising in the students' union or contacting the human resources department of large local companies. A friend or work colleague may recommend someone, but it is advisable to steer clear of letting to friends or relatives – it can lead to a breakdown in relationships.

However you find your prospective tenants, it is a wise precaution not to be alone when you show them round the property. Make separate appointments with each applicant. Have all the information you may need to provide (about the property, its management and the area) at the ready. Remember, you are selling the property, so present it well and concentrate on emphasising its best features. Insist that you see references (ideally from a previous landlord and a character witness) and always follow them up, doing the best you can to check they are genuine. Ask to see proof of their regular employment (letter from employer, pay-slips). Although it is impossible to protect yourself completely against the wiliest of con men, you can take as many precautionary measures as possible. Keep a note of each prospective tenant's details so that you can remember them clearly when it comes to making your choice, and contact them when you have made your decision.

Having chosen your tenant and ascertained when he wants to move in, you should go through the tenancy agreement with him. The deposit is payable on signature. For your own security, insist the tenancy begins after the deposit is safely in your hands (any cheque must be cleared) and, if you can, have the rent paid by standing order. It is the most reliable and trouble-free method, and infinitely preferable to banging on the door and asking for cash or chasing cheques that have slipped your tenant's mind. When receiving money, make sure to give a receipt for both parties' records.

When the tenant moves in, take the trouble to show him exactly how everything works, leaving instruction manuals wherever possible. Go through the inventory and sign it together. Read the meters together so the new tenant can write to the supplier giving them the details at the beginning of the tenancy and notifying them that he is now responsible for the bills. If there is anything you particularly want him to pay attention to, such as watering the garden, not sticking drawing pins in the walls, not chopping directly on the work surfaces or regularly cleaning the oven, now is the moment. You might also want to tell him about the nearest doctor's surgery, shops, leisure centre, cinema or restaurants. Give him a key and keep one for yourself. You must respect your tenant's right to privacy. If you need to get into the flat to repair or replace something or to inspect it, you should give him at least twenty-four hours notice (the time could be specified in the agreement).

DURING THE TENANCY

Unless you are using a letting agent, your work is not over once your tenant moves in. To begin with, you may be inundated with queries about how things work, or complaints when they do not. Try to establish good communications and be as patient as you can, helping or repairing things as quickly as possible. If you do not know a good all-round handyman for the more complicated jobs, or for those that have to be done while you are at work, then it is a good idea to build up a folder of reliable tradesmen's details. If you are going on holiday, it might be worth arranging for someone to stand-by in your absence in case of emergency, giving them your folder and providing your tenant with their contact number.

When a problem is raised, decide if it is a potential safety hazard. If it is, ask the tenant to take emergency action (eg turning off the water or gas at the mains immediately) while you get round to inspect or arrange for emergency repairs. For something more minor, assess the problem and agree which of you is responsible for its repair (this should be specified in the lease).

Do not assume everything will go according to plan. Keep an eye on your bank account to check that the rent is being paid. Before the situation gets out of hand, write to the tenant reminding him payment is overdue. If they continue to default, you may have to ask your solicitor or letting agent to intervene. If you do end up exchanging any correspondence, keep copies of all your letters. If things look like they are going to get difficult, take notes of any telephone calls so you can be quite clear as to what was said when and to whom.

Make arrangements to inspect the property regularly so that you can check everything is in good repair and nothing is being neglected. It will also give you the opportunity to get to know the tenant and to discuss any mutual problems. Make arrangements with your tenant to visit every three or four months. When you do, you are quite within your rights to inspect every room and appliance, but you have absolutely no right whatsoever to pry into his belongings. If a drawer needs fixing or a cupboard door fixing, ask him to show it to you. If anything worries you about the way your property is being treated mention it immediately and follow up with a letter for the record. The responsibility for particular repairs and their payment should be specified in the tenancy agreement. In the unfortunate case of the tenant deliberately damaging part of the property whether wilfully or through neglect, your responsibility for payment may be fairly shifted to the tenant although you will probably need a qualified, independent witness to assess the nature of the damage in writing.

If the neighbours complain about your tenant, you will have to listen to them, investigate both sides of the story and make a decision as to what course of action to take, informing all parties. It is essential that you remain objective, remember your responsibilities and make a well-reasoned decision, again confirming it in writing, trying to effect an amicable solution.

THE END OF THE TENANCY

If you want your tenant to leave, the agreed notice must be served on a periodic and a fixed-term lease. If your tenant wants to renew the lease, you must renegotiate terms where necessary.

Before your tenant leaves, contact your solicitor about terminating the agreement. Make a final inspection and plan for any work or redecoration that will need to be done before the next tenant can move in. About a month before he is due to move out, begin the process of finding a new tenant, replacing fittings and furniture and, if necessary, book a steam clean for the carpets, upholstery and curtains. If the place will be left in a tip, and you have not the time to fix it yourself, book a cleaning company to clean it from top to toe.

This is the opportunity to improve your property so that you can increase its value, let it more easily or attract a different sort of tenant. If the surrounding area has changed, it may be time to rethink your target market and their demands.

If there is no need for any major overhaul, then ask your tenant if he will mind you showing prospective new tenants around the place before he leaves. Assuming he has no objections, arrange times when it would be mutually convenient.

Once the tenant has moved out and before you have repaid the deposit, check the inventory, assess the redecoration costs, take the final meter readings and make sure he has taken everything with him. If the tenant can go through this with you, it can save a lot of trouble. Any disagreements or queries over damaged items can be ironed out there and then. At the least, questions can be asked, even if the problem cannot immediately be resolved. Make sure you get the keys back, although it may be sensible to change the locks for security reasons. Also ask him for a forwarding address so you can pass on any bills and mail. In any event you will have to detail what you are deducting from the deposit. If the costs exceed the deposit, you should let the tenant have copies of the estimates or bills and try to settle it reasonably. Otherwise ask your solicitor for advice as how best to pursue the matter.

REFERENCES

Assuming you have worked to maintain good relations with your tenant, he may ask you for a reference to help him find a new place to live. Include the length of time he rented your property, the standard of care lavished on it and his record of reliability in paying the rent. If relations are truly amicable, ask him to write you a reference as a landlord. If he is prepared to take the resultant phone calls he could be doing you a great favour.

WHAT CAN GO WRONG

Sub-letting

If you do not want your tenant to sub-let to someone else, you should specify it in the tenancy agreement. A sub-let removes your control over who is living in the property unless you have made it clear in the agreement that your written approval is necessary. If the tenant sub-lets the property, you can terminate the agreement immediately.

Refusal to leave

If the tenant refuses to leave the property at the end of the term of the tenancy agreement and you as landlord do not wish to renew it, you must seek the advice of your solicitor or letting agent. Having served the correct notices to the tenant, you will be required to get a court order before you can repossess the property.

Non-payment of rent/damage to property

If the tenant is in arrears with his rent or has broken any of the terms of the letting arrangement (for example, by not caring for the property) and you wish to terminate the tenancy, you will almost certainly need a court order to gain repossession. You may pursue your tenant for payment for repairs or for the arrears but, if he has left without warning, it probably will not be worth the time and effort. It is important that you carry out regular inspections and react swiftly to any signs of damage or neglect or non-payment of rent so that you stand to lose as little as possible.

Leaving early

If your tenant tries to leave before the agreed term is up, he is liable to pay you the rent due on the remaining months.

Death

If a tenant dies, the remaining joint tenants have the right to continue the tenancy under the existing agreement. In the case of a sole tenancy, it can be passed on to whoever is named in the will.

JO AND SIMON MILES, THAMES VALLEY

Wanted: 'Our ideal house would have four bedrooms, two reception rooms, hopefully a nice den, and a big kitchen. I think we haven't found a house yet because we're waiting for one that we walk into to say, 'Buy me,' straight away. We haven't been willing to compromise yet. Our budget could reach £500,000.'

Commuting from London to Reading was an impossibility for Simon Miles, so he and his wife, Jo, had sold their north London home and been renting in Henley-on-Thames for four months while they house-hunted in the Thames Valley. Jo Miles runs a picture-framing business from home and had found the time to view over forty houses. Despite their generous budget, Henley could not offer a house that fitted their criteria for that price. It was time to find something outside the town but within commuting distance of Reading for Simon, who works for a software company. Once they found their perfect home, they were in an ideal bargaining position, being chain-free cash buyers with the desire to move quickly.

The village of Boxford is idyllic, with a pub and a nearby shop. Here, a thatched four-bedroom timber-framed cottage was on the market for £435,000. It even offered a light workshop that Jo could use as a studio. Inside, the rooms were good sizes, the original beams had been left unpainted, there was a fine wood floor in the living room, attractive stone work in the kitchen and superb views. Any thoughts of creating a larger kitchen by knocking down walls were likely to be thwarted because the house was a Grade II listed building. The thatch put Jo off immediately and completely.

> TIP: Look at the ridge on a thatched roof for signs of rot. Bear in mind replacement costs and insurance premiums.

Staying in the country, they looked next at a property in Whitchurch-on-Thames, a twenty-minute commute from work for Simon and just across the river from the important shops and village life. An eighteenth-century blacksmith's forge offered four bedrooms, four bathrooms and many original features including the blacksmith's original branding panel, at an asking price of £425,000. First impressions were good. The double-height living room and huge chimney made an impressive start. Jo was not won over by the very pink bathrooms, though conceded that the double garage could be used as a studio. Simon could see the potential but Jo just did not feel it was right for her.

Looking at the neighbouring village of Pangbourne, they saw a house that had been on the market for just a day. A splendid half-timbered riverside house built in the 1890s, it offered four huge reception rooms, four large bedrooms and a double garage that could be used as a studio. The period features such as the main fireplace and the cornicing were particularly striking as was the vast bath. Simon loved it. 'This has everything we wanted – high ceilings, great windows. It's bright and it's airy.' But Jo was less convinced, especially by the noise from the road outside.

> TIP: Check the local plan thoroughly and quiz the neighbours for an honest appraisal of the property.

Only three minutes walk from Odiham, a renovation project was underway. Once home to the boss of the old chalk quarry, The Chalkmaster's House had also been a Napoleonic prison and a pub. Structurally sound and with mains services, the house would eventually have five bedrooms, and four living rooms. The asking price was £315,000 with £20,000 fitting out costs. Donning hard hats, they went inside. The prospect of taking on something as big as this might be scary, but with experts to put their design ideas into effect, it seemed less daunting. On a project this size it was vital they weigh up the advantages of getting the house of their dreams and its potential as an investment with the uncertainty, the time it would take and the eventual cost. Once in, there would be no going back. Paying £500,000 and having to live in a caravan for a year would not be everybody's idea of money well spent. Even Jo looked a little uncertain.

> TIP: A retention clause can be used in a contract to enable the buyer to retain money until works promised by the vendor are complete.

Finally they visited Sherfield-on-Loddon, half an hour south of Reading, where the converted coach house and stables of the former rectory was on the market for £500,000. It had four large bedrooms, a living room converted from where the coach was once kept, a conservatory, a walled garden, a courtyard and a workshop that had a great sense of light and space. At last, they had found a property that both of them responded to wholeheartedly.

LOCATION LOCATION LOCATION

They decided to revisit both the coach house and The Chalkmaster's House before finally making up their minds. Visiting at a different time of day showed them that the rush hour traffic roaring past The Chalkmaster's House would be intolerable. So it was the coach house or nothing. Both Jo and Simon responded to the house equally warmly as when they first visited. They noticed the seal on the double-glazing in the conservatory was not watertight, but this was a problem the vendor should agree to rectify before the sale went through. They decided that the roof should be checked for loose slates and faulty flashings and that the workshop would need to be insulated at an estimated cost of £3,000.

> **TIP: Look out for slipped tiles and lead flashings that have come apart.**

Bearing these things in mind, and confident of their strong position as buyers, they made an offer of £480,000. That evening they heard to their delight that it had been accepted and the house was theirs.

KEEPING THE NOISE DOWN

Noise is a common problem in many properties, whether from passing traffic, building works, the flat upstairs or the television in the next room. One person's music is frequently someone else's nightmare. Noise is one thing that can destroy good relationships between neighbours. If you are buying a property but are worried you may be disturbed by noise travelling through floors or walls, there are a number of things you can do:

➤ Draughtproof all windows and doors.
➤ Use heavy, lined curtains.

➤ Move your bedroom to the back of the house so as not to be disturbed by traffic noise at the front.

➤ Carpet floorboards so less noise travels upwards or downwards.

➤ Talk to your neighbours to see if some sort of compromise can be reached.

If the problem is or is likely to be persistent, there are more drastic measures that can be taken:

➤ Double glazing can disguise outside background noise such as traffic.

➤ Secondary glazing is more effective than double glazing. A second window is fitted inside the existing one. The cavity between the panes is larger. The glass can be thicker than standard glass, laminated or acoustic laminated to reduce the noise further. Used with acoustic tiles in the reveal and draught proofing, it should keep the noise down and reduce heating costs.

➤ Glass fibre or mineral wool insulation placed between floor joists can provide effective soundproofing.

➤ There are various types of acoustic underlay suitable for laying under different types of floors.

➤ Add a floating floor above the existing one. Particularly useful between a bedroom and a noisy room below.

➤ A floating ceiling will only be really effective if it is attached to new joists spanning the room, otherwise the noise will transfer from the existing joists to the ceiling itself. Not a great solution if it reduces the height of the room too much.

➤ A stud wall, filled with mineral wool and finished with two layers of plasterboard, their joins not coinciding, must not touch the existing wall so the path of vibrations is interrupted.

These measures should soundproof your home satisfactorily so that you and your family can go about their business without unduly disturbing one another or being driven mad by outside noise. They should also help flat dwellers, particularly in old, less well-sound-proofed conversions, live amicably side by side.

JACKIE THOMPSON, YORK

Wanted: 'I'm not looking for a specific type of property. I'm just looking for somewhere with real character. I was thinking of spending around £200,000, however I decided I would really push the boat out if I found the perfect property that had real investment potential. If I do, I'll spend up to £300,000.'

A broad price range meant a wide variety of properties were available to Jackie Thompson, a high flyer in the world of computer software. She was house-hunting in the city of York, an architectural oasis surrounded by thriving commercial centres where property is highly desirable. A vibrant university town, business is brisk, investments increasing and house prices are on the up. York still retains its charms and history of prosperity built on traditional heavy industries, and it is best known as the home of Terry's and Rowntree-Nestlé chocolate. Newly promoted, Jackie had just sold her current flat and was looking for somewhere special to live. 'I work an average of a sixty-hour week and by the time it comes to Friday, I want to kick the shoes off, get rid of the suit and enjoy myself. I enjoy having a good time. I'm quite noisy as a result of having parties and I think it's about time I gave my wonderful neighbours a bit of peace and quiet.'

The pretty suburb of Acomb is fifteen minutes north-west of the city centre. Here, a four-bedroom end-of-terrace house in Front Street, built around 1810, had come on to the market at £199,500. The rooms were all of a similar size and retained many period features. Downstairs there were three reception rooms, one leading into the biggest room of all, the kitchen. The drawback of this traditional layout was that the house was a bit of a warren, with smallish rooms and low ceilings. Jackie's idea of knocking through one of the reception rooms into another was thwarted by the mighty chimney-breast that extended through the bedroom and attic above. To remove it downstairs would involve taking it out all the way through the house, starting at the top. Alternatively, the upper two floors would have to be supported – at an estimated cost of £10-12,000. On the plus side, there was a beautifully kept garden with a driveway to the side where Jackie could safely keep her beloved sports car. Modifying the house to meet Jackie's needs would be pricey and sacrifice the house's period charm. 'To make it the house I need, I would have to knock down one of the walls, and it's a shame because it's a house with great character.' It was better to move on to something else.

Fifteen minutes south of the city in Fulford was a massive five-bedroom Victorian townhouse in St Oswalds Road. At £315,000, it was over Jackie's budget but came complete with a self-contained basement flat that could be let out. Buying this would put a slightly different spin on the purchase because some of the money Jackie would have to borrow would come under a slightly more expensive buy-to-let scheme. The main house was impressive, with large rooms, although the kitchen ceiling had been lowered in the 1970s but, if desired, it would only be a day's work to take it out. Upstairs, the real highlights were the jacuzzi and sauna in the main bathroom. Jackie warmed to the property but the added responsibility of being a landlady was something she needed to mull over.

> TIP: Buying a partially renovated house can be an excellent opportunity to involve yourself in the finishing decorative touches.

Period was not something Jackie was hooked on, so she was keen to see a riverside loft conversion at Woodsmill Quay. The original beams of the wood mill had been kept and although it had just been renovated, the overall finish was rather basic. What she would be paying for was the sensational view down the banks of the Ouse which she had to set against the lack of living space – in particular, the kitchen. This was definitely a case of style over content. 'It's a great flat with real character but I don't think it's for me. Two bedrooms, so less living space.'

However, the next property she saw, architect-designed Downie House just fifteen minutes across town, took her breath away. At £335,000, it was a stunning open-plan property that oozed contemporary chic – wood floors, white walls, open staircase, underfloor heating, a sleek modern kitchen, so much light and space and a precious parking spot. Although over her budget, it was possible the developer would consider a lower offer. 'I loved the house, and it was probably quite obvious when I looked around that I could imagine myself living there.'

> TIP: Consider possible drawbacks with open-plan living: the lack of privacy, light and noise.

Finally, Jackie looked at a three-bedroom property in Scott Street, just round the corner from where she went to school. Stylishly renovated, there was still some work to be done in the attic and basement. The concrete floor in the basement would lend one of its three rooms to Jackie's gym equipment, and another featured a mid-nineteenth century kitchen range. Again, these basement rooms could be rented out as a separate flat.

Upstairs she particularly liked the kitchen, a large room with terracotta floor tiles and wood units. However, the unfitted units were not included in the sale price and would have to be part of a separate negotiation. Upstairs, she was surprised by the elegant blue and white master bedroom with long windows admitting plenty of light, while the dramatic, opulent bathroom successfully caught her imagination. 'I think the house has real potential and I could see myself making some money over the longer term.'

Torn between Downie House and Scott Street, Jackie decided to look at them again with her mother. 'I'm still in a dilemma about them both. They offer such different things and I've got to start to clarify what I want.' Downie Street was as striking as before but she had to look behind its seductive veneer and imagine what it might look like with her own furniture in it.

> **TIP: Try to look past the contents of a house and imagine your own possessions in place.**

She also had to consider the drawbacks of open-plan living. She might be kept awake by the light without blackout blinds and noise from visitors downstairs might be disturbing. But for Jackie all that was disturbing was the price. Scott Street was undoubtedly the more practical option. Although decorating the basement and attic rooms could be expensive, Jackie could talk to the estate agent, find to what degree it will be finished and involve herself in the choices. It would also be worth her considering another bathroom with a mansard window into the top floor. Other houses had similar extensions, so planning permission was likely to be forthcoming.

> **TIP: Look at other properties in the area to see what precedents have been set in terms of extensions and exterior alterations.**

The only negative point she could find was that the small paved courtyard would have to double as a parking space. This was a problem too big to overcome so Jackie ultimately decided to put in an offer of £280,000 on Downie Street. 'It's a one shot and if not, I'll never go around thinking "what if". I'll simply walk away thinking it was not to be.' Unfortunately, her offer was rejected so that is exactly what she had to do before beginning her search anew.

OPEN-PLAN LIVING

Positives:

➤ Communal living for the family.

➤ A stylish, unified look.

➤ Makes a feature of individual pieces of furniture.

➤ Adaptable, multi-purpose space that can be divided by screens.

➤ When cooking, the cook can remain involved with guests or family.

➤ Knocking small rooms into one open plan area can provide much greater light and a feeling of greater space.

➤ Different wall colours can define the different living areas.

➤ The space is flexible and can be arranged with emphasis on particular living areas to suit the owner.

➤ Easier to clean.

Negatives:

➤ The space needs to be kept tidy for optimum effect.

➤ Gives no quarter to lazy housekeepers.

➤ Not being able to get away on one's own.

➤ Lack of privacy.

➤ Average-sized furniture can appear dwarfed.

➤ More difficult to heat.

➤ Cooking smells throughout living area unless you have a powerful extractor.

CHECKLIST 1: MORTGAGES

Compare available mortgages:

Name of lender	Sum lent	Type	Terms of repayment	Cost per month	LTV (loan to value)	Comments

CHECKLIST 2: BUYER'S BUDGET

SAVINGS ☐

Mortgage borrowed ☐

TOTAL ☐

Purchase costs

Price of property ☐

Survey ☐

Mortgage company's valuation fee ☐

Solicitor's fees (inc those covering his acting for the mortgage lender) ☐

Local searches ☐

Other searches ☐

Stamp Duty ☐

Land Registry Fee ☐

Mortgage arrangement fee ☐

Mortgage Indemnity Guarantee ☐

Insurance ☐

Other ☐

TOTAL ☐

Moving costs

Removal van

Gas connection/ installation fee ☐

Electricity connection/ installation fee ☐

Telephone installation fee ☐

Costs for disconnecting/ connecting appliances ☐

Mail redirection ☐

Change of address cards ☐

Change of locks ☐

Redecoration costs ☐

Curtains and carpets ☐

New parking permits ☐

Pets boarding fee ☐

Other ☐

TOTAL ☐

Possible renovation costs

Professional consultants' fees

Architect ☐

Depending on nature of work

Party wall surveyor ☐

Structural engineer ☐

Soil engineer ☐

Planning consultants ☐

Quantity surveyor ☐

Building contractor

Specialist subcontractors

Damp proofing ☐

Infestation treatment ☐

Chimney sweep ☐

Drainage company ☐

Tree surgeon ☐

Security alarm company ☐

Garden landscaping ☐

Fees for applications for statutory authorities including:

Planning ☐

Building control ☐

Temporary accommodation ☐

Other ☐

TOTAL ☐

CHECKLIST 3: BUYER'S CHECKLIST

Take with you:
- ❏ Notebook
- ❏ Checklist
- ❏ Tape measure
- ❏ Measurements of large pieces of furniture

CHECK
- ❏ Estate agent
- ❏ Owner's name
- ❏ Address
- ❏ Asking price

Number of bedrooms ▢

Number of bathrooms ▢

Number of reception rooms ▢

Kitchen – size and condition ▢

Layout ▢

Decorative state ▢

Central heating ▢

Lighting and other services ▢

Direction house faces ▢

Age of property ▢

Condition of property – interior and exterior ▢

Queries for surveyor ▢

Garden – size and direction ▢

Garage ▢

Additional extras ▢

WATCH OUT FOR
- ❏ Damp
- ❏ Cracks
- ❏ Badly fitting doors and windows
- ❏ Wood rot
- ❏ Sagging floors
- ❏ What is under carpets
- ❏ Outside noise

- ❏ Slipped or broken roof tiles
- ❏ Absent or cracked flashings
- ❏ Condition of pipes and guttering
- ❏ Bulging walls
- ❏ Damp proof course
- ❏ Trees close to property

ASK

Why is owner moving? ▢

When does owner hope to move? ▢

Is owner in chain? ▢

How long has property been on the market? ▢

Has it been under offer before? If so, what went wrong? ▢

What is included in the price? – see Checklist 4 ▢

Loft insulation? ▢

Restrictive covenants? ▢

Rights of access? ▢

Guarantees and warranties for work carried out ▢

Fuel bills ▢

Council tax band ▢

IN A FLAT:

Who owns the freehold? ▢

Are they reliable? ▢

Service charge ▢

Sinking fund ▢

Ground rent ▢

CHECKLIST 3: BUYER'S CHECKLIST

Take with you:
- ☐ Notebook
- ☐ Checklist
- ☐ Tape measure
- ☐ Measurements of large pieces of furniture

CHECK
- ☐ Estate agent
- ☐ Owner's name
- ☐ Address
- ☐ Asking price

Number of bedrooms ☐
Number of bathrooms ☐
Number of reception rooms ☐
Kitchen – size and condition ☐
Layout ☐
Decorative state ☐
Central heating ☐
Lighting and other services ☐
Direction house faces ☐
Age of property ☐
Condition of property – interior and exterior ☐
Queries for surveyor ☐
Garden – size and direction ☐
Garage ☐
Additional extras ☐

WATCH OUT FOR
- ☐ Damp
- ☐ Cracks
- ☐ Badly fitting doors and windows
- ☐ Wood rot
- ☐ Sagging floors
- ☐ What is under carpets
- ☐ Outside noise

- ☐ Slipped or broken roof tiles
- ☐ Absent or cracked flashings
- ☐ Condition of pipes and guttering
- ☐ Bulging walls
- ☐ Damp proof course
- ☐ Trees close to property

ASK
Why is owner moving? ☐

When does owner hope to move? ☐

Is owner in chain? ☐
How long has property been on the market? ☐
Has it been under offer before? If so, what went wrong? ☐

What is included in the price? – see Checklist 4 ☐

Loft insulation? ☐
Restrictive covenants? ☐
Rights of access? ☐
Guarantees and warranties for work carried out ☐
Fuel bills ☐
Council tax band ☐

IN A FLAT:
Who owns the freehold? ☐

Are they reliable? ☐
Service charge ☐
Sinking fund ☐
Ground rent ☐

CHECKLIST 3: BUYER'S CHECKLIST

Take with you:
- ☐ Notebook
- ☐ Checklist
- ☐ Tape measure
- ☐ Measurements of large pieces of furniture

CHECK
- ☐ Estate agent
- ☐ Owner's name
- ☐ Address
- ☐ Asking price

Number of bedrooms ☐
Number of bathrooms ☐
Number of reception rooms ☐
Kitchen – size and condition ☐
Layout ☐
Decorative state ☐
Central heating ☐
Lighting and other services ☐
Direction house faces ☐
Age of property ☐
Condition of property – interior and exterior ☐
Queries for surveyor ☐
Garden – size and direction ☐
Garage ☐
Additional extras ☐

WATCH OUT FOR
- ☐ Damp
- ☐ Cracks
- ☐ Badly fitting doors and windows
- ☐ Wood rot
- ☐ Sagging floors
- ☐ What is under carpets
- ☐ Outside noise

- ☐ Slipped or broken roof tiles
- ☐ Absent or cracked flashings
- ☐ Condition of pipes and guttering
- ☐ Bulging walls
- ☐ Damp proof course
- ☐ Trees close to property

ASK
Why is owner moving? ☐

When does owner hope to move? ☐

Is owner in chain? ☐
How long has property been on the market? ☐
Has it been under offer before? If so, what went wrong? ☐

What is included in the price? – see Checklist 4 ☐

Loft insulation? ☐
Restrictive covenants? ☐
Rights of access? ☐
Guarantees and warranties for work carried out ☐
Fuel bills ☐
Council tax band ☐

IN A FLAT:
Who owns the freehold? ☐

Are they reliable? ☐
Service charge ☐
Sinking fund ☐
Ground rent ☐

CHECKLIST 3: BUYER'S CHECKLIST

Take with you:
- ❏ Notebook
- ❏ Checklist
- ❏ Tape measure
- ❏ Measurements of large pieces of furniture

CHECK
- ❏ Estate agent
- ❏ Owner's name
- ❏ Address
- ❏ Asking price

Number of bedrooms [　　　　]
Number of bathrooms [　　　　]
Number of reception rooms [　　　　]
Kitchen – size and condition [　　　　]
Layout [　　　　]
Decorative state [　　　　]
Central heating [　　　　]
Lighting and other services [　　　　]
Direction house faces [　　　　]
Age of property [　　　　]
Condition of property – interior and exterior [　　　　]
Queries for surveyor [　　　　]
Garden – size and direction [　　　　]
Garage [　　　　]
Additional extras [　　　　]

WATCH OUT FOR
- ❏ Damp
- ❏ Cracks
- ❏ Badly fitting doors and windows
- ❏ Wood rot
- ❏ Sagging floors
- ❏ What is under carpets
- ❏ Outside noise

- ❏ Slipped or broken roof tiles
- ❏ Absent or cracked flashings
- ❏ Condition of pipes and guttering
- ❏ Bulging walls
- ❏ Damp proof course
- ❏ Trees close to property

ASK
Why is owner moving?
[　　　　　　　　　　　]

When does owner hope to move?
[　　　　　　　　　　　]

Is owner in chain? [　　　　]
How long has property been on the market? [　　　　]
Has it been under offer before?
If so, what went wrong? [　　　　]
[　　　　　　　　　　　]

What is included in the price?
– see Checklist 4
[　　　　　　　　　　　]

Loft insulation? [　　　　]
Restrictive covenants? [　　　　]
Rights of access? [　　　　]
Guarantees and warranties for work carried out [　　　　]
Fuel bills [　　　　]
Council tax band [　　　　]

IN A FLAT:
Who owns the freehold?
[　　　　　　　　　　　]

Are they reliable? [　　　　]
Service charge [　　　　]
Sinking fund [　　　　]
Ground rent [　　　　]

269

CHECKLIST 3: BUYER'S CHECKLIST

Take with you:
- ☐ Notebook
- ☐ Checklist
- ☐ Tape measure
- ☐ Measurements of large pieces of furniture

- ☐ Slipped or broken roof tiles
- ☐ Absent or cracked flashings
- ☐ Condition of pipes and guttering
- ☐ Bulging walls
- ☐ Damp proof course
- ☐ Trees close to property

CHECK
- ☐ Estate agent
- ☐ Owner's name
- ☐ Address
- ☐ Asking price

Number of bedrooms

Number of bathrooms

Number of reception rooms

Kitchen – size and condition

Layout

Decorative state

Central heating

Lighting and other services

Direction house faces

Age of property

Condition of property – interior and exterior

Queries for surveyor

Garden – size and direction

Garage

Additional extras

WATCH OUT FOR
- ☐ Damp
- ☐ Cracks
- ☐ Badly fitting doors and windows
- ☐ Wood rot
- ☐ Sagging floors
- ☐ What is under carpets
- ☐ Outside noise

ASK

Why is owner moving?

When does owner hope to move?

Is owner in chain?

How long has property been on the market?

Has it been under offer before? If so, what went wrong?

What is included in the price? – see Checklist 4

Loft insulation?

Restrictive covenants?

Rights of access?

Guarantees and warranties for work carried out

Fuel bills

Council tax band

IN A FLAT:

Who owns the freehold?

Are they reliable?

Service charge

Sinking fund

Ground rent

CHECKLIST 3: BUYER'S CHECKLIST

Take with you:
- ❏ Notebook
- ❏ Checklist
- ❏ Tape measure
- ❏ Measurements of large pieces of furniture

CHECK
- ❏ Estate agent
- ❏ Owner's name
- ❏ Address
- ❏ Asking price

Number of bedrooms ☐
Number of bathrooms ☐
Number of reception rooms ☐
Kitchen – size and condition ☐
Layout ☐
Decorative state ☐
Central heating ☐
Lighting and other services ☐
Direction house faces ☐
Age of property ☐
Condition of property – interior and exterior ☐
Queries for surveyor ☐
Garden – size and direction ☐
Garage ☐
Additional extras ☐

WATCH OUT FOR
- ❏ Damp
- ❏ Cracks
- ❏ Badly fitting doors and windows
- ❏ Wood rot
- ❏ Sagging floors
- ❏ What is under carpets
- ❏ Outside noise

- ❏ Slipped or broken roof tiles
- ❏ Absent or cracked flashings
- ❏ Condition of pipes and guttering
- ❏ Bulging walls
- ❏ Damp proof course
- ❏ Trees close to property

ASK

Why is owner moving?
☐

When does owner hope to move?
☐

Is owner in chain? ☐
How long has property been on the market? ☐
Has it been under offer before? If so, what went wrong? ☐
☐

What is included in the price? – see Checklist 4
☐

Loft insulation? ☐
Restrictive covenants? ☐
Rights of access? ☐
Guarantees and warranties for work carried out ☐
Fuel bills ☐
Council tax band ☐

IN A FLAT:
Who owns the freehold?
☐

Are they reliable? ☐
Service charge ☐
Sinking fund ☐
Ground rent ☐

CHECKLIST 4: FIXTURES AND FITTINGS

What is included in the purchase price?

	Included	Excluded
Living room		
Carpets	☐	☐
Underlay	☐	☐
Curtains	☐	☐
Curtain rails & tracks	☐	☐
Blinds	☐	☐
Electrical fittings	☐	☐
Lamp shades	☐	☐
Light bulbs	☐	☐
Wall lights	☐	☐
Fireplaces	☐	☐
Heaters	☐	☐
Fitted mirrors	☐	☐
Book shelves	☐	☐
Items of furniture	☐	☐
Other	☐	☐
Dining room		
Carpets	☐	☐
Underlay	☐	☐
Curtains	☐	☐
Curtain rails & tracks	☐	☐
Blinds	☐	☐
Electrical fittings	☐	☐
Lamp shades	☐	☐
Light bulbs	☐	☐
Wall lights	☐	☐
Heaters	☐	☐
Fitted mirrors	☐	☐
Items of furniture	☐	☐
Other	☐	☐
Kitchen		
Cooker	☐	☐
Microwave	☐	☐

	Included	Excluded
Fridge	☐	☐
Freezer	☐	☐
Dishwasher	☐	☐
Washing machine	☐	☐
Kitchen units	☐	☐
Freestanding furniture	☐	☐
Shelving	☐	☐
Light fittings	☐	☐
Other	☐	☐
Bedroom 1		
Carpets	☐	☐
Underlay	☐	☐
Curtains	☐	☐
Curtain rails & tracks	☐	☐
Blinds	☐	☐
Electrical fittings	☐	☐
Lamp shades	☐	☐
Light bulbs	☐	☐
Wall lights	☐	☐
Heaters	☐	☐
Fitted mirrors	☐	☐
Book shelves	☐	☐
Wardrobe	☐	☐
Items of furniture	☐	☐
Other	☐	☐
Bedroom 2		
Carpets	☐	☐
Underlay	☐	☐
Curtains	☐	☐
Curtain rails & tracks	☐	☐
Blinds	☐	☐
Electrical fittings	☐	☐
Lamp shades	☐	☐
Light bulbs	☐	☐

	Included	Excluded		Included	Excluded
Wall lights	☐	☐	Wardrobe	☐	☐
Heaters	☐	☐	Items of furniture	☐	☐
Fitted mirrors	☐	☐	Other	☐	☐
Book shelves	☐	☐			
Wardrobe	☐	☐	**Bathroom**		
Items of furniture	☐	☐	Medicine cabinet	☐	☐
Other	☐	☐	Towel rail	☐	☐
			Light fittings	☐	☐
Bedroom 3			Other	☐	☐
Carpets	☐	☐			
Underlay	☐	☐	**General**		
Curtains	☐	☐	Door bell	☐	☐
Curtain rails & tracks	☐	☐	Door plates	☐	☐
Blinds	☐	☐	Other	☐	☐
Electrical fittings	☐	☐			
Lamp shades	☐	☐	**Garden**		
Light bulbs	☐	☐	Garden furniture	☐	☐
Wall lights	☐	☐	Garden ornaments	☐	☐
Heaters	☐	☐	Garden shed	☐	☐
Fitted mirrors	☐	☐	Window boxes	☐	☐
Book shelves	☐	☐	Other	☐	☐

Items offered by the owner	Items you want to negotiate for

CHECKLIST 5: COUNTDOWN TO THE MOVE

6 weeks to go
- ☐ Get removal firms' estimates/van hire rate
- ☐ Accept one estimate
- ☐ Confirm arrangements in writing
- ☐ Check insurance policy covers move
- ☐ Order change of address cards
- ☐ If renting, give notice
- ☐ Cancel all rental agreements to terminate on day of move

Current property:
- ☐ Arrange for final meter readings
- ☐ Arrange appliance disconnection
- ☐ Arrange for final telephone bill and closing of account
- ☐ Arrange carpet cleaning of those you are taking
- ☐ Arrange furniture re-upholstery/cleaning of pieces you are taking

New property:
- ☐ Arrange for taking over gas/electricity accounts
- ☐ Arrange for connection of electric/gas appliances
- ☐ Organise new telephone arrangements
- ☐ Organise a decorator if necessary
- ☐ Measure up and order new carpets/curtains

4 weeks to go
- ☐ Organise friends/helpers to be on hand
- ☐ Start going through belongings
- ☐ Get rid of unwanted belongings
- ☐ Confirm removal arrangements
- ☐ Order packing cases
- ☐ Buy labels
- ☐ Arrange for redirection of mail
- ☐ Make arrangements for children
- ☐ Make arrangements for pets

1 week to go
- ☐ Confirm removal arrangements
- ☐ Start packing
- ☐ Draw diagram of location of furniture in new home

- ☐ Send change of address cards
- ☐ Get your survival kit ready

Current property
- ☐ Close milk delivery account
- ☐ Close newspaper delivery account
- ☐ Check with buyer whether they want water/gas/electricity left on or off

New property
- ☐ Open milk account at new address
- ☐ Open newspaper delivery account at new address
- ☐ Ask vendor to leave water/gas/electricity on or off

24 hours to go
- ☐ Finish packing
- ☐ Put important documents safely together
- ☐ Make sandwiches and drinks for following day
- ☐ Put together survival kit (see page 132)
- ☐ If freezer contains food, switch temperature to maximum
- ☐ Defrost fridge
- ☐ Deliver children and pets
- ☐ Charge mobile phone
- ☐ Fill car with petrol and check tyres

Old property
- ☐ Confirm electricity/gas connection arrangements with buyer

New property
- ☐ Confirm electricity/gas disconnection arrangements with vendor

The big day
- ☐ Pack van
- ☐ Give removers directions
- ☐ Check nothing is left behind
- ☐ Turn off water, gas, electricity if arranged
- ☐ Shut windows, doors
- ☐ Leave keys
- ☐ Collect keys and MOVE

CHECKLIST 6: WHOM TO NOTIFY OF YOUR MOVE

Remember to add anyone or any company from whom you are expecting to hear.

☐ Leave a change of address card with new owner of the property.

Home
☐ Family
☐ Friends
☐ TV licence
☐ Rental firms
☐ Telephone
☐ Electricity
☐ Gas
☐ Schools
☐ Clubs/societies
☐ Mail order clubs
☐ Charities
☐ Council tax
☐ Public library
☐ Magazine subscriptions
☐ Mailing lists (theatre, holiday brochure etc)
☐ Milk deliveries
☐ Paper deliveries

Medical
☐ Doctor
☐ Optician
☐ Dentist
☐ Alternative practitioners, eg osteopath, homeopath,
☐ Private practitioners, eg gynaecologist, paediatrician

Work
☐ Employer
☐ Pension fund
☐ Trade Union
☐ Professional associations

Finance
☐ Bank
☐ Savings account holders
☐ Building societies
☐ Investments – contact company registrars (details on share certificates)
☐ Stockbroker
☐ Premium Bonds
☐ National Savings Accounts
☐ National Insurance
☐ Inland Revenue
☐ Accountant
☐ Book-keeper
☐ DSS – for pensions and benefits
☐ Credit card companies
☐ Store card companies
☐ Hire purchase companies
☐ Local authority
☐ Water authority

Insurance
☐ Insurance broker
☐ Life insurance
☐ Medical insurance
☐ Travel insurance
☐ House insurance
☐ Other insurers

Car
☐ DVLC – vehicle registration
☐ AA, RAC, other motoring organisations
☐ DVLA – driving licence

Other
☐
☐

CHECKLIST 7: BEFORE SELLING YOUR HOME

Prepare your house
☐ Kerb appeal
☐ Garden
☐ Front door
☐ Carry out essential repairs
☐ Finish all unfinished DIY jobs
☐ Maximise space and light
☐ Redecorate where necessary
☐ Get rid of unnecessary clutter
☐ Remove overwhelming evidence of your life and tastes
☐ Remove evidence of pets
☐ Remove evidence of children
☐ Tidy within an inch of your life – inside cupboards and out
☐ Clean, clean and clean again

Sell your house
☐ Valuation
☐ Appoint estate agent
☐ Agree terms in writing
☐ Alternatively, organise other means of sale
☐ List what is included in the price
☐ Dig out all warranties/guarantees
☐ Conduct viewings
☐ Remove valuables
☐ Give potential buyers your contact details
☐ Take their contact details
☐ Receive offer
☐ Negotiate
☐ Accept offer

☐ Contact solicitor
☐ Exchange contract
☐ Complete
☐ Move out

Selling a property in Scotland
☐ Appoint solicitor
☐ Set 'offers above' price
☐ Invite offers and viewings
☐ Conduct viewings
☐ Receive notice of interest from buyers
☐ Allow surveys
☐ Receive offers
☐ Set closing date
☐ Accept of reject offers
☐ Missives
☐ Conclusion of missives
☐ Settlement
☐ Move out

USEFUL CONTACTS

**Architecture and Surveying
Institute**
St Mary House
15 St Mary Street
Chippenham
Wiltshire
SN15 3WD
Tel: 01249 444505
Fax: 01249 443602
www.asi.org.uk

**Architectural Association and
School of Architecture**
34-36 Bedford Square
London
WC1B 3ES
Tel: 020 7887 4000
Fax: 020 7414 0782
www.aaschool.ac.uk

Association of British Insurers
51 Gresham Street
London
EC2V 7HQ
Tel: 020 7600 3333
Fax: 020 7696 8999
www.abi.org.uk

**Association of Building
Engineers**
Lutyens House
Billing Brook Road
Northampton
NN3 8NW
Tel: 01604 404 121
Fax: 01604 784 220
www.abe.org.uk

**Association of Plumbing and
Heating Contractors**
14 Ensign House
Ensign Business Centre
Westwood Way
Coventry
CV4 8JA
Tel: 024 7647 0626
Fax: 024 7647 0942
www.aphc.co.uk

**Association of Relocation
Agents**
PO Box 189
Diss
Norfolk
IP22 1PE

Tel: 08700 73 74 75
Fax: 08700 71 87 19
www.relocationagents.com

**Association of Residential
Letting Agents**
Maple House
53–55 Woodside Road
Amersham
Bucks
HP6 6AA
Tel: 0845 345 5752
Fax: 01494 431 530
www.avla.co.uk

**Association of Residentital
Managing Agents**
178 Battersea Park Road
London
SW11 4ND
Tel: 020 7978 2607
Fax: 020 7498 6153
www.arma.org.uk

British Association of Removers
3 Churchill Court
58 Station Road
North Harrow
Middlesex
HA2 7SA
Tel: 020 8861 3331
Fax: 020 8861 3332
www.barmovers.com

**British Wood Preserving and
Damp-proofing Association**
1 Gleneagles House
Vernon Gate
Derby
DE1 1UP

Tel: 01332 225 100
Fax: 01332 225 101
www.bwpda.co.uk

Building Societies Association
3 Savile Row
London
W15 3PB
Tel: 020 7437 0655
Fax: 020 7734 6416
www.bsa.org.uk

**CORGI (Council for Registered
Gas Installers)**
1 Elmwood
Chineham Business Park
Crockford Lane
Basingstoke
Hampshire
RG24 8WG
Tel: 01256 372200
Fax: 01256 708144
www.corgi-gas.com

**Council for Licensed
Conveyancers**
16 Glebe Road
Chelmsford
Essex
CM1 1QG
Tel: 01245 349 599
Fax: 01245 341 300
www.conveyancers.gov.uk

**Department of the Environment,
Transport and the Regions**
Eland House
Bressington Place
London SW1E 5PV
Tel: 020 7944 3000

Electrical Contractors' Association
ESCA House
34 Palace Court
London W2 4HY
Tel: 020 7313 4800
Fax: 020 7221 7344
www.eca.co.uk

English Heritage
23 Savile Row
London
W1S 2ET
Tel: 020 7973 3000
Fax: 020 7973 3001
www.english-heritage.org.uk

Federation of Master Builders
14-15 Great James Street
London
WC1N 3DP
Tel: 020 7242 7583
Fax: 020 7404 0296
www.fmb.org.uk

Heating and Ventilating Contractors' Association
ESCA House
34 Palace Court
London
W2 4JG
Tel: 020 7313 4900
Fax: 020 7727 9268
www.hvca.org.uk

Incorporated Society of Valuers and Auctioneers
3 Cadogan Gate
London
SW1X 0AS
Fax: 020 7235 4390

Independent Schools Information Service
Grosvenor Gardens House
35-37 Grosvenor Gardens
London
SW1W 0BS
Tel: 020 7798 150
Fax: 020 7798 1531
www.isis.org.uk

The Institute of Plumbing
64 Station Lane
Hornchurch
Essex
RM12 6NB
Tel: 01708 472 791
Fax: 01708 448 987
www.registeredplumber.com

The Leasehold Advisory Service
70–74 City Road
London
EC1Y 2BJ
Tel: 0845 345 1993
Fax: 020 7253 2043
www.lease-advice.org

National Approved Council for Security Systems
Queensgate House
14 Cookham Road
Maidenhead
Berkshire
SL6 8AJ
Tel: 01628 637 512
Fax: 01628 773 367
ww.nsi.org.uk

National Association of Estate Agents
Arbon House
21 Jury Street
Warwick
CV34 4EH
Tel: 01926 496 800
Fax: 01926 400 953
www.naea.co.uk

National Federation of Builders
Construction House
56-64 Leonard Street
London
EC2A 4JX
Tel: 020 7608 5150
Fax: 020 7608 5151
www.builders.org.uk

National House Building Council
Buildmark House
Chiltern Avenue
Amersham
Bucks
HP6 5AP
Tel: 01494 735 363
www.nhbc.co.uk

National Land Information Service
Local Government
Information House
Layden House
76-86 Turnmill Street
London
EC1M 5LG
Tel: 01279 451 625
www.nlis.org

National Replacement Window Advisory Service (NRWAS)
National Conservatory Advisory Service (NCAS)
Customer Relations NRWAS
Head Office Call Centre:
1 Crossgreen
Carrickfergus Co. Antrim
Northern Ireland BT38 8DN
Tel: 028 9335 5234
Fax: 028 9336 9893
Customer Freephone:
0800 0285809
E-mail: relations@nrwas.com
www.nrwas.com

Office for the Ombudsman of Estate Agents
Beckett House
4 Bridge Street
Salisbury
Wilts
SP1 2LX
Tel: 01722 333 306
Fax: 01722 332 296
www.oea.co.uk

Royal Institute of British Architects
66 Portland Place
London W1B 1AD
Tel: 020 7580 5533
Fax: 020 7255 1541
www.architecture.com

Royal Institute of Chartered Surveyors Contact Centre
Syrveyor Court
Westwood Way
Coventry
CV4 8JE
Tel: 020 7222 7000
www.rics.org

Royal Institute of Chartered Surveyors in Scotland
9 Manor Place
Edinburgh
EH3 7DN
Tel: 0131 225 7078
Fax: 0131 240 0830
www.rics-scotland.org.uk

Royal Society of Architects in Wales
Bute Building
King Edward VII Avenue
Cathays Park
Cardiff
CF10 3NB
Tel: 029 2087 4753
Fax: 029 2087 4926
www.architecture-wales.com

Royal Society of Ulster Architects
2 Mount Charles
Belfast
BT7 1NZ
Tel: 028 9032 3760
Fax: 028 9033 7313
www.rsua.org.uk

Property search websites:
www.assertahome.co.uk
www.easier.co.uk
www.espc.co.uk
www.findaproperty.com
www.fish4.co.uk
www.homes-on-line.com
www.homepages.co.uk
www.hometrack.co.uk
www.move.co.uk
www.new-homes.co.uk
www.periodproperty.com
www.primelocation.com
www.propertyfinder.co.uk
www.propertylive.co.uk
www.propertyworld.com
www.reapit.com
www.rightmove.co.uk
www.sequencehome.co.uk
www.teamprop.co.uk
www.thisislondon.co.uk
www.wotproperty.co.uk

Home search companies:
Kirmir Property Search
www.kirmir.com
Garrington Home Finders
www.garrington.co.uk

Regional information:
www.bramich.demon.co.uk
www.travelengland.org.uk
www.scotourist.org.uk
www.townpages.so.uk
www.rural.co.uk
www.visitbritain.com
www.visitwales.com

Road maps:
www.directions.ltd.uk
www.streetmap.co.uk

Useful building society sites:
www.abbeynational.co.uk
www.halifax.co.uk
www.nationwide.co.uk

Useful government sites:
Local Government Association, www.lgan.gov.uk
Greater London Authority, www.london.gov.uk
The Environment Agency, www.environment-agency.gov.uk
Department of Transport Local Government and the Regions,
www.dtlr.co.uk

**Useful online mortgage
search sites:**
www.about-mortgages.co.uk
www.charcolonline.co.uk
www.moneyfacts.co.uk
www.moneysupermarket.co.uk
www.moneynet.co.uk
www.yourmortgage.co.uk

Insurance:
British Insurance and Investment Brokers Association, www.biba.co.uk
www.theinsurancecentre.co.uk

Renting and Letting:
Association of Residential Letting Agents, www.arla.co.uk
www.buytolet.co.uk

General:
www.themovechannel.com

GLOSSARY

A

Administration fee – the cost of not taking a building and contents insurance policy that comes as part of a mortgage lender's package.

Agency sales fee – the fixed percentage of the property's sale price that is payable to the estate agent.

Agent – a person who acts on behalf of another, eg estate agent, letting agent.

Aggregated site – a website that carries particulars from a number of different agencies.

Agreement in principal – a document provided by a mortgage lender showing the prospective buyer will, subject to valuation of the property, be eligible for a mortgage.

Air brick – perforated brick for aiding ventilation in enclosed spaces.

APR – Annual Percentage Rate. Intended to reflect the true cost of borrowing, taking into account the costs of taking out a mortgage. Always quoted with any mortgage rate. Helps borrower compare one loan with another.

Arbitration – the method by which disputes over services provided or work done is resolved.

ARLA – Association of Residential Letting Agents

Arrangement fee – the fee charged by a mortgage lender on completing the mortgage arrangements. Usually charged when competitive rates are offered.

Arrears – overdue payments whether rental, mortgage, ground rent etc.

Asking price – the price the seller hopes to achieve for his property.

Assignment – the transfer of property from one person to another, eg a lease or an insurance policy on an endowment policy.

Assured shorthold tenancy – the usual tenancy for domestic lets whereby the landlord can repossess the property after six months provided he has given the correct notices.

Assured tenancy – a tenancy agreement whereby the landlord does not have the right to repossess after six months.

Auction – the process of acquiring a property by bidding against other potential buyers. Surveys and estimates should be obtained first.

B

Balance outstanding – the amount still owed on a loan.

Bank of England base rate – the rate of interest set by the Bank of England and usually followed by lenders.

Banker's draft – the payment of funds guaranteed by a bank. More secure than a personal cheque.

BAR – The British Association of Removers

Blind bids – sealed best offers that are made in Scotland after surveys and estimates. They are made in ignorance of what other interested parties may have offered.

Boundaries – the limits of the property or the land surrounding it.

Bridging loan – a loan enabling a buyer to complete the purchase of a property before he has received the proceeds from the sale of his old one.

Buildings insurance – this gives financial cover for the structure of a property. It should cover the replacement costs if the building is destroyed.

Buildmark – a structural guarantee from the NHBC given on most new homes.

Buyer's market – the state of a falling property market when sellers will reduce their price to sell the property.

Buyer's position – describes the position of a buyer, whether he is a cash buyer, a first-time buyer, a buyer who has not put his own property on the market, in a chain etc.

Buy-to-let mortgage – a mortgage designed to encourage investors into buying property to let out.

C

Cap-and-collar mortgage – a mortgage with top and bottom limits set for the interest rate.

Capital – the mortgage loan (aka advance or principal).

Capital gains tax – tax payable on the profit arising from the sale of a property.

Capped-rate mortgage – a mortgage with a top limit set for the interest rate.

Cashback mortgages – these give a lump sum cash payment to the buyer when the mortgage transaction is complete.

Cash buyer – someone who is not in the position of having to sell his house before buying.

Cavity wall – a common building method for modern properties whereby two walls are built with a small gap between that can be used for insulation.

Chain – a number of people dependent on one another's property sale and purchase before they can complete on their own.

Clear title – the title to a property unencumbered by legal charges regarding its ownership.

Commission – the percentage of the selling price received by the seller's agent.

Completion date – the date the property transaction is concluded and the property changes hands.

Conclusion of missives (Scotland) – the point at which the property sale becomes binding.

Conditions of sale – standard terms in the contract of a property sale stipulating what has to be done before the transaction is completed. If they are not fulfilled the aggrieved party can withdraw from the deal.

Contract – the agreement to sell a property that becomes binding when buyer and seller exchange.

Conveyance – the written document that conveys the unregistered property from the seller to the buyer.

Conveyancing – the legal and administrative process involved in transferring property from the seller to the buyer.

Covenant – a promise in a deed to undertake or to abstain from specific things.

CRA – Credit Reference Agency

Creditor – the lender or someone owed money.

Current account mortgage (CAM) – a flexible mortgage whereby the outstanding balance of your current account is offset against the outstanding balance of the mortgage.

D

Dado – strip of raised wood fixed to wall once used to prevent damage from chairbacks.

Defects – aspects of the property that may affect its present value.

Deposit – a lump sum (usually 5%–10%) paid on exchange of contract; a lump sum (usually 4–6 weeks rent) paid on signing a tenancy agreement.

Disbursements – expenses incurred by a solicitor on your behalf during conveyancing (eg local searches, land registry fees etc).

Discount period – the period of reduced payments at the beginning of the span of a mortgage.

Discounted mortgages – a guaranteed deduction in the SVR over an agreed period.

Draft contract – legal document setting out the terms of sale used as a starting point for negotiation between solicitors handling a property transaction.

E

Early redemption – paying off a mortgage before the end of its term.

Early redemption penalty (ERP) – financial penalty levied to cover administration costs when a loan is repaid early.

Easement – the legal right of a property owner to use a facility on someone else's land such as a right of way.

Egg and dart – a patterned moulding alternating egg shapes and darts.

Endowment mortgage – a loan on which the interest only is paid throughout the term. It is linked to an endowment policy and the capital is paid off in a lump sum at the end of the term.

Endowment policy – an investment, including life insurance, linked to a mortgage loan to pay off the loan at the end of its term.

Engrossment – the final executed deed.

Equity – the amount of your deposit on your new property.

Excess – applies to an insurance claim and represents the initial amount of money to be paid by yourself.

Exchange of contracts – the process by which the sale and purchase of the house becomes legally binding.

Extended redemption penalty – when the redemption penalty extends beyond the period of the fixed or capped rate period.

F

Fixed rate – interest charged on a mortgage as a fixed amount over a set period.

Fixtures and fittings – the immovable items (whether stuck, glued or screwed etc) in a property that are judged part of its fabric.

Flashing – metal or cement seal to prevent a roof leaking at a joint.

Flaunching – the cement round the base of the chimney that lets the rain run off.

Flexible mortgage – a loan allowing overpayment or underpayment that can be set against a current account.

Freehold – outright ownership of property and the land on which it stands.

Full structural survey – the most comprehensive survey available to examine all aspects of a property.

G

Gazumping – when a seller drops a buyer, having accepted his offer on the property, in favour of someone offering more.

Gazundering – when the buyer drops his price at the last moment before exchange and threatens to renege on the deal if it is not accepted.

Ground rent – an annual sum paid by a leaseholder to a freeholder.

Guarantor – the person who assumes responsibility for defaulted payments.

Guide price – an estimate of the eventual selling price.

H

Homebuy schemes – schemes run by Housing Associations to sell off their property.

Homebuyer's report – a less detailed survey than a full structural survey but more thorough than a valuation.

Homesearch agency – an agency who will search for a property that suits your specific criteria.

Household insurance – an insurance policy combining buildings and contents policies.

Housing Association – a non-profit-making organisation providing low rent accommodation.

I

Index map search – a search to find out if the ownership of a property is registered at the Land Registry.

Index tracker mortgage – a rate of interest that is at a fixed margin above the Bank of England base rate and follows its fluctuations.

Insulation – material used to retain warmth in the structure of the property.

Interest-only mortgage – monthly repayments are made to pay off the interest on the loan with contributions paid to another investment to pay off the capital at the end of the term.

Interest rate – this is the percentage charged each year by the mortgage lender for the privilege of borrowing the loan.

Inventory – a comprehensive list of possessions that have gone into storage or are owned by a landlord in a rented-out property. They should be jointly checked and signed by the owner and representative of the removal/storage company or tenant respectively.

ISA mortgage – a mortgage with a repayment vehicle in the form of an Individual Savings Account (ISA).

ISVA – The Incorporated Society of Valuers and Auctioneers

J

Joint mortgage – a mortgage obtained between two people who are equally liable for its repayment.

Joint sole agency – two estate agents market the property together and split the commission.

Joint tenants – two or more people holding property as co-owners.

L

Land certificate – a certificate issued by the Land Registry confirming the ownership of a property.

Land Registry – government department responsible for keeping a register of all the properties in England and Wales which have registered titles.

Leasehold – ownership of a lease for a limited number of years after which the ownership returns to the freeholder.

Legal charge – a mortgage (more or less).

Loan to Value (LTV) – the percentage of the property's value being borrowed as a mortgage.

Local search – an application to local authorities for information on a property and its surrounds.

Lock-out agreement – an agreement by which the seller takes the property off the market for a certain time during which contracts must be exchanged.

Low-cost endowment mortgage – a mortgage secured by an endowment policy. The annual bonuses ensure, without guaranteeing, that the loan will be paid off at the end of the term.

Low-start mortgage – a mortgage with low initial repayments that rise to a set percentage each year until the full level premium is reached.

M

Missives – the exchange of letters between solicitors to confirm the deal is binding under Scottish law.

Mortgage – a loan for which the property is the security. The lender assumes certain rights including the power to sell the property if the repayments are not made.

Mortgage Indemnity Guarantee (MIG) – a form of insurance levied by mortgage lenders to protect themselves against any losses incurred on a loan above 75% of the purchase price. This charge is passed on to the borrower to be paid before they begin their mortgage repayments.

Mortgage protection policy – insurance to protect the owner against inability to make repayments due to redundancy, sickness, accident or disability.

Multiple agency – a number of estate agencies market a property and the one that sells it gets the commission.

N

NAEA – National Association of Estate Agents

Negative equity – this occurs when the value of your property is less than the amount you borrowed to buy it.

NHBC – the National House Building Council

Non-profit endowment – this type of mortgage is guaranteed to repay the loan but because there is no benefit, other than life cover, it is not regarded as the best way of repaying a mortgage.

Notice – the official request from the landlord or freeholder asking the tenant to vacate the property.

O

Offer – the price named by the buyer for the property.

Off-plan – the process of buying the property from the floor plan, brochures and show house before it is built.

Overhang – this occurs when the ERP continues beyond the fixed or capped rate period.

P

Part-exchange – a developer sells your home for you in part-exchange for a new home.

Payment protection insurance – if unable to work for a time, this insurance covers your mortgage repayments.

Pension mortgage – a mortgage where the repayment vehicle takes the form of a pension plan.

Permitted development rights – the right to carry out certain alterations to a property without planning permission.

Preliminary enquiries – the questions asked by the buyer's solicitor before contracts are exchanged.

Premium – payment for an insurance policy in one-off or regular instalments.

Principal – the loan against which interest is calculated.

Private treaty – the most common way of selling property in England and Wales whereby an estate agent advertises the property and quotes a definitive asking price.

R

Redemption – paying off a loan.

Redemption fee – a fee often payable when you pay off a mortgage early and take out a further mortgage with the same lender.

Redemption penalties – see ERP

Remortgage – when a second mortgage is taken out against the capital in the first property.

Repayment mortgage – loan repayments cover both the loan and the interest throughout the period of the loan.

RIBA – Royal Institute of British Architects

RICS – Royal Institute of Chartered Surveyors

Rising damp – capillary action causing damp to rise up a wall leading to wood rot and plaster decay.

S

Sealed bids – best bids.

Seller's market – when demand is high and and sellers can command top prices.

Seller's pack – if the government's scheme goes through, a seller's pack will contain information invaluable to the buyer, eg leases, deed, searches and homebuyer's report.

Seller's property information form – a form completed by the seller and his solicitor, giving relevant information to the buyer after their offer has been accepted.

Service charges – charges applied to leaseholders to cover maintenance, insurance and repair of the building.

Shared ownership scheme – a way of buying property from a registered social landlord.

Show home – a model home built on the site of a new development to demonstrate the sort of property on offer. Make sure you check your own specifications.

Sinking fund – a sum of money built up through leaseholders' payments to cover large or unforeseen repair work to the building.

Sitting tenant – a tenant who cannot be evicted because they are keeping to the tenancy agreement.

Sole agency – the agreement to sell your property through one estate agent.

Stamp duty – a fee levied by the government on properties that change hands for over £60,000.

Standard variable rate (SVR) – the standard interest rate on a mortgage which is usually a point above or below the base rate and moves up and down with it.

Subject to contract – words that should appear in every correspondence between buyer and seller (or their solicitors) before contracts are exchanged.

Sum insured – the amount that is paid out when a term insurance policy matures or the event insured for occurs.

T

Tenants in common – two or more people who share ownership of a property so that when one of them dies, their share does not automatically pass on to the other owner but can be left to whomever they choose.

Title deeds – the documents proving ownership of land. The title deed in registered land transactions is the land certificate.

Title number – the number allocated to each property by the land registry.

Top-up mortgage – a second mortgage when the first lender is not prepared to lend enough for the purchase of the property.

Tracker mortgage – mortgage with an interest rate that tracks the Bank of England base rate.

U

Upset price (Scotland) – the price fixed by the seller and his solicitor as a minimum price.

Utilities – the companies providing gas, electricity, telephone etc.

V

Valuation – the price put on the property by an estate agent and also by the building society when assessing whether it is sufficient security for the loan they have been asked to lend.

Variable rate mortgage – monthly payments are made at the mortgage lender's standard variable rate (SVR).

VAT – value added tax.

Vendor – the seller.

W

With profits policy – a policy often used with an endowment mortgage whereby the bonuses from a life insurance policy are added to the original sum assured paid when the policy matures.

Writ – method of stating legal action against a third party.

INDEX

NOTES

NOTES

NOTES

NOTES

NOTES